ACT® Mastery Science

Student Workbook

4th Edition

MasteryPrep

Inquiries concerning this publication should be mailed to:

MasteryPrep
7117 Florida Blvd.
Baton Rouge, LA 70806

ISBN-13: 978-1-948846-07-3

Table of Contents

Get ready to master the ACT® test!

You are about to take part in the most effective and broadly used ACT prep program in the nation! With ACT Mastery, you will learn the most frequently tested content on the ACT test and develop the skills and strategies necessary to achieve the score you desire.

With practice in all four subjects, you will be fully prepared.

The ACT Mastery Science workbook is just one part of a larger program that includes four core subject books, each in line with a subtest found on the ACT: English, math, reading, and science. Each book works to build your mastery of the content most frequently tested on the ACT by providing thorough subject reviews and hundreds of ACT practice questions. By completing this book, you will be prepared for the science subtest; the rest of the program will prepare you for the English, math, and reading subtests.

Test prep is a team effort.

Although you may be tempted to jump ahead, this workbook should be used in conjunction with a teacher's instructions and is not intended for self-guided practice. Each lesson is designed so that the majority of the direction and some of the content is delivered by an instructor either verbally or visually by way of slide presentations or whiteboards. Working ahead will limit your understanding of the ACT content and may actually lead to confusion. Follow the teacher's instructions during the lesson and only work on practice as directed. This will maximize your understanding of the material and, ultimately, your score.

The score you want is within your reach!

The ACT test is a rigorous, challenging marathon of an exam. It can be intimidating. Of the more than two million students who take the test each year, many feel that it is uncoachable—that whatever score they earn on the test is the best they can do. The ACT Mastery program has proven this assumption to be completely false. Students dedicated to the program routinely see substantial improvement on their test scores. It will take hard work and determination, but with the content and strategies available to you, anything is possible.

You *can* master the ACT test.

The keys to success with ACT preparation are content, practice, and strategy. As your teacher leads you through the lessons, focus on the content. Take notes on all of the definitions and rules, ask questions to clarify any points of confusion, and participate in all of the activities.

Once you begin to master the content, practice the problems in your workbook. Give your best effort on every question no matter how hard or easy it may seem. Complete any homework your teacher assigns and make sure you ask questions if you do not fully understand a concept.

Finally, as you develop content mastery and practice the ACT questions, work on building your test-day strategy. Look for trends in the questions and answer choices, determine your strongest and weakest areas, and decide how you will pace yourself on the day of the test.

Good luck!

Select Data and Features Part 1

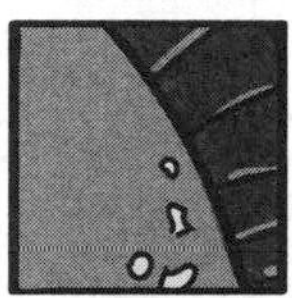

Pie I have eaten

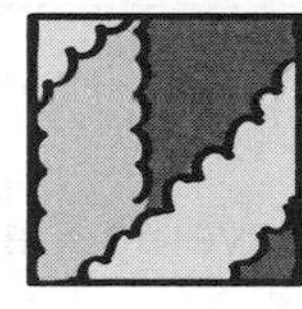

Pie I have not yet eaten

CAPTION:

1.1 Entrance Ticket

Answer the questions below.

This year, Elena, Jared, Tiana, Darren, Marisela, and Kyu each recorded the average temperature of the city where they live in March and September.

Table 1

	Average March temperature (°F)	Average September temperature (°F)
Jacksonville, Florida	74	71
Portland, Oregon	52	47
Los Angeles, California	69	61
Cleveland, Ohio	39	64
Burlington, Vermont	35	59
Austin, Texas	62	82

Elena's city had a higher average temperature in March than in September.

Does Elena live in Austin, Texas, or Portland, Oregon? ______________________________

Darren's city had an average March temperature 4° lower than Marisela's city's average March temperature.

If Marisela lives in Cleveland, Ohio, does Darren live in Burlington, Vermont, or Jacksonville, Florida?

____

The average September temperature in Tiana's city was greater than 60°F.

Does Tiana live in Portland, Oregon, or Los Angeles, California? ______________________

1.2 Learning Targets

1. Find basic data represented on charts, graphs, tables, and figures

2. Quickly answer science questions using charts and graphs presented in the ACT science test

Self-Assessment

Circle the number that corresponds to your confidence level in your knowledge of this subject before beginning the lesson. A score of 1 means you are completely lost, and a score of 4 means you have mastered the skills. After you finish the lesson, return to the bottom of this page and circle your new confidence level to show your improvement.

Before Lesson

1 2 3 4

After Lesson

1 2 3 4

1.3.1 Road Signs

Step #1 when approaching a science passage: ______________________________

Step #2 when approaching a science passage: ______________________________

____

Two measurements are taken of the water in a hot spring: the sulfur content and the temperature. Both of these measurements can be affected by water flow.

Sulfur content in hot springs is thought to have medicinal and therapeutic effects for those relaxing in the springs. Figure 1 shows the sulfur levels in parts per million (ppm) on 5 collection days at two different hot springs, Spring 1 and Spring 2.

Table 1 shows the temperature in Fahrenheit of the water in Spring 1 and Spring 2 on each of the 5 collection days. Table 2 shows the average water temperature in Fahrenheit of Spring 1 and Spring 2 during this time.

Figure 2 shows the water flow of each spring in cubic feet per second on the 5 collection days.

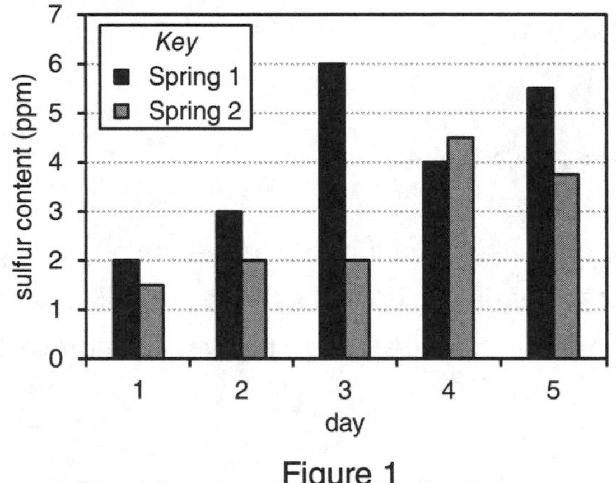

Figure 1

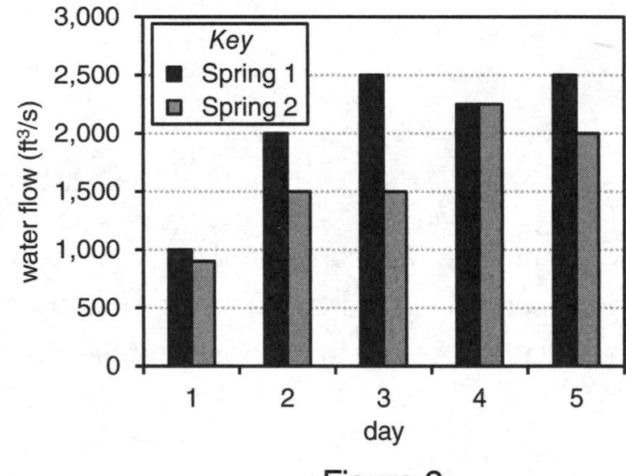

Figure 2

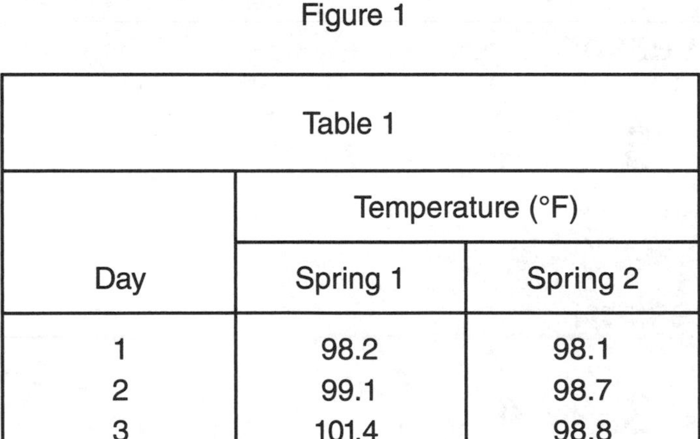

Table 1		
	Temperature (°F)	
Day	Spring 1	Spring 2
1	98.2	98.1
2	99.1	98.7
3	101.4	98.8
4	99.7	99.9
5	100.1	99.6

Table 2	
Spring	Average Temperature (°F)
Spring 1	99.7
Spring 2	99.0

1.3.1 Road Signs

Three metal alloys contain varying levels of chromium, which is known to help prevent corrosion, or rust. When rust forms on metals, hydroxide ions are produced as a byproduct.

Table 1 shows the concentration of hydroxide [OH⁻] produced over time by samples of three metal alloys with varying chromium content.

The first trial was then repeated four additional times, each with a constant concentration of one of four different potential corrosion inhibitor candidates. The results of these additional trials are shown in Figure 1.

Table 1

Metal alloy	Chromium content (%)	Volume of ions [OH⁻] produced (μM)			
		Day 2	Day 4	Day 6	Day 8
1	9.0	19	42	86	131
2	10.5	2	4	8	12
3	11.0	1	3	5	7

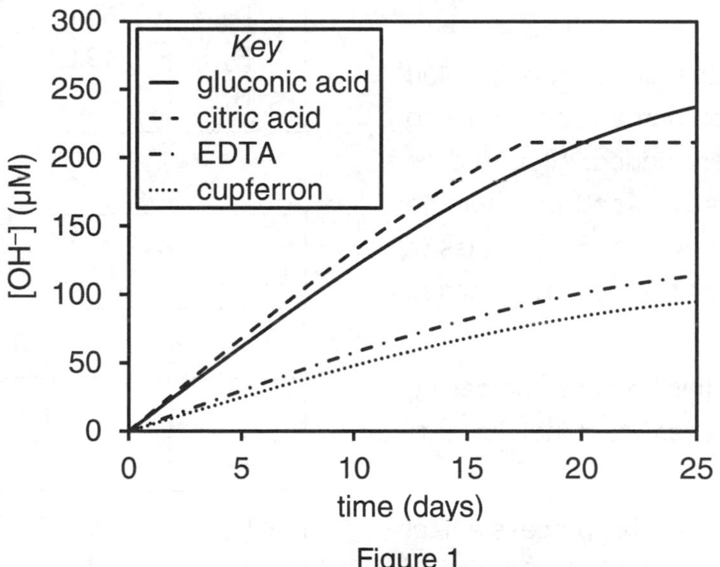

Figure 1

1.3.1 Road Signs

High-salt environments cause blueberry bushes to grow poorly. This effect is brought about by two distinct conditions:

- An increased concentration of Na^+ ions in the cytoplasm
- Decreased water absorption by the plant cells

Arabidopsis thaliana, a small flowering plant, carries the gene AtNHX1, whose product, VAC, increases the uptake and removal of Na^+.

A group of researchers bred four identical lines of blueberry bushes (B_1–B_4). They then isolated the AtNHX1 gene from the *Arabidopsis thaliana* and inserted two copies of this gene into the B_1 genome. They repeated this process for B_2 and B_3, changing the AtNHX1 alleles for each so that B_1, B_2, and B_3 had distinct AtNHX1 genotypes. They then performed an experiment on the growth of lines B_1–B_4.

Experiment

Seedlings from each of the lines were planted and watered with 10 L of nutrient solution into which 2 grams of NaCl were added. After 90 days of growth, the researchers recorded the average height, average mass, and average berry mass of each line. The results of their findings are recorded in Table 1.

The researchers repeated this process, increasing the mass of NaCl to 8 g. The results of their findings are recorded in Table 2.

The researchers then repeated this process a final time, increasing the mass of NaCl to 64 g. The results of their findings are recorded in Table 3.

Table 1

2 g NaCl / 10 L nutrient solution			
Line	Height (cm)	Mass (kg)	Berry mass (g)
B_1	60.9	0.7	0.80
B_2	61.2	0.7	0.81
B_3	59.8	0.7	0.79
B_4	60.4	0.7	0.80

Table 2

8 g NaCl / 10 L nutrient solution			
Line	Height (cm)	Mass (kg)	Berry mass (g)
B_1	58.5	0.6	0.75
B_2	59.6	0.6	0.77
B_3	42.3	0.4	0.51
B_4	40.6	0.4	0.49

Table 3

64 g NaCl / 10 L nutrient solution			
Line	Height (cm)	Mass (kg)	Berry mass (g)
B_1	58.3	0.6	0.74
B_2	58.9	0.6	0.78
B_3	21.2	0.2	0.00
B_4	20.5	0.2	0.00

1.3.1 Road Signs

1. Based on Table 1, the average percent of regions inhabited by at least 1 predator in Zones A–E of the study area was closest to:
   A. 25%.
   B. 35%.
   C. 55%.
   D. 75%.

Road Signs: ____

____

2. Based on the results of Experiment 1, which of the following produced the fastest decomposition of HgO at 175°C?
   A. KCl
   B. KOH
   C. $KHCO_3$
   D. K_2O

Road Signs: ____

____

1.3.1 Road Signs

3. Based on Study 1, the potassium content of Solution A, after undergoing the 12-hour treatment in Study 3, was most likely:

A. less than 5%.
B. between 5% and 10%.
C. between 10% and 25%.
D. greater than 25%.

Road Signs: ____

____

4. According to Figures 1 and 2, Solutions A and B have the same boiling point of:

A. 57°C.
B. 67°C.
C. 73°C.
D. The figures do not show that Solutions A and B share a boiling point.

Road Signs: ____

____

Science Tip

Road Signs: Almost every question on the ACT science test will give you the information you need to locate the answer in the passage. Be sure to underline all of these road signs and use them to answer the questions.

1.3.2 Road Race

Table 1

Successional time (yr)	1	5	15	20	25	35	60	100	150
Bird species \ Dominant plants	weeds	grasses	shrubs		small trees				canopy trees
ground thrush	■	■							
boatbill		■	■						
cicada bird			■	■					
cockatoo			■	■	■				
friarbird			■	■					
quail			■	■					
scrubwren					■	■	■	■	
noisy pitta					■	■	■	■	
wompoo pigeon					■	■	■	■	
brown pigeon						■	■	■	
sacred ibis						■	■	■	
straw-necked ibis						■	■	■	■
yellow-faced honeyeater						■	■	■	
spotless crake								■	■
dollarbird							■	■	■
channel-billed cuckoo								■	■
black-faced cuckoo shrike								■	■
darter								■	■
emerald dove									■

A shaded box indicates that birds were present in a density of at least one pair per 20 acres.

1.3.2 Road Race

Table 2

Week	Weekly average light intensity			Weekly average air temperature (°C)		
	Section 1	Section 2	Section 3	Section 1	Section 2	Section 3
1	290.3	84.9	120.3	19.68	19.08	18.65
2	307.1	79.8	80.7	20.11	19.23	18.48
3	315.2	76.9	76.8	20.75	19.19	18.64
4	305.3	73.9	69.6	21.02	19.51	18.98
5	312.2	70.2	75.1	21.15	19.61	19.12

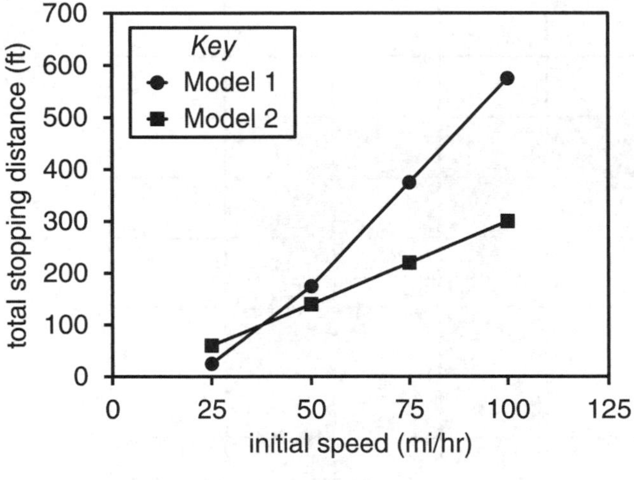

Figure 1

Science Tip

Use the Figures: The majority of the questions on the ACT science test do not require you to read or understand the passage. After you preview the passage and figures, start answering questions based on the road signs that refer to figures and use the passage text only if necessary.

This page is intentionally left blank.

1.4.1 Set One

Passage I

Both solids and liquids typically have the property of expanding when heated. Two experiments were conducted by chemists to study the expansion of various substances. In the first experiment, five 1-meter wires were hung vertically from the ceiling. An electric current was passed through each wire to heat them from 0°C to 120°C. The length of each wire was measured and recorded in 20-degree increments. The results of this study are shown in Figure 1.

In the second experiment, designed to test the expansion of various liquids, four different solutions were placed in 1-meter tall, graduated burets. The liquids were heated at the same rate from 20°C to 60°C, and the increase in volume was measured in 5-degree increments. The results of this experiment are shown in Figure 2.

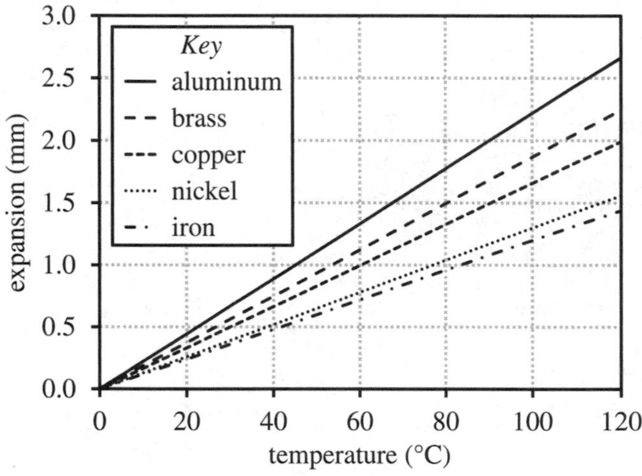

Figure 1

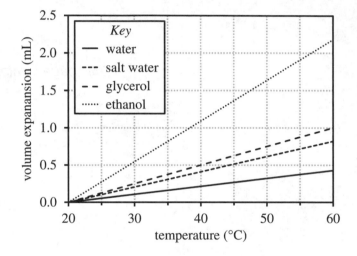

Figure 2

1. About how many millimeters did the brass wire stretch at 60°C?

   A. 0.9 mm
   B. 1.0 mm
   C. 1.1 mm
   D. 1.3 mm

2. Which of the following wires expanded the least at 80°C?

   F. Brass
   G. Nickel
   H. Copper
   J. Aluminum

3. Which liquids expanded by less than 1 mL at 50°C?

   A. Ethanol only
   B. Water only
   C. Water and salt water only
   D. Water, salt water, and glycerol only

4. What was the largest amount of expansion measured on a wire in Figure 1?

   F. 1.9 mm
   G. 2.2 mm
   H. 2.7 mm
   J. 3.0 mm

5. What was the smallest amount of volume expansion measured for a liquid at 60°C in Figure 2?

   A. 0.4 mL
   B. 0.8 mL
   C. 1.0 mL
   D. 2.2 mL

END OF SET ONE
STOP! DO NOT GO ON TO THE NEXT PAGE
UNTIL TOLD TO DO SO.

1.4.2 Set Two

Passage II

Scientists categorized Japan's native species. Where possible, they determined each species' risk of extinction and then placed that species in 1 of 4 different risk categories. If the species was not at risk of extinction, it was not included in these categories. Table 1 shows the breakdown of the scientists' categorizations.

Table 1

Group	Native species	Extinct	Endangered	Vulnerable	Rare	Total
Vertebrate						
Mammal	188	5	3	11	36	55
Bird	665	13	27	27	65	132
Reptile	87	–	1	2	13	16
Amphibian	59	–	2	4	8	14
Freshwater fish	200	2	16	6	17	41
Subtotal	1,199	20	49	50	139	258
Invertebrate						
Insect	28,720	2	23	15	166	206
Land/freshwater decapod	192	–	–	7	45	52
Land/freshwater snail	824	–	34	39	54	127
Other	4,040	–	4	3	11	18
Subtotal	33,776	2	61	64	276	403

The small Indian mongoose is a non-native species that was introduced into Japan at various points in the twentieth century. They affect a variety of native species in the area, including the native Amami rabbit population. Table 2 shows the population details of nine different regions. Figure 1 shows the number of Amami rabbits as estimated in 1993–94 and 2002–03 in these various regions of Japan.

Table 2

Region	1993–1994 area (ha)	Density (/100 ha)	Population size	2002–2003 area (ha)	Density (/100 ha)	Population size
A	771	1.1–2.5	8–19	599	2.6–6.1	16–36
B	1,504	2.5–5.8	37–88	344	0.4–0.8	1–3
C	2,932	12–30	360–880	3,123	3.2–7.5	98–230
D	1,797	3.9–9.1	69–160	1,715	2.0–4.6	34–79
E	6,496	3.2–7.8	210–500	6,496	4.5–11	290–700
F	2,419	4.6–11	110–270	1,950	5.8–14	110–270
G	6,226	11–25	670–1,600	6,656	12–29	810–1,900
H	6,904	12–29	810–1,900	4,991	8.7–21	430–1,000
I	4,420	5.5–13	240–570	4,263	5.6–13	240–560
Total	33,469	7.5–18	2,500–6,100	30,137	6.8–16	2,000–4,800

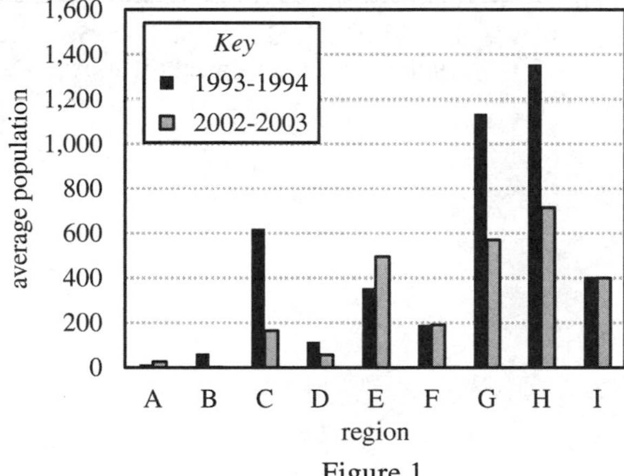

Figure 1

6. Based on Table 1, how many endangered freshwater fish species were tallied for Japan?

F. 2
G. 16
H. 41
J. 49

7. In Figure 1, in which of the following regions does the population of Amami rabbits NOT decrease from 1993–1994 to 2002–2003?

A. Region B
B. Region C
C. Region D
D. Region F

8. In Table 1, the number of endangered and vulnerable species was the same for which group?

F. Mammals
G. Birds
H. Insects
J. Amphibians

9. According to Table 1, how many invertebrates that did not fit into the insect, land/freshwater decapods, and land/freshwater snails categories are listed as vulnerable?

A. 3
B. 11
C. 64
D. This cannot be determined from the given information.

10. Based on Figure 1, what was the population of Amami rabbits in Region C in 1993–1994?

F. 80
G. 100
H. 300
J. 620

END OF SET TWO

STOP! DO NOT GO ON TO THE NEXT PAGE UNTIL TOLD TO DO SO.

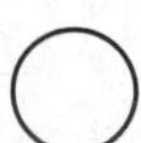

4 ○ ○ ○ ○ ○ ○ ○ ○ ○ 4

1.4.3 Set Three

Passage III

A chemical reaction associated with energy production in humans can be summarized by the following chemical equation:

$C_6H_{12}O_6 + 6O_2 \rightarrow 6CO_2 + 6H_2O + \text{energy}$

Table 1 gives an approximate breakdown of how glucose from a meal containing 90 grams of glucose was distributed.

Table 1

Location	Glucose (g)
liver	17
brain	15
kidneys	8
muscles	48
fat	2

Figure 1 shows the relative levels of glucose and insulin in a normal person's blood over the course of the day.

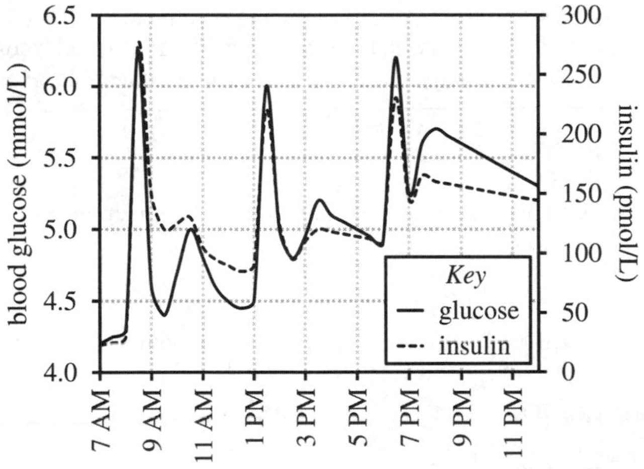

Figure 1

Figure 2 shows the changes in blood glucose after a single meal for a normal person and for a diabetic person.

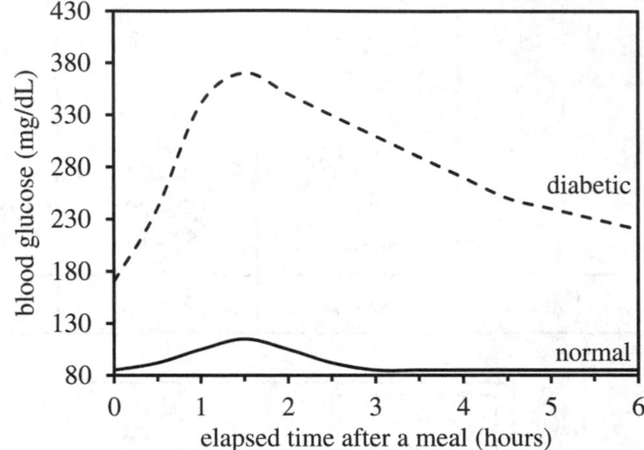

Figure 2

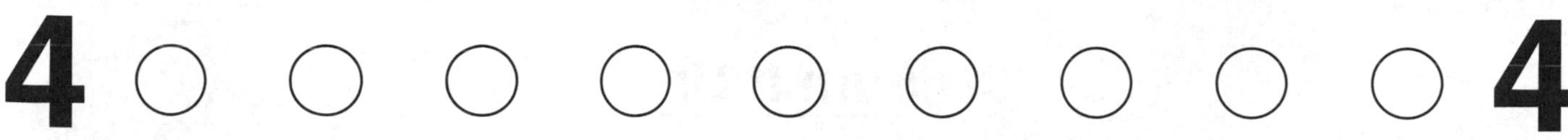

11. Based on Figure 1, at approximately which time of day does a person's brain receive the greatest influx of glucose?

A. 8:30 AM
B. 10:30 AM
C. 1:30 PM
D. 6:30 PM

12. In Figure 2, at which of the following times does a normal person's blood glucose concentration reach its maximum after eating?

F. 30 minutes after eating
G. 1 hour after eating
H. 1.5 hours after eating
J. 2 hours after eating

13. According to Figure 2, within an hour after a meal, the blood glucose concentration of a normal person typically:

A. decreases.
B. increases.
C. stays the same.
D. The figure provides no information about the relationship between blood glucose concentration and the time following meals.

14. According to Figure 1, the lowest concentration of glucose in a person's blood during the day was:

F. 4.00 mmol/L.
G. 4.25 mmol/L.
H. 4.50 mmol/L.
J. 4.75 mmol/L.

15. According to Table 1, the part of a person's body that received the least amount of glucose was the:

A. liver.
B. brain.
C. kidneys.
D. fat.

END OF SET THREE
STOP! DO NOT GO ON TO THE NEXT PAGE UNTIL TOLD TO DO SO.

Sum It Up

Tips and Techniques

Road Signs: Almost every question on the ACT science test will give you the information you need to locate the answer in the passage. Be sure to underline all of these road signs and use them to answer the questions.

Use the Figures: The majority of the questions on the ACT science test do not require you to read or understand the passage. Answer questions based on the road signs that refer to figures and use the passage text only if necessary.

Select Data and Features Part 2

CAPTION:

2.1 Entrance Ticket

Think of a time when you could not get somewhere directly and describe the in-between steps you had to take to arrive at your destination. It can be a physical destination or something metaphorical such as a goal you wanted to achieve.

2.2 Learning Targets

1. Read charts and graphs to answer ACT questions

2. Find information in the science passages and experimental descriptions needed to read complex charts and graphs

3. Relate information given in the passage to the terminology used in the question items

Self-Assessment

Circle the number that corresponds to your confidence level in your knowledge of this subject before beginning the lesson. A score of 1 means you are completely lost, and a score of 4 means you have mastered the skills. After you finish the lesson, return to the bottom of this page and circle your new confidence level to show your improvement.

Before Lesson

1 2 3 4

After Lesson

1 2 3 4

2.3.1 Making the Connection

Scientists have found that carbon monoxide gas (CO) is toxic when it exceeds concentrations of 0.1% by volume. In urban areas, automobiles are a significant source of CO. Studies have shown that CO levels in cities are higher during colder weather. A group of students hypothesized that cars emit more CO in colder air temperatures than in warmer air temperatures during the first 18 minutes after they are started. The students then performed two experiments to test their hypothesis.

Experiment 1

A hose was connected to the tailpipe of a car. After the engine was started, the exhaust was collected in a leak-proof bag. From there, a 10-mL sample was taken from the bag with a syringe and injected into a *gas chromatograph*, which separates mixed gases into their individual components. The students then were able to determine the percentage by volume of CO present in the exhaust. Samples were taken at 3-minute intervals, with the last sample taken 18 minutes after the engine was started. This experiment was conducted on four different vehicles with an external air temperature of –7°C. The results of this experiment are shown in Table 1.

Experiment 2

The same study was conducted on the same four cars at an external temperature of 22°C. The results of this experiment are shown in Table 2.

Table 1

Time after starting (min)	% of CO in exhaust at –7°C			
	1980 Model A	1980 Model B	2008 Model A	2008 Model B
3	3.4	3.3	1.3	0.2
6	4.1	7.2	1.1	1.3
9	4.4	11.1	0.6	2.6
12	3.8	7.3	0.5	3.2
15	3.3	6.9	0.4	1.9
18	3.0	6.8	0.4	1.7

2.3.1 Making the Connection

Table 2				
Time after starting (min)	% of CO in exhaust at 22°C			
	1980 Model A	1980 Model B	2008 Model A	2008 Model B
3	2.1	2.0	0.4	1.0
6	3.5	6.3	0.4	1.5
9	1.5	7.1	0.3	0.8
12	1.0	6.1	0.1	0.3
15	1.0	4.9	0.1	0.3
18	0.9	4.7	0.1	0.2

1. What percent of CO was present in the exhaust of the 1980 Model A at –7°C after 6 minutes?

A. 3.3%
B. 4.1%
C. 4.4%
D. 7.2%

2. What vehicle had the lowest level of CO present in the exhaust after 18 minutes at –7°C?

F. 1980 Model A
G. 1980 Model B
H. 2008 Model A
J. 2008 Model B

3. What vehicle had a time period with a higher level of CO in the exhaust at 22°C than at –7°C?

A. 1980 Model A
B. 1980 Model B
C. 2008 Model A
D. 2008 Model B

4. What vehicle had the lowest level of CO in the exhaust compared to the other vehicles?

F. 1980 Model A
G. 1980 Model B
H. 2008 Model A
J. 2008 Model B

5. At what minute mark did the CO percentage of the exhaust reach 0.5 in the 2008 Model A at –7°C?

A. 6 minutes
B. 9 minutes
C. 12 minutes
D. 15 minutes

2.3.1 Making the Connection

Several recent health studies point to excessive sodium intake as a contributing factor to various health problems. Sodium is typically added to food in the form of table salt (NaCl). Students performed two experiments to measure the sodium levels of various canned goods.

Experiment 1

Four solutions, each containing a different amount of dissolved NaCl, were prepared in water. A coloring agent that reacts with sodium to form a blue compound that strongly absorbs light of a specific wavelength was added to each solution before they were all diluted to 100 mL with water. A control solution was also prepared with no NaCl added. The students used a *colorimeter* (a device used to measure how much light of a selected wavelength is absorbed by a sample) in order to determine the *absorbance* of each solution. The absorbances were then corrected by subtracting the absorbance of the control solution from each reading. The results are shown in Table 1.

Experiment 2

After being drained, 50-g samples of various canned vegetables were ground in a blender with 50 mL of water. The resulting mixture was filtered and then diluted to 100 mL with water. The students added the coloring agent to each solution. Then they measured the absorbance of each solution using the colorimeter, with the results shown in Table 2.

Table 1

Concentration of Na^+ (ppm)	Measured absorbance	Corrected absorbance
0.0	0.1	0.0
1.0	0.2	0.1
2.0	0.3	0.2
4.0	0.5	0.4
8.0	0.9	0.8

Table 2

Canned goods	Corrected absorbance	Concentration of Na^+ (ppm)
green beans	0.552	5.52
corn	0.439	4.39
carrots	0.024	0.24
mixed vegetables	0.123	1.23

2.3.1 Making the Connection

1. What was the measured absorbance of the solution of sodium at 4 ppm?

   A. 0.1
   B. 0.2
   C. 0.5
   D. 0.9

2. What was the corrected absorbance of the solution of sodium at 8 ppm?

   F. 0.0
   G. 0.1
   H. 0.2
   J. 0.8

3. If another sodium solution had a measured absorbance of 0.3, what would its corrected absorbance be?

   A. 0.0
   B. 0.1
   C. 0.2
   D. 0.5

4. According to Table 1, what is the predicted corrected absorbance of a sodium solution with a concentration of 8 ppm?

   F. 0.4
   G. 0.5
   H. 0.8
   J. 0.9

5. Which canned good had the highest concentration of Na^+?

   A. Green beans
   B. Corn
   C. Carrots
   D. Mixed vegetables

2.3.1 Making the Connection

Direct

Table 1			
Sample	Molarity of sample (mol/L)	Volume of solution (L)	Moles of solute (mol)
EXP.001	2.677	0.538	1.44
EXP.002	4.286	0.700	3.00
EXP.003	5.120	0.250	1.28
EXP.004	3.285	0.825	2.71

1. In Experiment 2, which of the following samples had the largest moles of solute per liter of solution?

A. EXP.001

B. EXP.002

C. EXP.003

D. EXP.004

2.3.1 Making the Connection

Connection Needed

Bacterial inhibition, by acidic or alkaline environments, can affect the efficacy of antimicrobial treatments. Two types of bacteria were measured for their levels of inhibition when acid and alkali content varied. The stronger the alkali or acid, the greater the inhibition on bacterial growth. Measurements of the diameter of the zone of inhibition in bacterial cultures, regions where there is no bacterial growth, were used to determine bacterial growth inhibition levels.

Table 1

Bacteria type	Concentration of acid (%)	Zone of inhibition (mm)	Concentration of alkali (%)	Zone of Inhibition (mm)
Micrococcus luteus	3	4.1	3	3.2
Micrococcus luteus	6	7.3	6	5.0
Micrococcus luteus	9	10.4	9	8.6
Serratia marcescens	3	2.7	3	1.4
Serratia marcescens	6	4.8	6	3.3
Serratia marcescens	9	9.1	9	7.8

2. In Table 1, which of the following values corresponds to the bacterium that has the greatest inhibition under alkaline conditions?

F. 7.3
G. 7.8
H. 8.6
J. 9.1

---

1. Direct questions: These questions require you to ______________________ from a ______________________.

2. Indirect questions: These questions require you to ______________________ a figure, chart, or graph using information found in the ______________________. They require critical thinking to determine the ______________________ information.

2.3.2 Connection Practice

Table 1				
	Simple distillation		Fractional distillation	
	Cyclohexane relative percentage (%)	Toluene relative percentage (%)	Cyclohexane relative percentage (%)	Toluene relative percentage (%)
Fraction 1 (2nd mL)	97.79	2.121	98.27	1.378
Fraction 2 (10th mL)	1.419	95.31	0.3792	99.27

In Table 1, simple and fractional distillation refer to techniques used to separate chemical mixtures by boiling point. Purification of compounds is also achieved during the distillation process. During distillation, compounds are separated into different parts called fractions. *Relative percentages* are calculated to determine the percentage of a given compound and level of purity in a fraction. A higher relative percentage indicates higher purity.

1. When comparing simple and fractional distillations, which of the following relative percentages is classified as the purest fraction of toluene?

A. 1.378%
B. 2.121%
C. 95.31%
D. 99.27%

Science Tip

Choose the Obvious Answer: If you are stuck on a science question, always choose the obvious answer choice—the one that stands out among the answer choices or is directly connected to information in the figures and passage. Resist the urge to "over-think" it.

2.3.2 Connection Practice

Table 1		
Band	Band color/description	Distance traveled (mm)
1	faint blue, thin band	41
2	pink, thick band	36
3	dark blue, thick band	20
4	faint blue, thin band	15

1. Based on Table 1, what band most likely corresponds to the smallest DNA fragment?

A. Band 1
B. Band 2
C. Band 3
D. Band 4

2.3.2 Connection Practice

A

DNA fragments are short sections of DNA that are recognized on an agarose gel as a band.

#1

B

Smaller fragments travel at a farther distance and faster pace than larger fragments.

2.3.2 Connection Practice

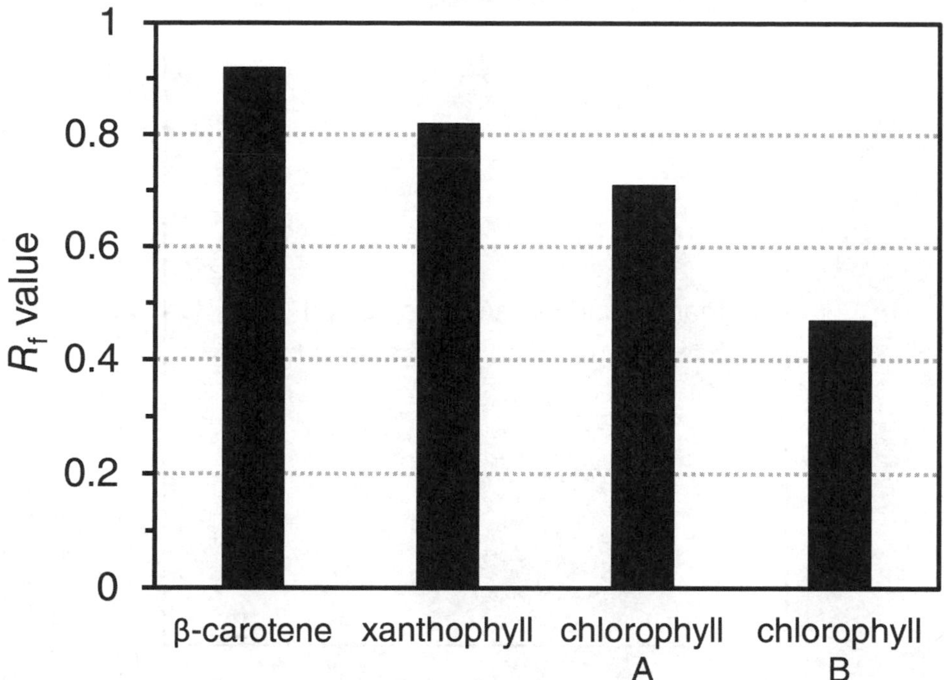

Figure 1

2. Given Figure 1, which of the following pigments migrated the fastest?

A. β-carotene only
B. Chlorophyll A and chlorophyll B
C. Xanthophyll only
D. Chlorophyll B and β-carotene

2.3.2 Connection Practice

A

Plant pigments can be separated using a technique called chromatography.

#2

B

The R_f value is directly proportional to the speed of migration for varying pigments.

2.3.2 Connection Practice

Table 1			
Compound	Molecular formula	Molecular mass (g/mol)	Branching classification
methanol	CH_4O	32.04	unbranched
ethylene	C_2H_4	28.05	unbranched
3-methylheptane	C_8H_{18}	114.23	branched
acetone	C_3H_6O	58.08	unbranched
isobutane	C_4H_{10}	58.12	branched

3. Given Table 1, which of the following compounds has the lowest boiling point, based on molecular mass?

A. Acetone
B. Isobutane
C. Ethylene
D. Methanol

2.3.2 Connection Practice

A

Boiling point is the temperature at which a compound changes phases from a liquid to a vapor (gas).

#3

B

Boiling points are generally higher for linear organic compounds that have higher molecular weights.

This page is intentionally left blank.

2.4.1 Set One

Passage I

Cloud type refers to the different names a cloud can be given depending on its shape or height in the sky. The effect of cloud types on solar radiation can be determined by measuring *cloud radiative forcing*, which is the ratio of radiation energy in a clear sky versus a cloudy sky. Table 1 shows the percentage of clouds, based on type, as well as their effect on cloud radiative forcing (LWCRF, SWCRF, and NETCRF). The NETCRF represents the overall effect on cloud radiative forcing. Figures 1–3 explain how much the constrained (predicting clear sky data) and unconstrained (using national data to determine clear sky data) models, used to predict cloud radiative forcing, vary on a monthly basis.

Table 1

Cloud types	Cloud amount (%)	LWCRF (W/m^2)	SWCRF (W/m^2)	NETCRF (W/m^2)
cumulus	5.97	1.98	–0.93	1.03
stratocumulus	3.11	1.71	–5.01	–3.30
altocumulus	6.70	2.50	–4.71	–2.22
altostratus	4.97	2.51	–9.20	–6.69
nimbostratus	1.80	–0.58	–3.32	–3.90
cirrus	21.04	25.26	–18.48	6.77
deep convective	4.06	11.36	–17.44	–6.08

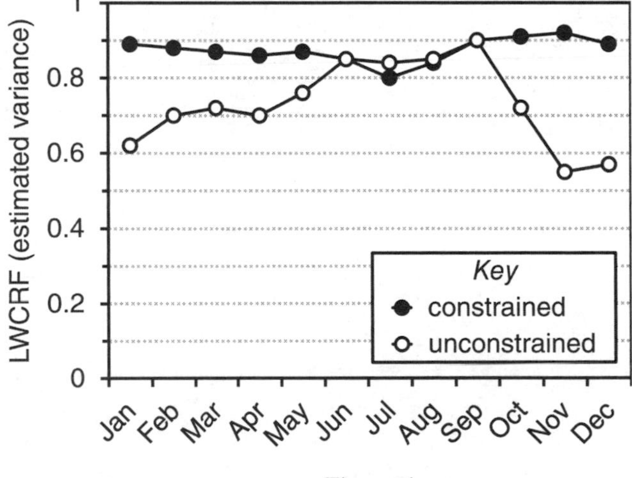

Figure 1

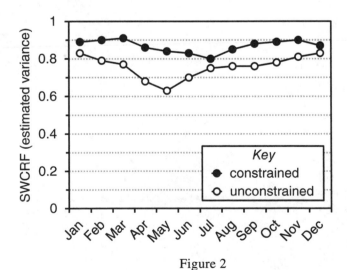

Figure 2

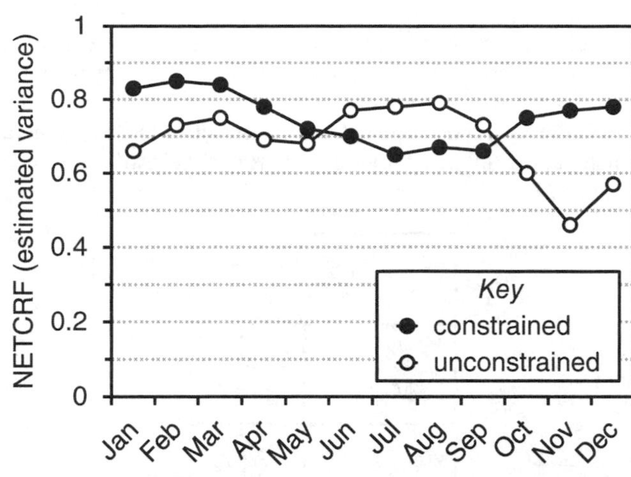

Figure 3

1. The estimated variance for the unconstrained model of cloud radiative forcing (NETCRF) in March was closest to which of the following?

   A. 0.65
   B. 0.74
   C. 0.83
   D. 0.91

2. Based on Figures 1 and 2, the lowest peak of estimated variance, in the unconstrained LWCRF and SWCRF models, correspond to which of the following months?

	LWCRF	SWCRF
F.	November	May
G.	June	September
H.	February	April
J.	August	December

3. In Figure 3, the estimated variance in the unconstrained model was about 0.45 for which of the following months?

   A. March
   B. April
   C. July
   D. November

4. Based on Figure 1, one of the points at which the constrained and unconstrained LWCRF models intersect corresponds to which month?

   F. February
   G. July
   H. September
   J. December

5. In Table 1, which cloud type had the greatest effect on cloud radiative forcing?

   A. Cirrus only
   B. Deep convective only
   C. Altostratus and deep convective
   D. Stratocumulus and nimbostratus

END OF SET ONE

STOP! DO NOT GO ON TO THE NEXT PAGE UNTIL TOLD TO DO SO.

     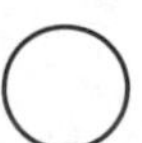     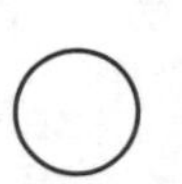

2.4.2 Set Two

Passage II

Researchers performed the following experiments in order to determine the density of five unknown metals.

Experiment 1

The water displacement method was used to determine the density of two unknown metals. A graduated cylinder was filled with 25 mL of water. An unknown metal was weighed on a balance to determine the mass. Once the metal was added to the beaker, the volume of water increased. The difference in volume was recorded, the mass of the metal was noted, and the density was calculated (see Table 1).

Table 1

Metal number	3	7
Mass (g)	14.10	12.75
Volume (mL)	8.20	1.50
Density (g/mL)	1.72	8.50

Experiment 2

The density of three unknown metals was determined using the water displacement method. A graduated cylinder was filled with 25 mL of water. The mass of the unknown metal was measured on a balance prior to its placement in the graduated cylinder. Once added, the difference in initial and final volume was noted. This volume difference and the mass of the metals were used to calculate the density (see Table 2).

Table 2

Metal number	5	2	8
Mass (g)	13.48	9.47	12.86
Volume (mL)	1.40	3.60	1.70
Density (g/mL)	9.63	2.63	7.56

Experiment 3

Given the density calculated for each unknown metal in Experiments 1 and 2, classification of metal type could be determined. The density of known metals was provided (see Table 3). Comparing calculated densities to known metal densities, the unknown metal was properly classified.

Table 3

Metal	Density (g/cm^3)
zinc	7.130
magnesium	1.738
tin	7.287
mercury	13.61
silicon	2.330
bismuth	9.807
lead	11.34
gold	19.32
iron	7.860
cobalt	8.860
aluminum	2.699
copper	8.960

6. In Experiment 1, the density, in g/mL, of the metal that increased the volume to 33.2 mL was found to be:

   F. 1.72
   G. 7.57
   H. 9.63
   J. 8.57

7. Based on Experiment 1, if the volume of Metal 7 was doubled and the mass was held constant, the calculated density would be:

   A. decreased by $\frac{1}{4}$.
   B. decreased by $\frac{1}{2}$.
   C. unaffected.
   D. increased by $\frac{1}{2}$.

8. According to Experiment 3, the metal bismuth corresponds most closely to which unknown metal?

   F. 3
   G. 5
   H. 7
   J. 8

9. In Experiment 2, if the density of a new unknown metal were 5.26 g/mL and the same mass as metal 2 were used, what would be the corresponding volume?

   A. 0.6 mL
   B. 1.8 mL
   C. 3.6 mL
   D. 49.8 mL

10. Table 1 lists the volume for two unknown metals. According to Experiment 1, what does this volume represent?

   F. The decrease in volume after the metal is added to the beaker
   G. The inverse amount of the density for the given unknown metal
   H. The difference between the initial and final volumes of water
   J. The ratio for the mass and density of each unknown metal

END OF SET TWO
STOP! DO NOT GO ON TO THE NEXT PAGE
UNTIL TOLD TO DO SO.

2.4.3 Set Three

Passage III

Different types of pigments in autotrophic organisms (such as plants) can affect the *rate of photosynthesis*, which is the energy absorbed from light over time. Researchers performed two experiments to study the relationship between pigmentation and photosynthesis. A chromatography analysis, where pigments were separated by size and solubility, was performed. A spectrophotometer was used to measure the percentage of light absorbed for varying pigment types.

Experiment 1

Filter paper was cut into small sections and marked with a pencil line on both ends. These marked lines were not more than 1 cm away from each end. Additionally a 25-mL beaker was filled with approximately 1 mL of an alcohol solvent (see Figure 1).

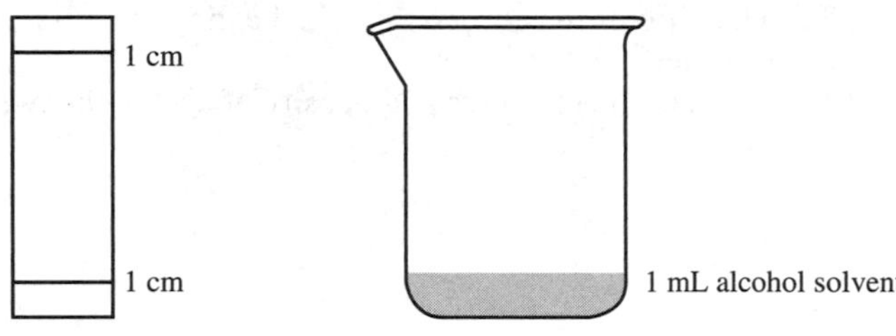

Figure 1

A leaf was cut into several different sections. Each section was individually placed on top of the filter paper, smearing its green color across the paper. The process of smearing the leaf sections was repeated each time. However, new leaf sections were used for each repeated process.

Following smearing, the tip of the filter paper was placed in the beaker containing the alcohol solvent. Careful attention was given to the filter paper ensuring it did not touch the sides of the beaker. The solvent (containing the green pigment) was allowed to travel up the filter paper toward the pencil mark. The distance traveled for the solvent band and different pigment bands, for each color observed, are displayed in Table 1.

Table 1

Bands	Distance traveled (mm)	Band color
1	0	colorless
2	10	brown
3	32	green
4	45	yellow

Experiment 2

Differences in pigmentation can affect the amount of light absorbed. To investigate the effect pigmentation has on photosynthesis, the percent absorbance of several treated leaf samples were measured at four different wavelengths (λ). This data is summarized in Table 2.

Table 2

Cuvette	Samples	λ_1	λ_2	λ_3	λ_4
1	solvent	0%	0%	0%	0%
2	unboiled/dark	22%	29%	21%	25%
3	unboiled/light	15%	20%	17%	14%
4	boiled/light	35%	39%	32%	33%
5	no chloroplasts	49%	52%	58%	47%

11. Based on Table 1, which of the following pigment colors falls within the measured distance traveled range of 30–37 mm?

    A. Colorless
    B. Yellow
    C. Brown
    D. Green

12. What is the correct distance traveled, in mm, for the solvent band in Experiment 1?

    F. 0
    G. 10
    H. 32
    J. 45

13. According to Table 2, which samples absorbed the smallest percentage of light at wavelength λ_3 compared to their measurements at the other three wavelengths?

    A. unboiled/dark and unboiled/light
    B. unboiled/dark and boiled/light
    C. boiled/light and no chloroplasts
    D. unboiled/dark and no chlorplasts

14. According to Experiment 2, at wavelength λ_2, what sample had a percent absorbance greater than 45%?

    F. No chloroplasts
    G. Unboiled/dark
    H. Boiled/light
    J. Unboiled/light

15. Table 1 lists the distance each pigment band traveled following chromatographic analysis of a leaf. What most likely caused Band 4 to travel at a farther distance than Band 2?

    A. Size of filter paper
    B. Solubility
    C. Pigment odor
    D. Time

END OF SET THREE

STOP! DO NOT GO ON TO THE NEXT PAGE UNTIL TOLD TO DO SO.

Sum It Up

Select Data and Features Part 2

Direct questions
Questions that require you to read information from a figure, chart, or graph.

Indirect questions
Questions that require you to interpret a figure, chart, or graph using information found in the passage. These questions require critical thinking to determine the missing connecting information.

Tips and Techniques

Choose the Obvious Answer: If you are stuck on a science question, always choose the obvious answer choice—the one that stands out among the answer choices or is directly connected to information in the figures and passage. Resist the urge to "over-think" it.

Lesson 3

Support of Hypotheses Part 1

CAPTION:

3.1 Entrance Ticket

Answer the questions below.

The melanic peppered moth's dark coloring is passed to its progeny and thus is an inheritable trait. This moth is shown in Figure 1.

Figure 1

Researchers have studied the melanic peppered moth in both Britain and the United States from the late 1950s to the mid-1990s. These researchers have monitored both the population of the melanic peppered moth and the levels of soot pollution in an attempt to correlate the two values.

Study 1

Researchers calculated the percentage of melanic moths at sites in both Britain and the United States and tabulated this data over a course of more than 30 years. This calculation is shown in Figure 2 (top). To account for any change in the percentage of melanic moths, the total number of moths during June and July were also observed during the same course of more than 30 years. This calculation is also shown in Figure 2 (bottom).

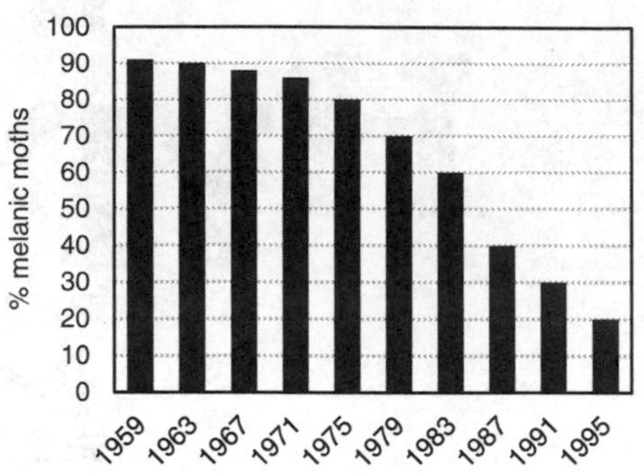

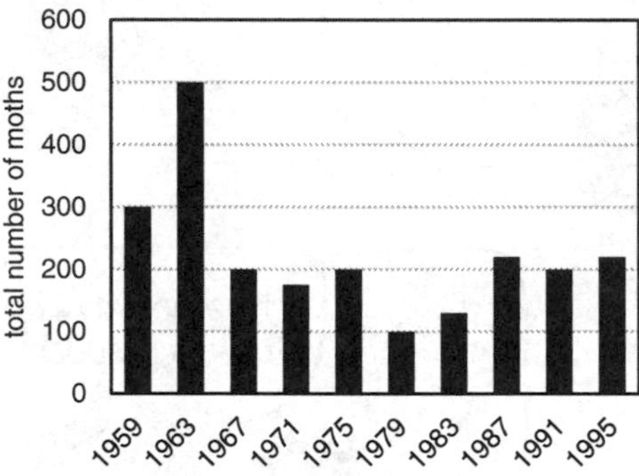

Figure 2

Study 2

After analyzing the results from Study 1, the researchers then looked at the pollution levels in both the United States and in Britain. The pollution levels from Detroit (US) over a span of 26 years is shown in Figure 3 (top). Accordingly, the pollution levels from a site in Britain over a span of 26 years is shown in Figure 3 (bottom).

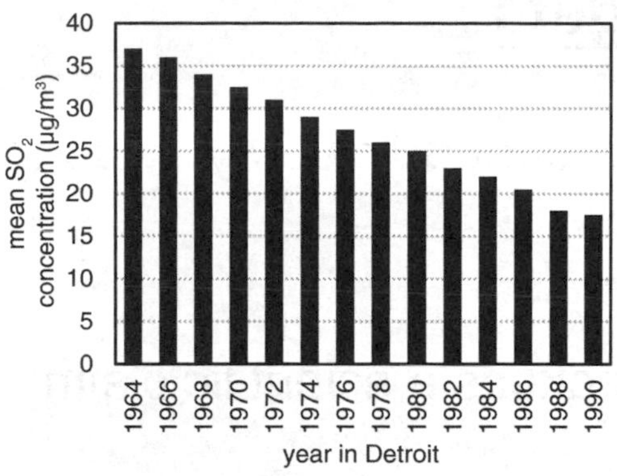

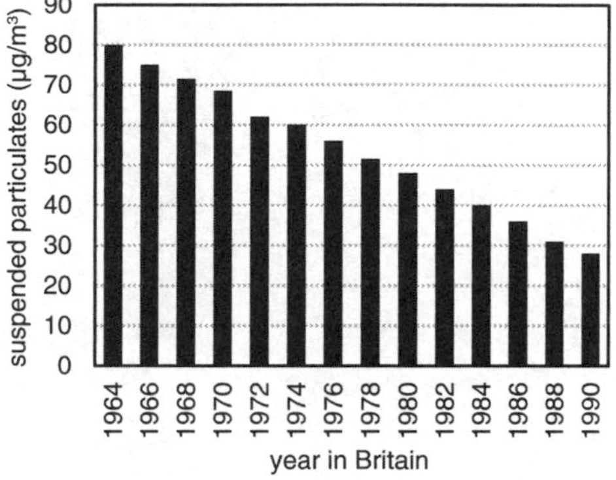

Figure 3

1. The scientists hypothesized that the population of the melanic peppered moth decreased with the decrease of particulate air pollution because the moths were then more susceptible to predation and thus could not pass their genes on to the next generation. Do Figures 2 and 3 support this hypothesis?

A. No; the decrease of the peppered moth population correlates with the overall decrease of moth numbers.

B. Yes; the decrease of the peppered moth population correlates with the decrease of SO_2 and particulate pollution.

C. No; there was no noticeable decrease in the numbers of the peppered moth population.

D. Yes; the decrease of the peppered moth population and the total moth population correlate with the decrease of SO_2 and particulate pollution.

2. Suppose it is discovered that rising pollution levels of certain carbon compounds not tested in this study led to an increase in the overall percentage of melanic moths in the general moth population. This discovery would most strongly contradict which of the following figures?

F. Figure 2, top

G. Figure 2, bottom

H. Figure 3, top

J. Figure 3, bottom

3. Suppose a separate study confirms that the percentage of melanic moths decreases with decreasing levels of pollution. Do the results of Study 2 support the statement "The number of melanic moths fell in Detroit, but increased in Great Britain"?

A. Yes, because the graphs show decreasing levels of pollution in Detroit, but increasing levels of pollution in Great Britain.

B. Yes, because the graphs show a relatively stable amount of melanic moths in Detroit but a sharp drop in melanic moths in Great Britain.

C. No, because pollution levels in both Detroit and Great Britain fell, which would indicate a decrease in the percentage of melanic moths for both countries.

D. No, because pollution levels in Great Britain decreased, while the pollution levels in Detroit increased, which would indicate that the number of melanic moths increased in Detroit and fell in Great Britain.

3.2 Learning Targets

1. Identify which hypothesis is supported or contradicted by evidence in a science experiment

2. Identify what information supports or weakens a scientific claim

Self-Assessment

Circle the number that corresponds to your confidence level in your knowledge of this subject before beginning the lesson. A score of 1 means you are completely lost, and a score of 4 means you have mastered the skills. After you finish the lesson, return to the bottom of this page and circle your new confidence level to show your improvement.

Before Lesson

1 2 3 4

After Lesson

1 2 3 4

3.3.1 Determining Support

Substances that absorb light are called pigments. Different pigments show maximum absorption of light at different wavelengths, reflecting the unabsorbed wavelengths. Varying forms of chlorophyll in plants lead to a large variety in the coloring of plant leaves due to discrete absorption profiles.

Figure 1 shows the absorption spectra for chlorophyll *a*, chlorophyll *b*, and β-carotene, important compounds in photosynthesis. These spectra show the relative absorption of light by each compound as a function of wavelength.

Figure 2 shows how the rate of photosynthesis varies with the wavelength of absorbed light for chlorophyll *a*.

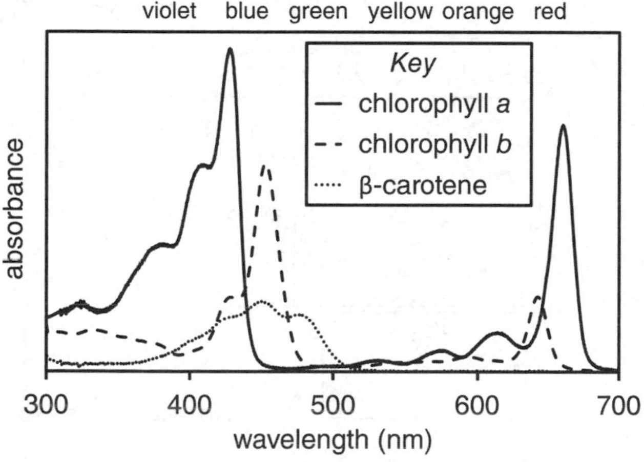

Figure 1

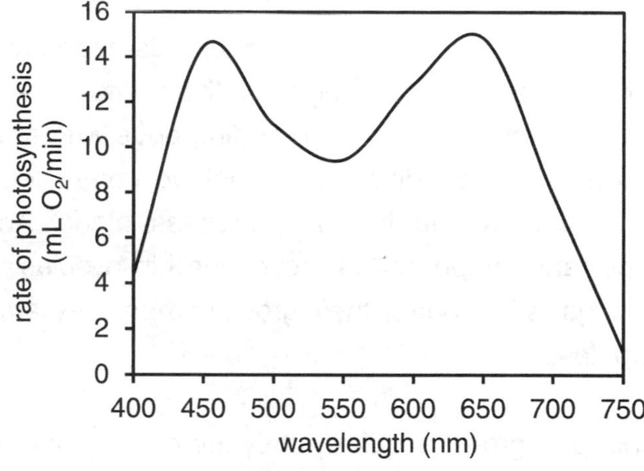

Figure 2

1. Which of the following is best supported by Figure 1?
   A. Chlorophyll *a* absorbs the most light at blue and red wavelengths.
   B. Chlorophyll *a* absorbs the most light at green and yellow wavelengths.
   C. Chlorophyll *a* absorbs the most light at violet and green wavelengths.
   D. Chlorophyll *a* absorbs the most light at yellow and orange wavelengths.

3.3.1 Determining Support

Hip dysplasia is a common concern for large breed dogs. It causes pain and joint damage and can greatly reduce a dog's quality of life. While breeders attempt to avoid breeding dogs who are prone to this condition, it cannot be completely eliminated by the breeding process alone. An important component of preventing hip dysplasia in dogs is to control their growth when they are puppies.

If puppies grow too quickly, they are more prone to hip dysplasia. The aim for puppies is to have slow, steady growth until they reach their adult size. One of the ways this is accomplished is by feeding large breed dogs specially formulated foods with carefully balanced calcium (Ca) and phosphorus (P) content.

A study followed the growth of two different breeds of puppies who were fed different dog food formulas over the course of one year. The puppies were weighed at the beginning of the study. The figures give the average weight of both breeds of dog from month to month for twelve months.

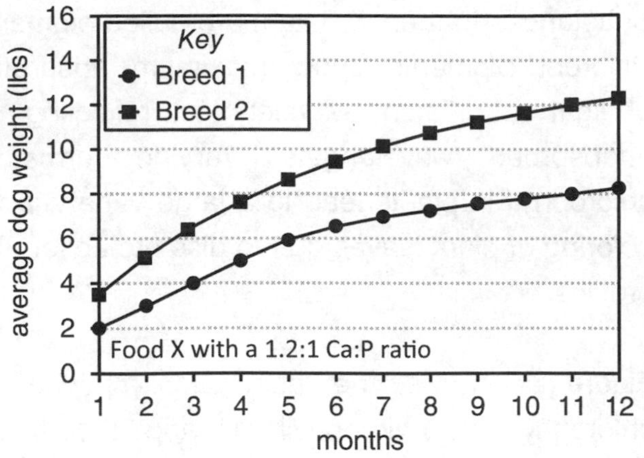

Figure 1

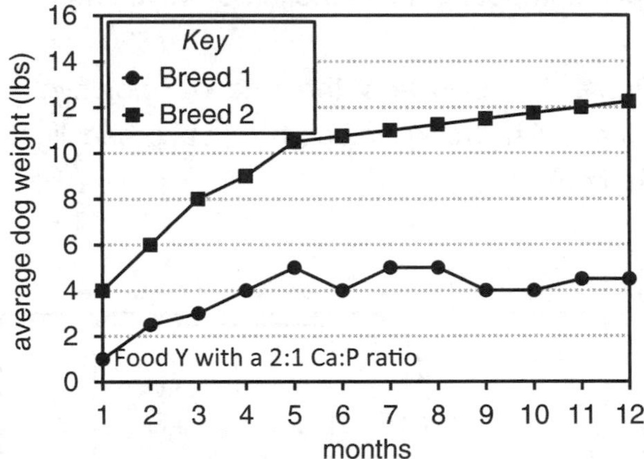

Figure 2

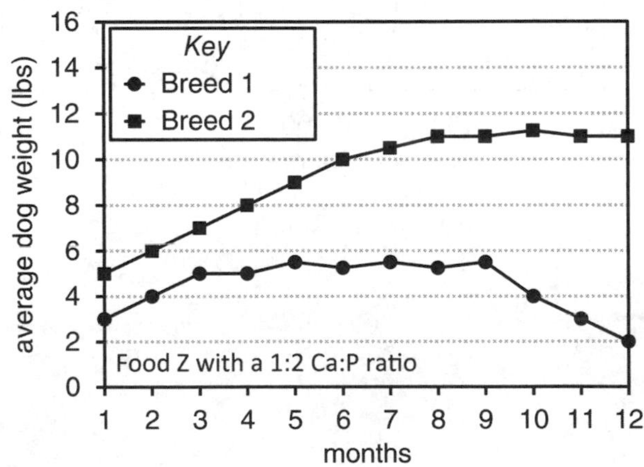

Figure 3

3.3.1 Determining Support

1. Which of the following statements about the Ca:P ratio in various dog foods is best supported by the information in Figures 1–3? Over the course of 12 months:

A. a 1.2:1 Ca:P ratio resulted in the smallest total weight change for Breed 1 puppies.

B. a 2:1 Ca:P ratio resulted in the smallest total weight change for Breed 1 puppies.

C. a 1:2 Ca:P ratio resulted in the smallest total weight change for Breed 1 puppies.

D. all foods resulted in the same total change in weight for Breed 1 puppies.

2. Which of the following statements about Breed 2 puppies is best supported by the information from Figures 1–3?

F. Breed 2 puppies fed the 2:1 Ca:P ratio food showed the most growth.

G. Breed 2 puppies fed the 1.2:1 Ca:P ratio food showed the most growth.

H. Breed 2 puppies fed the 1.2:1 Ca:P ratio food showed the least growth.

J. Food choice did not affect Breed 2 puppy growth.

3.3.2 Introducing New Information

Are boys or girls better able to kiss their own elbows?

Scientist 1: Girls are better than boys at kissing their own elbows.

Class Experiment:
☐ supports
☐ weakens

New Discovery:
☐ supports
☐ weakens

Scientist 2: Boys and girls have the same ability to kiss their own elbows.

Class Experiment:
☐ supports
☐ weakens

New Discovery:
☐ supports
☐ weakens

Scientist 3: No one can kiss their own elbow.

New Discovery:
☐ supports
☐ weakens

Science Tip

Keep Your Pencil Moving: When you are reading a *conflicting viewpoints* passage, the key is to focus on the main point of each scientist. Most of the time the scientist's argument is in the first sentence. Underline it along with any other facts the scientist uses to prove the argument.

3.3.2 Introducing New Information

Visible light is part of the electromagnetic spectrum ranging from wavelengths of 390 to 740 nanometers (nm). See Figure 1 for the range of wavelengths attributed to different colors. In order to test the effect of the light's wavelength on plant growth, the following experiment was performed.

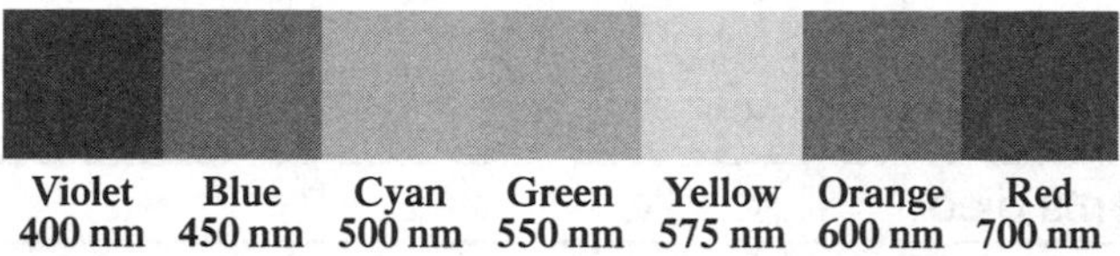

Figure 1

Experiment

Seedling tomato plants were placed in separate rooms under distinct lighting regimens, five plants to each set, and exposed to twelve hours of light each day. Lights that produce various wavelength ranges were placed in each room. The percentage of different emitted colors was quantified (Table 1). The plants were provided the same soil, temperature, and nutrient blend and were grown for 60 days. At the end of that time, the plants were harvested, separated, and dried, and the components were weighed (the average of each set is reported). Additionally, the fruit was evaluated for taste and general nutritional quality on a simplified 1–10 scale (Table 2).

Hypothesis 1

Ultraviolet light, while generally harmful to living creatures, has a beneficial effect on plant growth in small quantities.

Hypothesis 2

The color we see when looking at something is the wavelength of light that is being reflected back while the other wavelengths are being absorbed by the object we are viewing. Therefore, exposing a plant to predominantly green light will negatively affect its health.

Hypothesis 3

Some wavelengths will positively affect the growth of plants, some will negatively affect the growth of plants, and others will have no effect. The optimum color blend is one that eliminates the wavelengths that do nothing or harm the plant.

Table 1

Experiment	Percentage of colors			
	Ultraviolet	Blue	Green	Red
1	100	0	0	0
2	0	100	0	0
3	0	0	100	0
4	0	0	0	100
5	25	25	25	25
6	0	60	20	20
7	0	33	34	33
8	0	20	60	20
9	0	20	20	60
10	10	30	30	30

3.3.2 Introducing New Information

Table 2							
	Weight (mg)					Fruit quality	
Experiment	Roots	Stem	Leaves	Fruit	Total	Taste	Nutrition
1	Plants died						
2	1060	120	640	2180	4000	5	5
3	1254	171	304	2071	3800	5	5
4	1220	360	240	2180	4000	5	5
5	Plants died						
6	1485	190	600	2725	5000	7	7
7	1815	247.5	440	2997.5	5500	9	9
8	1650	225	400	2725	5000	7	7
9	1585	340	350	2725	5000	7	7
10	1815	247.5	440	2997.5	5500	10	10

1. Which of the hypotheses, if any, is strengthened by the results of Experiment 3?

A. Hypothesis 1
B. Hypothesis 2
C. Hypothesis 3
D. None of the hypotheses

2. Hypothesis 2 would be most weakened if which of the following observations had been made?

F. Experiment 1 had not resulted in plant death.
G. Experiment 3 had resulted in better-than-average plant growth.
H. Experiment 7 had resulted in the highest quality of fruit.
J. Experiment 10 had resulted in plant death.

This page is intentionally left blank.

3.4.1 Set One

Passage I

A *radioactive isotope* is a nuclide that decays spontaneously by releasing subatomic particles and energy. This decay can lead to a change in the number of protons, which transforms the nuclide into a different element. An example of this is radioactive carbon-14 (^{14}C), which decays into nitrogen-14 (^{14}N).

Radioactive isotopes have many scientific uses. One of these is to aid in the study of cell chemistry. Scientists use radioactive isotopes as markers to follow certain metabolic processes or to locate a compound within a cell or organism. This is known as radioactive labeling.

A science class is using radioactive isotopes to determine how heat impacts the rate at which cells make new copies of their DNA.

Student 1 hypothesizes that cells will make more DNA as temperature increases.

Student 2 hypothesizes that cells will make more DNA as temperature increases to a point, but then they will begin to make less DNA as temperature continues to increase.

Student 3 hypothesizes that cells will make less DNA as temperature increases.

To test these hypotheses, the following experimental steps were performed:

1. The students place cells in a dish that includes compounds necessary to synthesize DNA. They then label one of the compounds with ^{3}H, a radioactive isotope of hydrogen known as *tritium*. Any newly synthesized DNA will contain the ^{3}H marker.

2. Students then divide the cells into groups and incubate each group at a different temperature.

3. Students take samples from each group and test their DNA for radioactivity in a device called a scintillation counter. The DNA samples are placed in containers with a radiation-sensitive compound that emits a photon of light whenever it encounters radiation from the decay of ^{3}H. These photons are counted and plotted on a graph against the temperature at which the DNA was incubated (Figures 1–3).

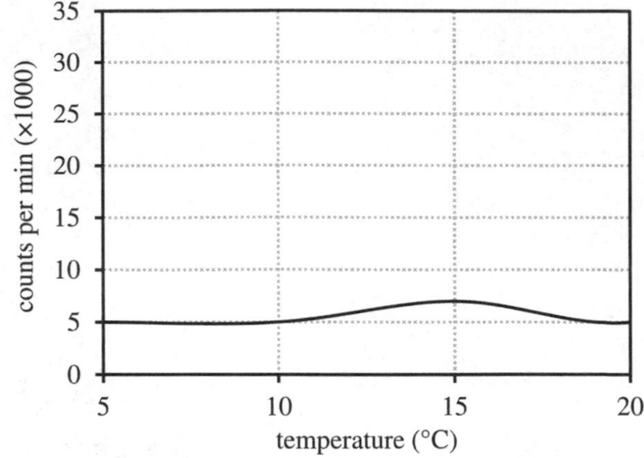

Figure 1

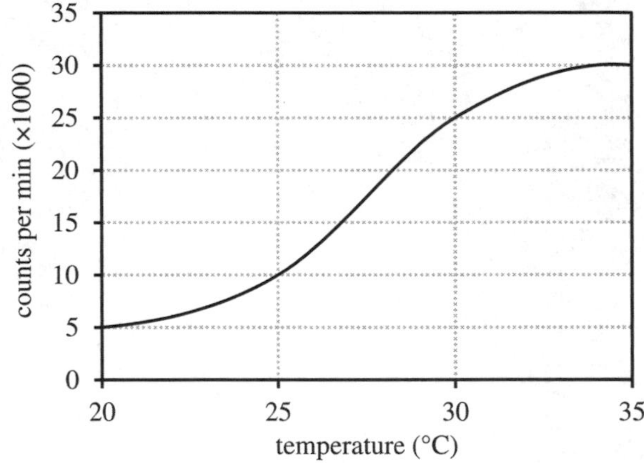

Figure 2

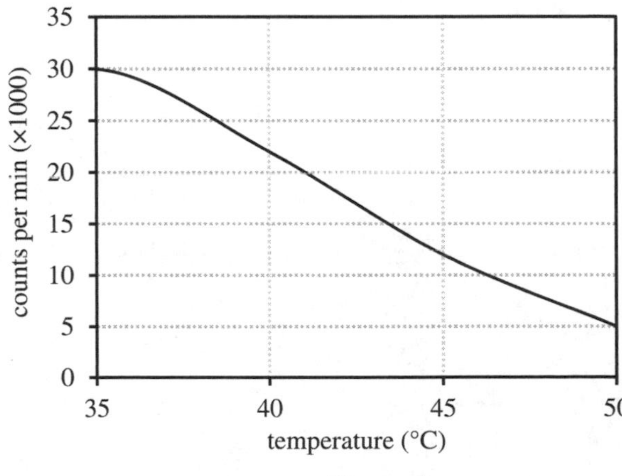

Figure 3

1. Which of the following statements about the effect of temperature on DNA production is best supported by Figures 2 and 3?

   A. DNA production increases only from 30°C to 45°C.
   B. DNA production decreases only from 30°C to 45°C.
   C. DNA production peaks at 35°C.
   D. DNA production peaks at 45°C.

2. Which of the following statements about the effect of temperature on DNA production is best supported by Figures 1–3?

   F. As incubation temperature increases, DNA production increases.
   G. As incubation temperature increases, DNA production decreases.
   H. As incubation temperature increases, DNA production increases then decreases.
   J. Incubation temperature has no impact on DNA production.

3. The scintillation counter registers 5,000 counts per minute at 10°C and 50°C. Which of the following conclusions about incubation temperature and DNA production can be supported by Figures 1 and 3?

   A. Very high and very low incubation temperatures both result in low DNA production.
   B. Very high and very low incubation temperatures both result in high DNA production.
   C. Very high incubation temperatures result in low DNA production, but very low incubation temperatures result in high DNA production.
   D. Very low incubation temperatures result in low DNA production, but very high incubation temperatures result in high DNA production.

4. Consider the 3 students' hypotheses on the effect of temperature on DNA production. Based on the results of the study, which student's prediction, if any, was correct?

   F. Student 1's only
   G. Student 2's only
   H. Student 3's only
   J. None of the hypotheses

5. Student 1 suggested that cells would produce more DNA as temperature increased. The results of Figure 2 provided which piece of evidence that supported the student's hypothesis?

   A. DNA production remained stable between 20°C and 30°C.
   B. DNA production decreased between 20°C and 30°C.
   C. DNA production increased between 20°C and 30°C.
   D. DNA production increased between 20°C and 30 °C and then decreased between 30°C and 40°C.

END OF SET ONE

STOP! DO NOT GO ON TO THE NEXT PAGE UNTIL TOLD TO DO SO.

3.4.2 Set Two

Passage II

Due to advances in medical science, human life expectancy is constantly increasing. As greater numbers of people live longer lives, researchers are becoming more familiar with complex signs of aging. However, while scientists understand the signs of aging, the molecular causes of aging remain a mystery.

Three scientists propose models to explain the human aging process.

Scientist 1

Aging is caused by an accumulation of mutations that cause damage to the body or prevent it from being repaired. This accumulation eventually causes death. Because most mammals do not live long enough in nature to worry about this process (having been killed by accident, disease, or predators), the body possesses few resources for addressing these mutations. What resources the body does possess are adapted to be most effective in youth, ensuring the animal lives long enough to propagate its species.

Scientist 2

Aging is caused by genetic tradeoffs, where a gene that provides a competitive advantage early in life exacts a negative effect later in life. Evolution is a race in which the fastest, strongest, most fertile creatures outbreed their competitors, causing their species to dominate, even if that speed, strength, and fertility comes at the cost of a shorter life. A gene that suppresses cancer might also suppress stem cells, thus providing better health early in life at the cost of the ability to replenish worn out cells. Modern genomic analysis has shown that most genes that cause aging are not mutations but are actually common across the species.

Scientist 3

Aging is caused by an accumulation of damage that eventually reaches the point of critical non-viability. While damage can be healed, the repaired cells are not always as functional as the original cells. As more and more cells lose effectiveness, the ability of the body to repair is decreased, reducing the effectiveness of repaired cells further, leading to a downward spiral that results in death. While some genes that cause aging show direct linkages to trade-offs in youth, many genes that cause aging do not. Similarly, while these genes have no discernable positive value—and considerable negative value—they are also common across the species, thus demonstrating they are not random mutations unique to the individual.

6. Scientist 1's model would be most weakened if which of the following observations were made?

F. A child possesses as many mutation clearing resources as an adult.
G. An adult possesses fewer mutation clearing resources than a child.
H. Age-causing genes do not possess positive tradeoffs in youth.
J. A child possesses the same ability to repair cells as an adult.

7. The scientist who describes the accumulated damage hypothesis implies that the mutation hypothesis is weakened by which of the following observations?

A. Genes that cause aging are common across species.
B. Genes that cause aging have no discernable positive value.
C. As the body ages, its ability to repair is decreased.
D. Repaired cells are sometimes not as effective as new cells.

8. Scientist 3's model would be most weakened by which of the following observations?

F. Cells with lower healing capacity are found in all species.
G. Genes are reproduced at a lower rate after cells repair damage.
H. Aging cells reproduce damaged genes while younger cells do not.
J. Repaired cells are found to be restored to full function after repairing damages.

9. Scientist 2's model would be best supported by which of the following observations?

A. Young cells have fewer mutations than old cells.
B. Old cells have fewer mutations than young cells.
C. A gene that increases cancer risk late in life increases fertility early in life.
D. Damaged cells are not as capable of reproducing as healthy cells.

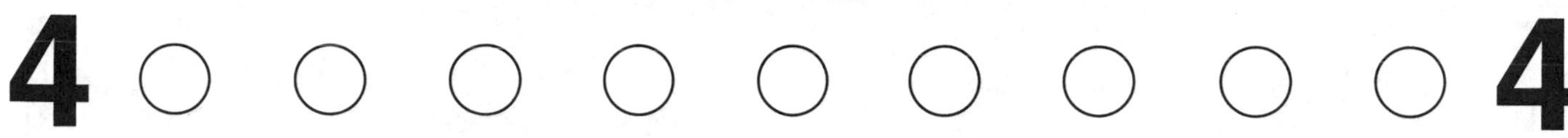

10. According to the genetic tradeoff hypothesis, which of the following observations provides the strongest evidence that aging is not caused by mutations?

F. Genes which have negative effects in older organisms are common across the species.
G. A cell has the fewest mutations when it is young.
H. Some genes responsible for aging show no positive value in youth.
J. A child has more ability to repair cells than an adult.

END OF SET TWO
STOP! DO NOT GO ON TO THE NEXT PAGE
UNTIL TOLD TO DO SO.

3.4.3 Set Three

Passage III

It has been proposed for several decades that plants found in rainforests and jungles may harbor compounds that act as natural antibiotics or natural inhibitors of virus replication. Viruses such as hepatitis C virus (HCV) are large contributors to illness and death around the world. HCV in particular is infamous for causing diseases of the liver, and HCV has no vaccine.

In a recent study, researchers isolated compounds from Brazilian plants such as *Maytenus ilicifolia* and *Peperomia blanda*. These compounds were then used to test if they inhibited HCV replication in at least two cell lines, the examples being a liver cell line (Huh 7.5 cells) and another cell line (JFH1 cells) used as a positive control.

In their experiment, researchers added several test compounds they isolated from the plants to the HCV-infected cell lines and tested to see if the HCV virus replicated in the cells 48 hours after incubation. The researchers experimented with several concentrations of the compounds to determine what concentration stopped HCV in 50% of the infected cell population—this value is known as EC_{50}. The researchers also found the maximum concentration for each compound where the maximum amount of HCV replication was stopped without adverse effects on the cell lines and the percent inhibition occurring at that maximum amount. This data is summarized in Table 1.

Table 1

Compound	EC_{50} (μM)	Maximum concentration (μM)	Huh 7.5 cells	JFH1 cells
			% Inhibition	
APS	2.3	50	100	96
3*43	4.0	12.5	92	100
3*20	8.2	25	87	100
5*362	38.9	50	68	38

11. APS was isolated from *Maytenus ilicifolia*, while the other 3 compounds were isolated from *Peperomia blanda*. A researcher hypothesized that the compound from *Maytenus ilicifolia* would be superior in stopping HCV replication in the liver for both the EC_{50} and the maximum concentration. Given the data in Table 1, is this hypothesis correct?

A. Yes; APS had both the lowest EC_{50} value and the lowest Huh 7.5 inhibition value at maximum concentration.
B. No; APS had the 2nd lowest EC_{50} value and the highest Huh 7.5 inhibition value at maximum concentration.
C. Yes; APS had the highest Huh 7.5 inhibition value at maximum concentration, and the lowest EC_{50} value.
D. No; APS had the highest EC_{50} value and the highest Huh 7.5 inhibition value at maximum concentration.

12. Do the results of the experiment support the hypothesis that the 5*362 compound inhibits Huh 7.5 cells more than JFH1 cells?

F Yes; the EC_{50} value of the 5*362 compound is 38.9, indicating that it affected the experimental variable more than the control variable.
G. Yes; the percent inhibition of Huh 7.5 cells is greater for the compound 5*362 than the inhibition of JFH1 cells for the same compound.
H. No; the maximum concentration of the 5*362 compound is the same as the control, indicating no effect on the inhibition of either cell.
J. No; the percent inhibition of JFH1 cells is greater than the percent inhibition of Huh 7.5 cells, contradicting the hypothesis.

13. Do the results of Table 1 support the hypothesis that HCV was affected by the compounds?

A. Yes, because HCV replication was inhibited.
B. Yes, because HCV replication was not inhibited.
C. No, because HCV replication was inhibited.
D. No, because HCV replication was not inhibited.

14. A set of researchers found that 50% of the infected cell population is only inhibited at a concentration—of any inhibiting compound—of 12.5 μM. This observation contradicts evidence in what part of the table?

F. The column labeled EC_{50}, which shows that different compounds stopped HCV in 50% of the infected cell population at different concentrations.
G. The column labeled EC_{50}, which shows that different compounds affect different percentages of the infected cell population, from 2.3% to 38.9%.
H. The column labeled maximum concentration, which shows that HCV is inhibited by most compounds at a concentration of 50 μM.
J. The column labeled maximum concentration, which shows that different compounds had different maximum concentrations where the maximum amount of HCV replication was stopped without adversely affecting the cells.

15. A student hypothesized that HCV was most adversely affected by the compound 5*362. Does the data in the table support this hypothesis?

A. Yes, because the table shows that the EC_{50} and maximum concentration of the compound 5*362 are the highest.
B. Yes, because the percent inhibition for both Huh 7.5 cells and JFH1 cells are highest in the row labeled 5*362.
C. No, because the table indicates that the compound APS most adversely affects HCV, not the compound 5*362.
D. No, because the table shows that a lower concentration of 5*362 is needed to stop HCV in 50% of the population than the other compounds.

END OF SET THREE
STOP! DO NOT GO ON TO THE NEXT PAGE
UNTIL TOLD TO DO SO.

Sum It Up

Support of Hypotheses Part 1

Statement
An expression in speech or writing

Conclusion
A judgment or decision

Claim
An assertion or statement, often without proof

Hypothesis
An explanation based on limited evidence, used as a starting point for further investigation

---

Prediction
A statement about what might happen or what will happen in the future

---

Evidence
Information supporting that something else exists or is true

Result
An outcome that is caused by something else

Data
Facts or information used to calculate, analyze, or plan something

Tips and Techniques

Keep Your Pencil Moving: When you are reading a *conflicting viewpoints* passage, the key is to focus on the main point of each scientist. Most of the time the scientist's argument is in the first sentence. Underline it along with any other facts the scientist uses to prove the argument.

Lesson 4

Support of Hypotheses Part 2

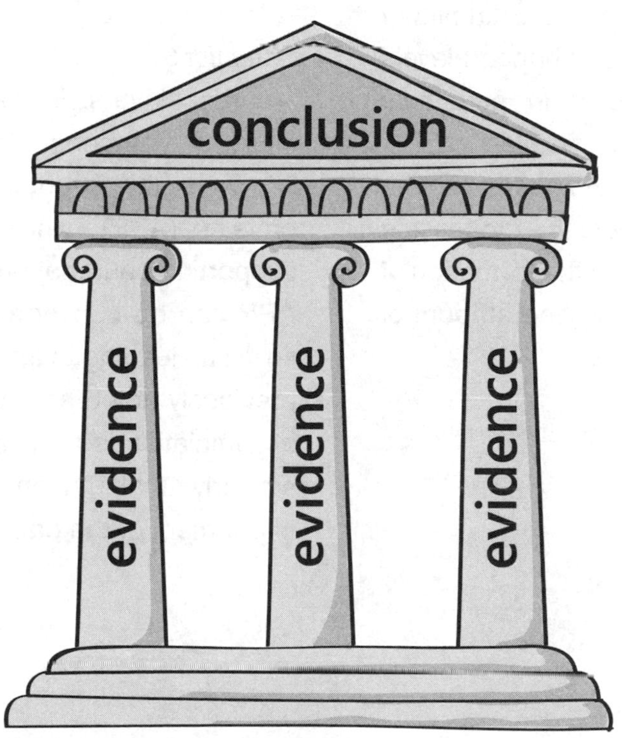

CAPTION:

4.1 Entrance Ticket

Solve the questions below.

Passage I

Due to advances in treatment of traumatic injuries, people are increasingly living to an age where neurodegenerative diseases become a concern. Although Alzheimer's disease is one of the most studied of this class of illnesses that most often affect the elderly, the exact causes of the disease remain a mystery to scientists.

Three scientists propose possible causes related to environmental factors.

Scientist 1

Alzheimer's is caused by exposure to aluminum in the environment of the patient. Enhanced levels of aluminum have been detected in pyramidal neurons containing neurofibrillar tangles (NFT), a major pathological feature of Alzheimer's. The aluminum binds to DNA and affects the processing of cytoskeletal proteins, resulting in the formation of NFT. As the levels of NFT increase, the amount of neurons lost increases.

Scientist 2

Alzheimer's is caused by improper diet and malnutrition. Chronic deficiencies in calcium and magnesium result in the development of NFT. Additionally, high levels of dietary cholesterol produce an increase in deposits of amyloid beta (AB), a precursor to amyloid plaques that are toxic to nerve cells. Thus, poor diet produces neurotoxicity and leads to Alzheimer's. Although many Alzheimer's patients do show increased levels of aluminum, recent studies have indicated the accumulation of aluminum to be a symptom of damaged brains, not a cause of the damage.

Scientist 3

Alzheimer's is caused by traumatic brain injury. A component of the brain's response to injury is the production of amyloid precursor proteins (APP), which maintain cell function by supporting neuronal growth and survival. However, APP can be converted to AB within the synaptic terminal, leading to an increase in amyloid plaques previously noted as toxic to nerve cells. Aluminum accumulation is a symptom of brain damage, and similarly, malnutrition is a result of the mental impairment of the patient.

4.1 Entrance Ticket

1. The scientist who describes the traumatic brain injury theory implies that the malnutrition theory is weakened by which of the following observations?
   - **A.** The disease causes mental impairment, which in turn causes the patient to have a poor diet.
   - **B.** Malnutrition leads to an increase in amyloid precursor proteins.
   - **C.** Amyloid plaques are a precursor to amyloid beta.
   - **D.** Amyloid beta leads to increased neurofibrillar tangles.

2. Which of the following observations would most weaken Scientist 1's theory?
   - **F.** People with increased accumulation of aluminum show the same number of neurofibrillar tangles as those without increased accumulation.
   - **G.** Elderly brains have more neurofibrillar tangles than young brains.
   - **H.** Patients with low cholesterol diets have greater accumulations of amyloid beta than patients with high cholesterol diets.
   - **J.** Patients with high cholesterol diets have greater accumulations of amyloid beta than patients with low cholesterol diets.

3. Which of the following observations would most strengthen Scientist 2's theory?
   - **A.** Because Alzheimer's patients are prone to mental impairment, their diets are low in calcium and magnesium.
   - **B.** Patients with high cholesterol diets have greater accumulations of amyloid beta than patients with low cholesterol diets.
   - **C.** Patients with low cholesterol diets have greater accumulations of amyloid beta than patients with high cholesterol diets.
   - **D.** Traumatic brain injuries do not increase production of amyloid precursor proteins.

4.2 Learning Targets

1. Determine whether new information supports or weakens given arguments

Self-Assessment

Circle the number that corresponds to your confidence level in your knowledge of this subject before beginning the lesson. A score of 1 means you are completely lost, and a score of 4 means you have mastered the skills. After you finish the lesson, return to the bottom of this page and circle your new confidence level to show your improvement.

Before Lesson

1 2 3 4

After Lesson

1 2 3 4

4.3.1 Supporting the Hypothesis

During combustion and other manmade and natural processes, various trace elements and compounds are introduced into the atmosphere as gases. Precipitation can retrieve these elements from the atmosphere and bring them back to Earth in a process known as wet deposition. Analyzing the water collected from areas around power plants (which can release metal and sulfide ions into the atmosphere) is useful in determining how much pollution is being emitted by the plant.

Study 1

Rain gauges were used to determine the average monthly amount of rainfall in the area containing a waste-to-energy plant (WEP) located in Northern Italy. Rain amounts were measured by rain gauges at 6 sites around the plant between the years of 2006–2009. The average monthly rain values (in mm) at the 6 sites are shown in Figure 1.

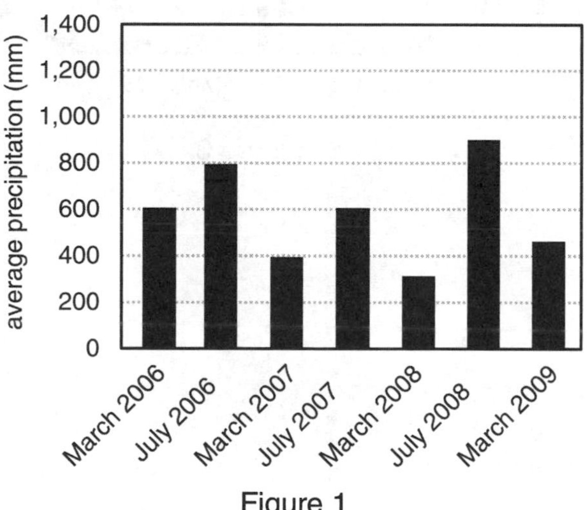

Figure 1

Study 2

Both water and leaves at the 6 areas around the WEP were analyzed for metal contaminants using a leeching test. The leaves and water were assessed for the concentration of 9 different metals. The aggregate quantity of metals in the water and leaves at the 6 different sites (A–F) are summarized in Figure 2.

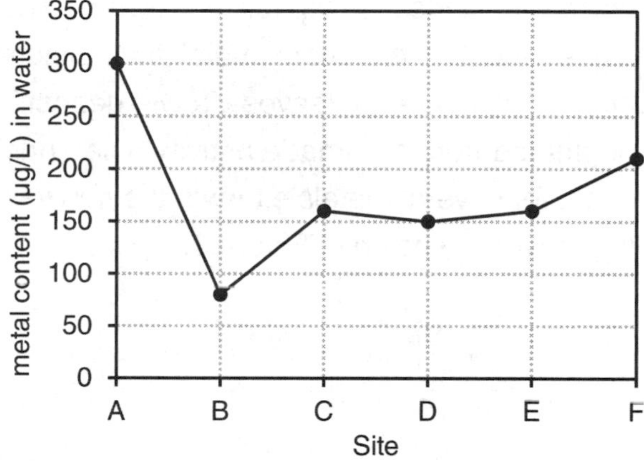

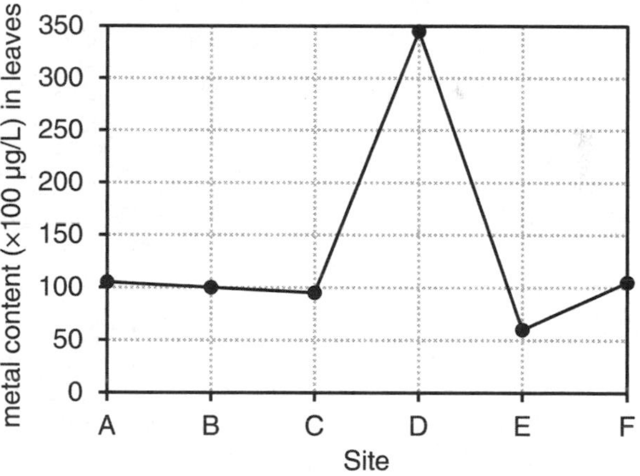

Figure 2

4.3.1 Supporting the Hypothesis

Study 3

There are trace amounts of heavy metals and other substances in the atmosphere. To determine whether the presence of these heavy metals in the leaves and water around the WEP is natural or manmade, the *enrichment factor* (EF) for several metals (in both water and leaves) was determined. The enrichment factor is a ratio of the concentration of the metal compared to the concentration that normally resides in topsoil (or water). Thus, the higher the EF, the more metal that accumulates either in the water or leaves via wet deposition that originated from manmade activity. The enrichment factor for several metals either in the rainwater or in the leaves is shown in Figure 3.

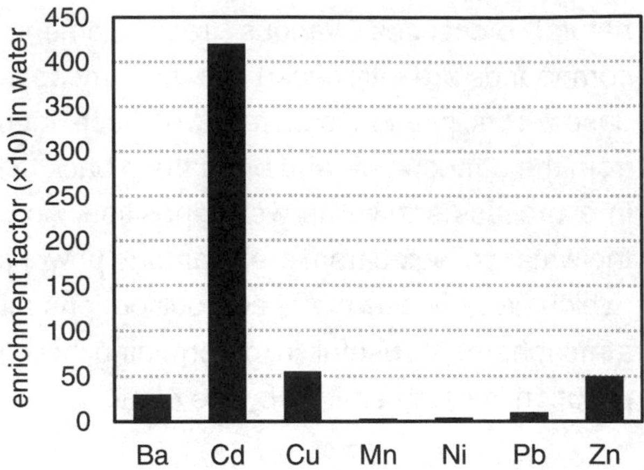

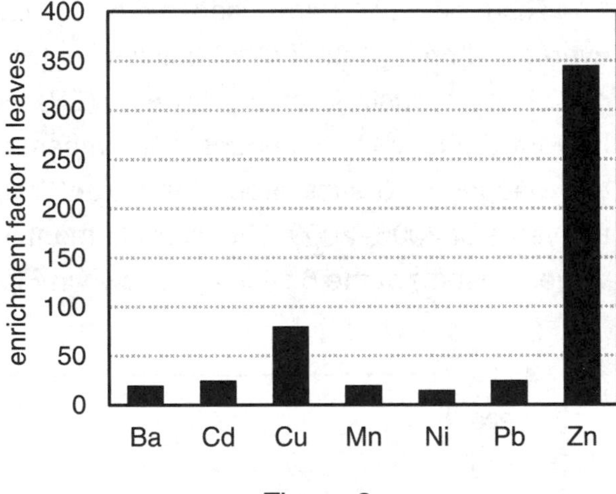

Figure 3

4.3.1 Supporting the Hypothesis

1. Is the statement, "The main metal pollutants from the WEP that are wet-deposited on the leaves of surrounding flora are zinc (Zn) and copper (Cu)" supported by the results in Study 3?
   A. No; because the top graph in Figure 3 shows that the main pollutant in the leaves is cadmium (Cd).
   B. Yes; because Zn and Cu had roughly equal EF values, higher than that of the other of the metals.
   C. No; because the bottom graph in Figure 3 shows that lead (Pb) is actually the main metal pollutant.
   D. Yes; because the EF for all the metals except (Zn) and (Cu) were near 0, and zinc and copper have significantly higher EF values.

2. Is the statement "The average rainfall in July is greater than the average rainfall in March of the same year" supported by the results of Study 1?
   F. Yes, because the data collected on average rainfall shows consistently higher values for July than March.
   G. Yes, because the data collected on average rainfall shows consistently higher values for March than July.
   H. No, because the data collected on average rainfall shows the highest amount of precipitation for July 2008.
   J. No, because the data collected on average rainfall shows relatively equal values for July and March.

Science Tip

Two by Two: On the ACT, the answer options often have two *yes* answers and two *no* answers. Eliminate any choice that contradicts the figures and then choose the one that makes the most sense. Often, you can eliminate all three wrong choices just based on the figures.

4.3.2 Weakening the Hypothesis

Acid-base titration is used quite frequently in research labs to titrate buffers or cell culture media to a desired pH. This is accomplished by adding acids (such as HCl) or bases (such as NaOH) to shift the pH of the solution either to be more acidic or more basic, respectively. The changes in pH achieved by the addition of the acid or base can be monitored in two ways. First, the pH shifts can be monitored chemically by adding an acid-base indicator, such as phenol red. Phenol red is a chemical which is normally red at around pH 7, but turns yellow at the lower pH of acidic environments. This is a quick way to check the health of cells (normally grown at around pH 7) in culture, as cellular waste products or contamination will turn the cell culture media yellow. The second way to monitor pH is by measuring the *conductivity*, or ability of solution to conduct electricity.

A student conducted the following titration experiment at room temperature (25°C). The solutions used were 0.1 M NaOH, 0.1 M NH_3, and 0.2 M HCl. The acid-base indicator used was phenol red, which is purple at pH above 8.2, yellow at pH 6.8 and below, and red between 8.2 and 6.8.

Experiment 1

First, several drops of phenol red were added to 100 mL of NaOH solution in an Erlenmeyer flask. This solution was then titrated with HCl while the conductivity was monitored. When adding a strong acid to a solution, it is important to add the acid slowly because the heat of hydration for H^+ ions is very high. The conductivity of the titrated solution was monitored continuously. Figure 1 shows the conductivity titration curve.

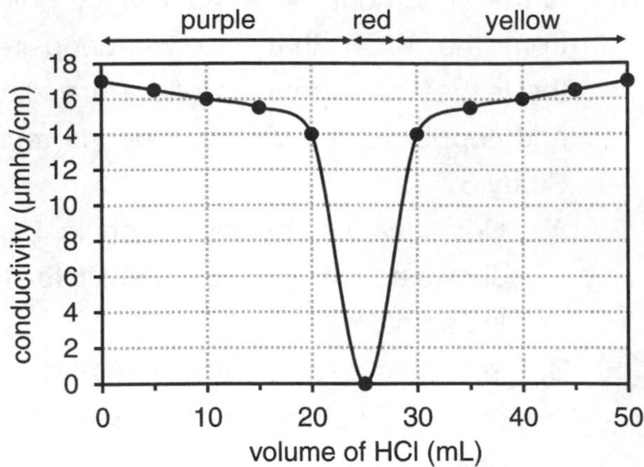

Figure 1

Experiment 2

The first experiment was repeated with a weak base, NH_3, instead of the NaOH solution, while every other condition remained the same. Figure 2 shows this conductivity titration curve.

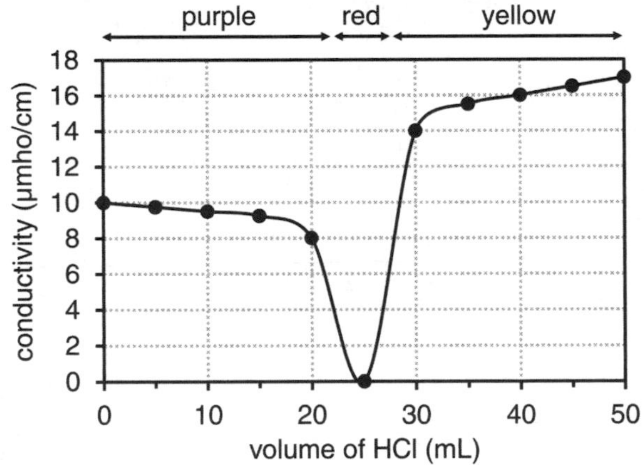

Figure 2

4.3.2 Weakening the Hypothesis

1. Another student claimed that the pH of the NH_3 solution required a greater volume of HCl to become acidic than the NaOH solution. Comparing Figures 1 and 2, is this claim accurate?
   A. Yes, because the yellow portion of the graphs start at different volumes of HCl.
   B. Yes, because the conductivity is different in both experiments after 30 mL.
   C. No, because the yellow portion of the graphs both start at the same point, near 30 mL.
   D. No, because the conductivity is the same in both experiments after 30 mL.

2. Is the hypothesis that conductivity always increases as the concentration of acid increases supported by the results of Experiment 1?
   F. Yes, because the experiment showed that the heat of hydration for H^+ ions increased over time, along with the conductivity of the solution.
   G. Yes, because the slope of the graph is positive as volume of HCl increases over time.
   H. No, because the conductivity of the solution initially decreased with the addition of acid.
   J. No, because the conductivity of the solution increased and decreased independently from the concentration of acid in the solution.

3. Suppose a scientist comes up with a theory that the conductivity of a solution is highest before any acid is added to it. Which of the experiments' results would most strongly contradict this theory?
   A. Experiment 1
   B. Experiment 2
   C. Both Experiment 1 and Experiment 2
   D. Neither Experiment 1 nor Experiment 2

Science Tip

50/50 Lifeline: You can use the process of elimination to narrow down the answer choices to two, getting rid of two answer choices with the wrong *yes/no* or two answer choices with the wrong supporting details. If you still feel stuck, mark and move.

This page is intentionally blank.

4.4.1 Set One

Passage I

Human cells have 2 sets of 23 chromosomes (46 chromosomes in all). This is known as being diploid (2*n*). Figure 1 is a genomic chromosomal map of the inherited pediatric cardiovascular disorders noted in modern scientific literature.

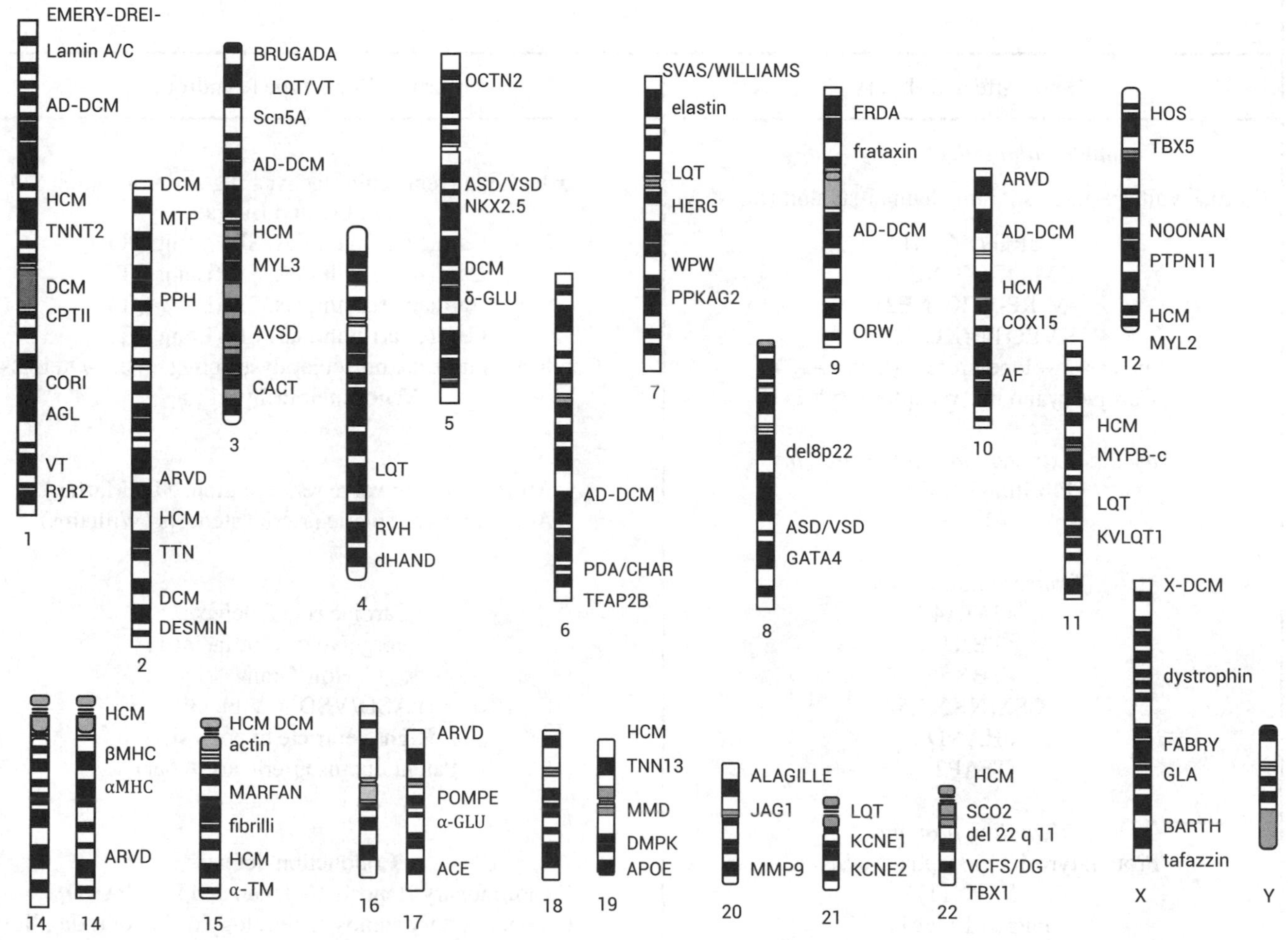

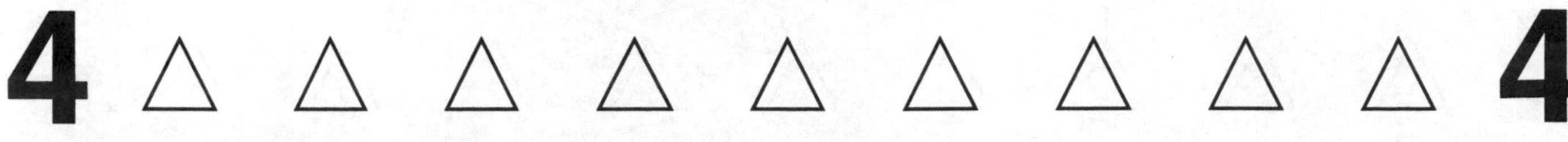

Genetics are important to study not only to learn more about modes of inheritance but also to learn more about genetic diseases. Often it is good to generate such maps to determine which genes are *linked*, physically close to each other on the same chromosome. Table 1 is a short list of cardiac issues and what genes affect them.

Table 1

Genes affected (Loci)	Cardiac Phenotype (Syndrome)
Channelopathies/electro-physiology	
Cardiac voltage-gated sodium channel-subunit (SCN5A)	Arrhythmia, ventricular tachycardia and fibrillation SD (Long QT and Brugada)
HERG (KCNH2)	Cardiac arrhythmias, SD (Long QT)
MinK (KCNE1)	Cardiac arrhythmias, SD (Long QT)
MiRP-1 (KCNE2)	Cardiac arrhythmias, SD (Long QT)
KVLQT1 (KCNQ1)	Cardiac arrhythmias, SD (Long QT)
Nuclear envelope protein (lamin A/C)	Conduction defects, muscular dystrophy (Emery-Dreifuss)
Cardiac ryanodine receptor (RyR2)	Ventricular tachycardia
Vascular extracellular matrix proteins	
Fibrillin-1 (FBN-1)	Mitral or aortic valve regurgitation, SD (Marfan)
Elastin	Aortic and systematic arterial stenosis (Williams)
Transcription Factors	
GATA4	Cardiac septal defects
TBX1	DiGeorge/velocardiofacial 17
TBX5	Holt-Oram
CSX/NKX2.5	ASD/VSD A-V block
dHAND	Right ventricle hypoplasia
TFAP2	Patent ductus arteriosus (Char)
Signaling proteins	
Protein tyrosine phosphatase SHP-2 (PTPN11)	Conduction defects Pulmonary stenosis (Noonan and LEOPARD)
Jagged 1 (Jag1)	Pulmonary artery stenosis, Tetralogy of Fallot (Alagille)
Myotonin protein kinase (DMPK)	Arrhythmias and conduction defects (myotonic muscular dystrophy)

1. On chromosome 1, there is the ryanodine receptor 2 gene (RyR2) and the Lamin A/C gene. If it was hypothesized that these genes are linked, according to this chromosome map, is that hypothesis correct?
   F. Yes; the genes are far enough away from each other that they are considered linked.
   G. No; the genes are in physical approximation with each other and as such are not linked.
   H. Yes; the genes are close enough to each other that they are considered linked.
   J. No; the genes are on opposite arms of the chromosome and thus are too far away to be linked.

2. A scientist claimed that the HERG (KCNH2) and MinK (KCNE1) genes can both cause cardiac arrhythmias. Does Table 1 support this claim?
   A. Yes, because the table shows that both genes are associated with mitral or aortic valve regurgitation, which in turn can lead to arrhythmias.
   B. Yes, because, along with MirP-1 (KCNE2) and KVLQT1 (KCNQ1), these are two of the genes that are associated with cardiac arrhythmias.
   C. No, because neither the HERG (KCNH2) nor the MinK (KCNE1) gene is associated with cardiac arrhythmias, according to the table.
   D. No, because only the MirP-1 (KCNE2) and KVLQT1 (KCNQ1) genes are associated with cardiac arrhythmias, based on the table.

3. Is the statement "genetic diseases are most likely to be found in Chromosome 1" supported by Figure 1?
   F. Yes, because Chromosome 1 is one of the longest chromosomes in the map, and so is more likely to have the most genetic mutations and resulting diseases.
   G. Yes, because the map shows that Chromosome 1 has some of the most significant mutations, including HCM, DCM, and AGL.
   H. No, because based on the map, Chromosomes 16, 17, 18, and 19 have the greatest density of genetic mutations.
   J. No, because the probability of disorders is not indicated by the figure.

4. A student predicted that cardiac septal defects are most likely to develop due to mutations in signaling proteins. Does the information in Table 1 support this conclusion?
   A. Yes, because the table shows that cardiac septal defects are associated with errors in signaling proteins like myotonin protein kinase (DMPK).
   B. Yes, because the table shows that cardiac septal defects are related to inborn errors like mutations in signaling proteins.
   C. No, because the table shows that cardiac septal defects are associated with errors in the transcription factor GATA4, not in signaling proteins.
   D. No, because the table shows that cardiac septal defects are not related to inborn errors, but to environmental factors.

5. A cardiac researcher discovers that right ventricle hypoplasia is actually caused by a variety of environmental factors including diet, exercise, and exposure to certain toxins. This discovery contradicts evidence stated in which figure?
   F. Figure 1, which shows that right ventricle hypoplasia is caused by a mutation to the JAG1 gene on Chromosome 20.
   G. Figure 1, which indicates that all cardiac abnormalities are caused by mutations in the chromosomes.
   H. Table 1, which shows that environmental factors only lead to cardiac issues like conduction defects.
   J. Table 1, which indicates that right ventricle hypoplasia is caused by a mutation affecting transcription factors.

END OF SET ONE

STOP! DO NOT GO ON TO THE NEXT PAGE UNTIL TOLD TO DO SO.

4.4.2 Set Two

Passage II

The Earth suffered the greatest mass extinction event in its history 252 million years ago (mya). The Permian-Triassic (P-Tr) Extinction Event, colloquially known as The Great Dying, resulted in the extinction of 93–97% of all species on the planet. While much is known about which species went extinct, the exact cause of the event remains a mystery. Due to the ongoing processes of plate tectonics and sea floor spreading, the sea floor is completely recycled every two hundred million years. Thus, much of the potential evidence that would support or weaken the many theories has been destroyed.

Two prominent theories involve the injection of sulfur (S) into the atmosphere, which blocks out the sun (lowering global temperatures) and, when combined with oxygen (O_2) and water (H_2O), forms sulfurous acid (H_2SO_4). The H_2SO_4 washes out of the atmosphere as acid rain. The acid rain lowered oxygen levels in the ocean and, combined with global cooling, set off the collapse of food chains across the globe.

Two scientists present their viewpoints.

Scientist 1

An extraterrestrial body (asteroid or comet) struck the earth 252 mya, instantly releasing an enormous cloud of sulfur into the atmosphere. In addition to the sulfur, the event would have thrown up materials common to extraterrestrial impacts: iridium, an element rare on earth but more common in meteorites; buckminsterfullerenes containing gases bearing extraterrestrial isotopes; shocked quartz, a form of quartz bearing deformations caused by short, intense bursts of pressure; and grains rich in iron, nickel, and silicon. While a period of intense volcanic activity did occur at the end of the Permian age, it was too prolonged to be responsible for the sudden extinction seen in The Great Dying. While greenhouse gases released by volcanic eruptions could raise the global temperature, the amount released by the Siberian Traps would have been insufficient to raise the temperature above the 5+ degrees necessary to trigger a mass extinction event.

Scientist 2

Around the time of The Great Dying, the largest known continental flood basalt province, known as the Siberian Traps, was forming in what is now Russia, near the Arctic Circle. In the Siberian Traps, large outpourings of lava covered vast areas of land. The extended period of volcanic activity in this area released sulfur and various greenhouse gases. As previously noted, the sulfur and ash lower global temperatures and produce acid rain. However, an impact event lacks the greenhouse gas component to explain the size and scope of the extinction event. Following a period of global cooling and oceanic oxygen depletion, greenhouse gases spike the global temperature. Species that were capable of surviving lowered temperatures are now subjected to higher temperatures at which they are not suited to survive. The combination of global cooling and warming is necessary to explain The Great Dying.

6. Suppose geological evidence found the concentration of iridium at the P-Tr boundary to be the same as most other points in the geological record. Which scientist would most likely use this information to support his or her view?

A. Scientist 1, because iridium is often found in extraterrestrial objects.
B. Scientist 1, because it would prove that greenhouse gases weren't necessary for the mass extinction.
C. Scientist 2, because iridium is a greenhouse gas that would raise the global temperature.
D. Scientist 2, because it would demonstrate that no abnormal extraterrestrial impacts occurred during this time frame.

7. The scientist who describes the Volcanic Hypothesis implies that the Impact Hypothesis is weakened by which of the following observations?

F. Buckminsterfullerenes do not contain greenhouse gases.
G. Acid rain leads to the reduction of dissolved oxygen in the ocean.
H. The amounts of shocked quartz around the P-Tr boundary are not sufficient to support a massive impact.
J. Extraterrestrial impacts do not produce greenhouse gas emissions.

8. Scientist 2's model would be most weakened if which of the following observations were made?

   A. Quartz deposits previously classified as shocked were determined to have been made by volcanic activity.
   B. The concentrations of iridium at the P-Tr boundary were considerably higher than at most other points in the geologic record.
   C. Acid rain did not reduce oceanic oxygen levels enough to endanger most species.
   D. An extraterrestrial impact set off the volcanic activity seen at the Siberian Traps.

9. According to the Impact Hypothesis, which of the following observations provides the strongest evidence the mass extinction was NOT caused by volcanic activity?

   F. Volcanic activity would not have produced shocked quartz at the P-Tr boundary.
   G. Volcanic eruptions do not produce greenhouse gas emissions.
   H. The volcanic eruptions did not produce sufficient global warming to trigger a mass extinction.
   J. Acid rain reducing oceanic oxygen levels was a primary cause of the mass extinction.

10. Suppose geological evidence indicates that volcanic eruptions at the equator have the potential to affect climate worldwide, but eruptions near the Earth's poles do not produce far enough ranging effects to alter global climate. Which scientist would use this information to support his or her view?

   A. Scientist 1, because the Siberian Traps are located near the Arctic Circle.
   B. Scientist 1, because volcanic eruptions do not produce sufficient greenhouse gases to affect global climate.
   C. Scientist 2, because it demonstrates that volcanic eruptions affect global climate.
   D. Scientist 2, because the Siberian Traps are located in an equatorial region.

END OF SET TWO
STOP! DO NOT GO ON TO THE NEXT PAGE
UNTIL TOLD TO DO SO.

4.4.3 Set Three

Passage III

One way to use the principle of density to isolate macromolecules from cell extracts is by separating out the various parts of a cellular extract using a density gradient.

Experiment 1

To make the density gradient, 6-mL aliquots for each *step* (a layer of liquid that has a different density than the other layers) of the density gradient were made by mixing together pure water with different amounts of 60% (wt/vol) iodixanol solution. The density of the 60% iodixanol solution is known (1.32 g/mL). See Table 1 for measurements of the various steps of the density gradient.

Table 1

Step	Mass of water (g)	Mass of iodixanol solution (g)	Total mass (g)	Density (g/mL)
1	0.00	8.10	8.10	1.35
2	0.91	6.87	7.78	1.30
3	1.69	5.81	7.50	1.25
4	2.48	4.73	7.21	1.20
5	3.00	4.05	7.05	1.18

Experiment 2

To make steps in the density gradient that are lower density than Step 5, a Falcon tube was tared on an electronic balance. Water and acetonitrile were added and weighed in the Falcon tube until the total volume in the Falcon tube was 6 mL. Several more steps of the density gradient were made by adding different masses of water and acetonitrile, the measurements for which are noted in Table 2.

Table 2

Step	Mass of water (g)	Mass of acetonitrile (g)	Total mass (g)	Density (g/mL)
6	6.00	0.00	6.00	1.00
7	5.00	0.78	5.78	0.96
8	4.00	1.56	5.56	0.93
9	3.00	2.35	5.35	0.89
10	2.00	3.13	5.13	0.85

Experiment 3

To determine the various densities of HPV virus fragments that are processed by the cell and by extracellular proteases, 293TT cells were infected with HPV and then harvested after 18 hours. To some of the cellular extracts, proteases such as trypsin, proteinase K, MMP-9, caspase-1, and caspase-5 were added and incubated with the extracts prior to loading them onto the density gradient. To locate where the HPV virus was on the gradient, it was "tagged" with GFP prior to infection—the virus will show up as a green band in one (or more) of the steps of the gradient. The locations of the HPV virus on the gradient after the various conditions are listed in Table 3. (+) means that GFP was detected in that step of the gradient, and (–) means GFP was not detected in that step of the density gradient.

Table 3

Condition	Step of the density gradient									
	1	2	3	4	5	6	7	8	9	10
virus only	+	+	–	–	–	–	–	–	–	–
virus + trypsin	–	–	–	–	–	+	+	+	+	+
virus + proteinase K	–	–	–	–	–	–	–	+	+	+
virus + MMP-9	+	+	–	–	–	–	–	–	–	–
virus + caspase-1	–	–	–	+	+	–	–	–	–	–
virus + caspase-5	–	–	–	–	+	+	–	–	–	–

11. The data from Table 3 was interpreted to mean that MMP-9 does not affect the location of the HPV virus on the gradient. Is that interpretation correct?

A. No; the GFP signal from the virus + MMP-9 condition is vastly different from that of virus alone.
B. Yes; the GFP signals from the virus alone and virus + MMP-9 conditions are the same.
C. No; the GFP signal from the virus + MMP-9 condition was seen in the steps of the gradient with the least density.
D. Yes; the GFP signal from virus + MMP-9 was similar to that of the virus + caspase-1 condition.

12. A student predicted that, if a solid with a known density of 2.33 g/mL were mixed with the solution from Step 5 of Experiment 1, the solid would float to the top. Based on the information in Table 1, is the student's prediction correct?

F. Yes, because the mass of the solid (2.33 g) is less than the mass of the Step 5 iodixanol solution (7.05 g).
G. Yes, because the density of the solid is less than the density of any of the solutions in the table.
H. No, because the solid would dissolve and create a homogenous solution.
J. No, because the density of the solid is greater than the density of the solution from Step 5.

13. Do the results of Experiment 2 indicate that the density of acetonitrile is less than the density of water?

A. Yes; the table indicates that only 3.13 g of acetonitrile can be added to the solution, while a maximum of 6 g of water can be added to the same solution.
B. Yes; as more acetonitrile and less water is added to the same volume of solution, the density goes down, indicating acetonitrile has a lower density.
C. No; the density of acetonitrile solutions goes down the more water is added, indicating that water has a lower density.
D. No; the mass of water added in each step goes down, while the density goes up, showing that acetonitrile has a higher density than water.

14. A student stated that the location of the HPV virus on the gradient is affected by each protease in different ways. Do the results of Experiment 3 verify this statement?

F. Yes, because the results of Table 3 show that the location of the virus was detected in different steps for each protease.
G. Yes, because the results of Table 3 show that the location of the virus was detected in the same steps for each protease.
H. No, because the results of Table 3 show that the location of the virus was detected in different steps for each protease.
J. No, because the results of Table 3 show that the location of the virus was detected in the same steps for each protease.

15. Is the statement "caspase-5 is denser than caspase-1" supported by the information in Table 3?

A. Yes, because caspase-5 reacts with the HPV virus at densities of 5 and 6, while caspase-1 reacts with the HPV virus at densities of 4 and 5.
B. Yes, because out of all of the proteases listed in the table, caspase-5 is the densest, as shown by its placement in Table 3 and its reaction with the HPV virus.
C. No, because caspase-5 reacts with the HPV virus at later steps of the gradient, indicating that it has a lower density than caspase-1.
D. No, because the table does not compare the densities of the various proteases, but instead shows how the relative densities of HPV virus fragments are produced by the different proteases.

END OF SET THREE
STOP! DO NOT GO ON TO THE NEXT PAGE
UNTIL TOLD TO DO SO.

Sum It Up

Support of Hypotheses Part 2

Support

Statements or evidence that allow a hypothesis to be true

Contradiction

A difference between two things so that both cannot be true

Tips and Techniques

Two by Two: On the ACT, the answer options often have two *yes* answers and two *no* answers. Eliminate any choice that contradicts the figures and then choose the one that makes the most sense. Often, you can eliminate all three wrong choices just based on the figures.

50/50 Lifeline: You can use the process of elimination to narrow down the answer choices to two, getting rid of two answer choices with the wrong *yes/no* or two answer choices with the wrong supporting details. If you still feel stuck, mark and move.

Lesson 5

Variables and Mathematical Relationships

CAPTION:

5.1 Entrance Ticket

Describe an important relationship in your life or in nature. Explain how both participants work together and how the actions of one affect the other.

5.2 Learning Targets

1. Identify relationships between variables
2. Determine the mathematical formula for the relationship between variables

Self-Assessment

Circle the number that corresponds to your confidence level in your knowledge of this subject before beginning the lesson. A score of 1 means you are completely lost, and a score of 4 means you have mastered the skills. After you finish the lesson, return to the bottom of this page and circle your new confidence level to show your improvement.

Before Lesson

1 2 3 4

After Lesson

1 2 3 4

5.3.1 Reading Variables

Experiment 1

A herd of dairy cattle were given various amounts of forage dry matter and grain as a percentage of their body weight, and their average milk output was measured.

Table 1

Forage dry matter intake (%)	Grain intake (%)	Average milk output (lb)
1.0	1.0	60
1.2	1.5	67
1.4	2.0	73

Experiment 2

Three herds of dairy cattle were each fed a constant amount of forage dry matter and a randomly assigned percentage of grain. Each herd's average milk output was measured.

Table 2

Herd	Grain intake (%)	Average milk output (lb)
A	3.0	60
B	2.5	63
C	2.0	71

5.3.1 Reading Variables

Table 1		
Trial	Current (mA)	Distance (cm)
1	5	9.68
2	10	5.74
3	15	4.19
4	20	3.29

Table 2			
Trial	Lake	Water temperature (°F)	Blue-green algae coverage (%)
5	A	80	5
6	B	82	11
7	C	85	28

5.3.1 Reading Variables

Table 1	
Time (s)	Temperature (°C)
0	100
200	90
400	80
1,200	70
2,400	60
3,600	50

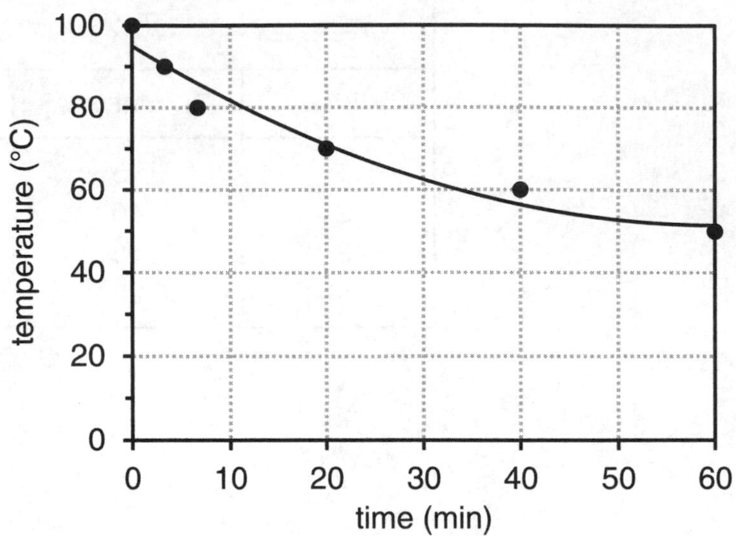

Figure 1

Table 2	
Time (s)	Temperature (°C)
400	50
800	60
1,000	70
1,400	80
2,400	90
3,200	100

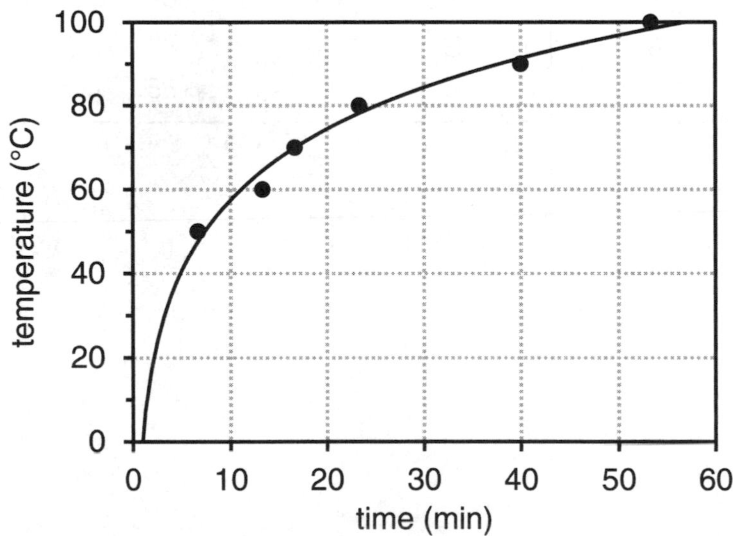

Figure 2

5.3.1 Reading Variables

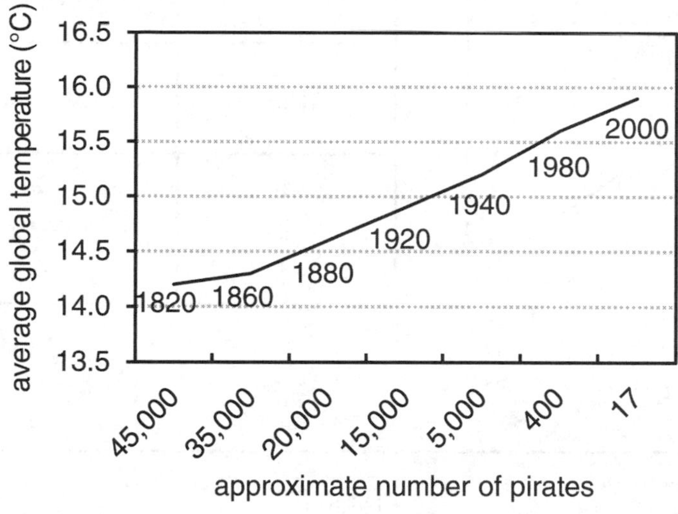

Figure 1

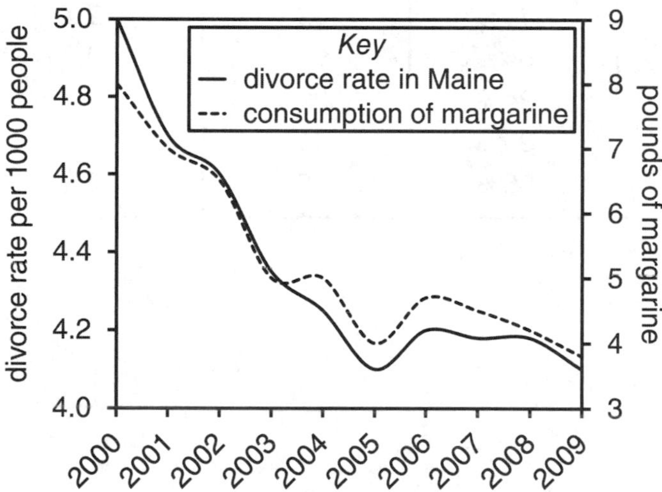

Figure 2

5.3.2 Careful Reading

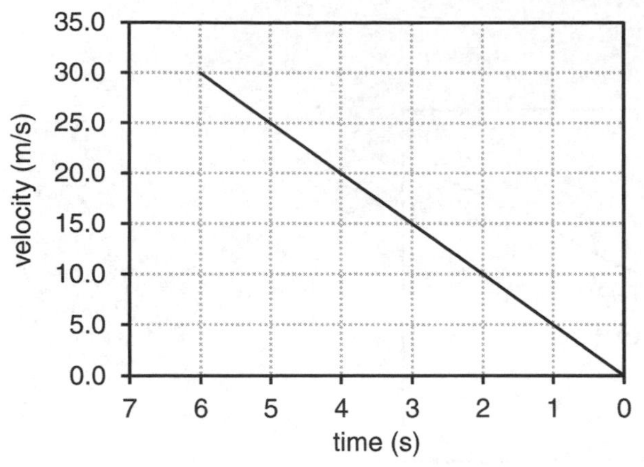

Figure 2

Table 1		
Trial	Temperature (°F)	Refrigerant pressure (psi)
1	–40	0.5
2	–35	2.6
3	–30	4.9

Table 2					
Zone	Population	Vaccination rate	Households exposed to measles	Average number of children per household	Number of cases of measles reported
A	70k	81%	92	2.1	36
B	300k	84%	57	2.2	21
C	180k	94%	22	2.4	7
D	240k	90%	19	1.7	5
E	115k	96%	3	2.2	0

Science Tip

Keep Your Pencil Moving: It is important to pay attention to details, such as axis labels and quantities, and to read tabulated data from top to bottom to ensure you are looking at the data correctly. Use your pencil to keep track of the information by underlining, circling, or writing down important facts, such as variables, units, or trends.

5.3.3 Calculating Relationships

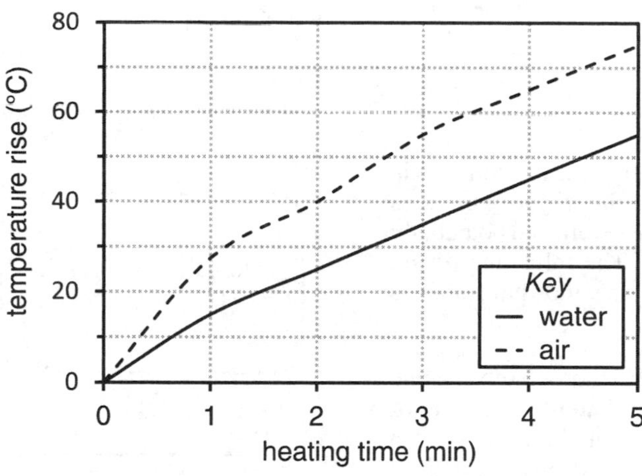

Figure 1

Based on the above figure, the relationship between water temperature rise (T) and heating time (t) is best represented by which of the following formulas?

A. $T = 11.6 \times t$

B. $T = \frac{11.6}{t}$

C. $T = 4.9 \times t$

D. $T = \frac{4.9}{t}$

Science Tip

Plug It In: For questions that ask you to identify which mathematical expression represents a relationship shown in a graph or table, you should plug data points from the figure into the answer choices to determine which one gives the correct value.

5.4.1 Set One

Passage I

West Nile is a virus that is transmitted to humans via bites from infected mosquitoes. While the majority of cases are mild and often go unnoticed, a more severe and potentially fatal neurological illness can develop. The following figure, Figure 1, describes the life cycle of the mosquito and its transmission of West Nile virus.

Exposure to West Nile virus is more likely in the midwestern and southern United States than in other areas of the country. A study looked at five regions in a midwestern state and divided them into five zones. People who lived within each study zone were tested monthly for West Nile virus. Table 1 shows the number of households in each study zone, as well as the percentage of the zone covered in standing water, the number of dead crows and blue jays, and the number of mosquitoes captured over the course of the week in each zone. In addition, the percentage of households within the zone that had at least one family member test positive for West Nile virus is also reported.

Life cycle of mosquitoes and the cycle of West Nile virus transmission

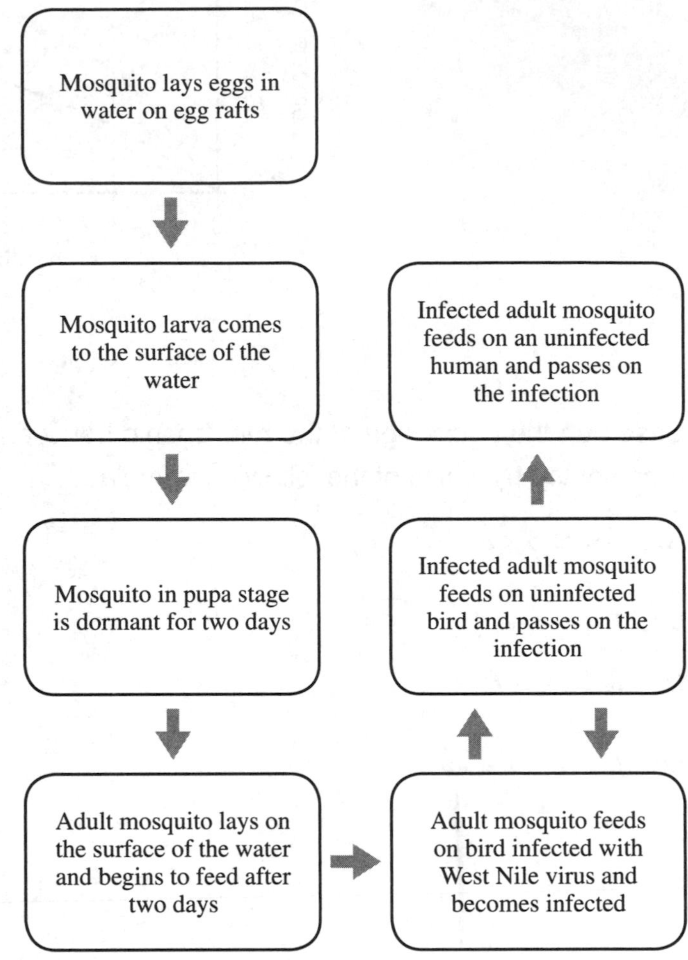

Figure 1

Table 1					
	Number of...				
Zone	Households	Trapped mosquitoes	Dead crows/ blue jays	Percent area with standing water	Percent house-holds with at least 1 case of West Nile virus
A	10	429	4	54	60
B	12	209	2	42	50
C	12	234	0	38	33
D	13	115	3	27	31
E	15	92	1	16	20

Figure 2 shows the number of cases of West Nile virus infection and the number of deaths reported in 2003 and 2004. It further illustrates how this data is distributed between West Nile virus infection with and without neurological complications.

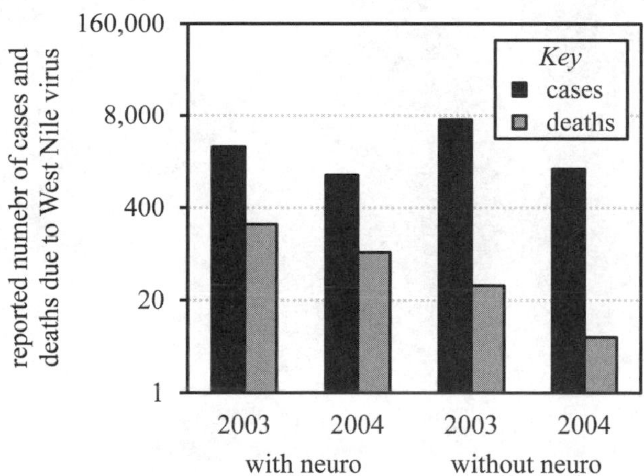

Figure 2

1. According to the information in Table 1, as the number of mosquitoes captured within a zone increased, the number of dead crows and blue jays:

   A. increased only.
   B. decreased only.
   C. decreased, then remained the same.
   D. varied.

2. According to the information in Table 1, as the percentage of area covered by water increased from 38% to 42%, the number of trapped mosquitoes:

   F. increased from 234 to 209.
   G. decreased from 234 to 209.
   H. increased from 209 to 234.
   J. decreased from 209 to 234.

3. According to the information in Figure 2, as reported cases of West Nile virus increase, deaths from West Nile virus:

   A. increase for West Nile virus both with and without neurological complications.
   B. increase for West Nile virus with neurological involvement and decrease for West Nile virus without neurological complications.
   C. decrease for West Nile virus both with and without neurological complications.
   D. remain the same for West Nile virus both with and without neurological complications.

4. In Table 1, as the percentage of area covered with standing water increased, the percentage of households in which one or more people were infected by West Nile virus:

   F. increased only.
   G. decreased only.
   H. varied, but with no general trend.
   J. remained constant.

5. According to Table 1, as the number of dead crows and blue jays increased from 0 to 4, the percentage of households in which one or more people were infected by West Nile virus:

   A. increased only.
   B. decreased only.
   C. increased, then decreased.
   D. alternated between decreasing and increasing.

END OF SET ONE

STOP! DO NOT GO ON TO THE NEXT PAGE UNTIL TOLD TO DO SO.

This page is intentionally left blank.

5.4.2 Set Two

Passage II

Photosynthesis is the process by which plants use light energy to convert carbon dioxide into chemical energy in the form of sugar. There are two stages in photosynthesis that, when both occur, result in this reduction reaction: light-dependent reactions and light-independent reactions. During *light-dependent reactions*, light energy is absorbed by chlorophyll in the chloroplast of plants. This energy is then converted into chemical energy as NADPH (a reducing agent) and ATP. The *light-independent reaction* is then able to proceed using the NADPH and high-energy ATP produced in the light-dependent reaction to reduce carbon dioxide to sugar.

In this study, students examined the rate of CO_2 reduction in chloroplasts. Students were asked to extract the chloroplasts from crushed spinach leaves. They used Table 1 to determine appropriate centrifuge settings to spin down a concentrated pellet of chloroplasts (Tube 1) for 10 min at 95 *g*.

The remaining liquid (supernatant) from Tube 1 was transferred to Tube 2. A small amount of DCPIP, a blue reducing agent that becomes colorless once it has been oxidized, was then added to both tubes, and the absorbance was recorded at each minute until both solutions became colorless (Figure 1).

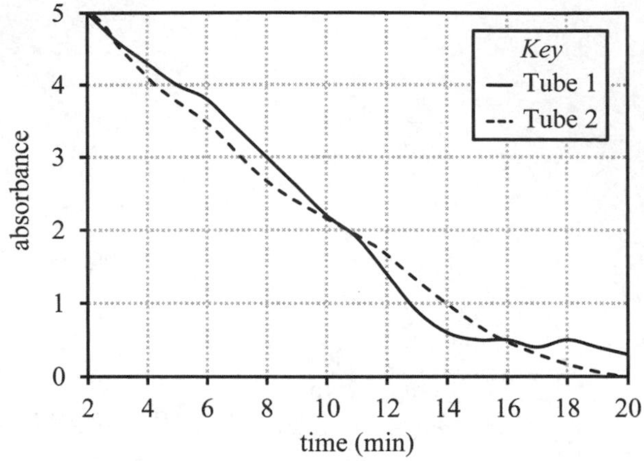

Figure 1

Table 1: *G*-force Experienced by the Sample in a Centrifuge ($g = 1.118 \times 10^{-5}\ RS^2$)										
Speed (rpm)	rotor radius from the center of the centrifuge to sample (cm)									
	4	5	6	7	8	9	10	11	12	13
1,000	45	56	67	78	89	101	112	123	134	145
1,500	101	126	151	176	201	226	252	277	302	327
2,000	179	224	268	313	358	402	447	492	537	581
2,500	280	349	419	489	559	629	699	769	839	908
3,000	402	503	604	704	805	906	1,006	1,107	1,207	1,308
3,500	548	685	822	959	1,096	1,233	1,370	1,507	1,643	1,780
4,000	716	894	1,073	1,252	1,431	1,610	1,789	1,968	2,147	2,325
4,500	906	1,132	1,358	1,585	1,811	2,038	2,264	2,490	2,717	2,943
5,000	1,118	1,398	1,677	1,957	2,236	2,516	2,795	3,075	3,354	3,634

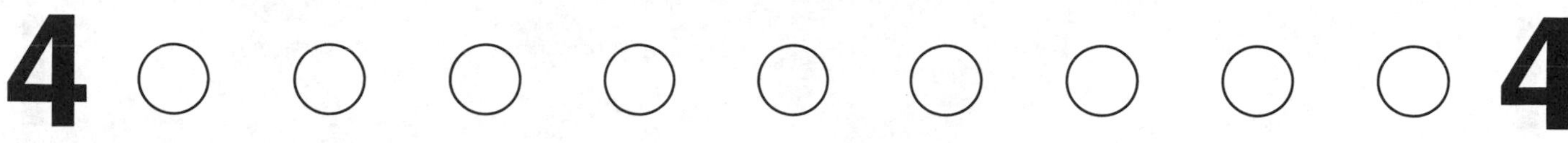

6. According to Table 1, as speed increases for any given rotor radius, the *g*-force felt by the sample:

F. increases only.
G. decreases only.
H. varies, but with no general trend.
J. remains constant.

7. A sample is spun in a centrifuge 9 cm from the center for 5 minutes, and it experiences a *g*-force of 906 *g*. It is spun a second time at 4 cm from the center for the same amount of time, and it experiences the same *g*-force. Between the first and second spins, the centrifuge speed:

A. increases only.
B. decreases only.
C. varies, but with no general trend.
D. remains constant.

8. According to Figure 1, for Tube 2, as time increases, absorption:

F. increases only.
G. increases, then decreases.
H. decreases only.
J. decreases, then increases.

9. In Figure 1, as time increases, absorption:

A. increases for Tube 1 and decreases for Tube 2.
B. increases for Tubes 1 and 2.
C. decreases for Tube 1 and increases for Tube 2.
D. decreases for both Tubes 1 and 2.

10. According to Table 1, as distance between the center of the rotor radius to the sample increases, the speed necessary to maintain the *g*-force:

F. increased only.
G. decreased only.
H. increased, then decreased.
J. alternated between decreasing and increasing.

END OF SET TWO
STOP! DO NOT GO ON TO THE NEXT PAGE
UNTIL TOLD TO DO SO.

5.4.3 Set Three

Passage III

The Carlingford Igneous Centre (CIC) was a site of volcanic activity in Ireland during the Ordovician Period that spanned 485 to 483 million years ago. This type of volcanism is an example of "bimodal volcanism" in which both basalt and rhyolite magma are found in the core of the volcano. This results in particularly violent eruptions. Scientists studied the geological makeup of the CIC and discovered that this bimodal volcanism may be caused by the geological features of the rocks underneath the volcano. Figure 1 illustrates a cross section of the rare earth element content of various CIC site. Figure 2 shows the relationship between the niobium (Nb) and zirconium (Zr) content of crustal rocks found at the CIC site.

Volcanic activity can influence global climate and trigger cold events. The injection of sulfur dioxide gas (SO_2), which is ultimately converted to sulfuric acid aerosol particles (H_2SO_4), scatters shortwave solar radiation and absorbs near-infrared solar radiation and outgoing longwave terrestrial radiation. This results in cooling of the troposphere and heating of the stratosphere. Figure 3 shows the results of a study that examined the effect of erupting volcanoes on the number of cold events in Ireland.

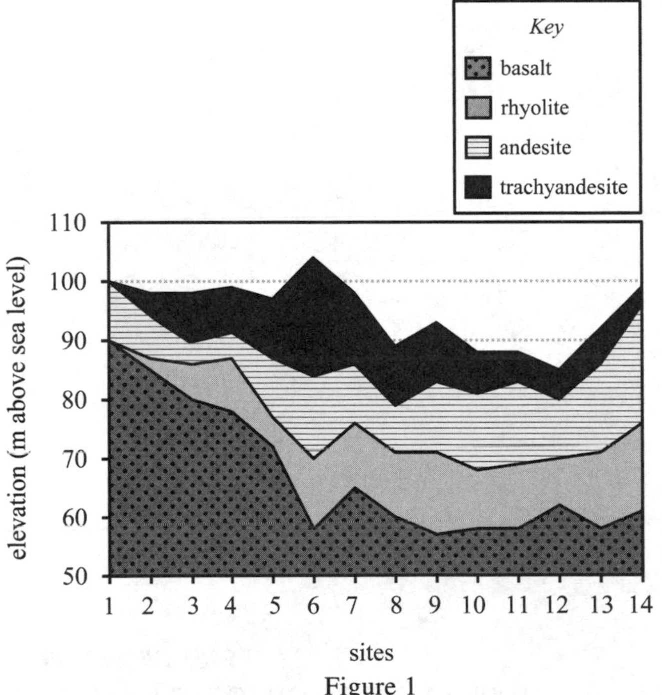

Figure 1

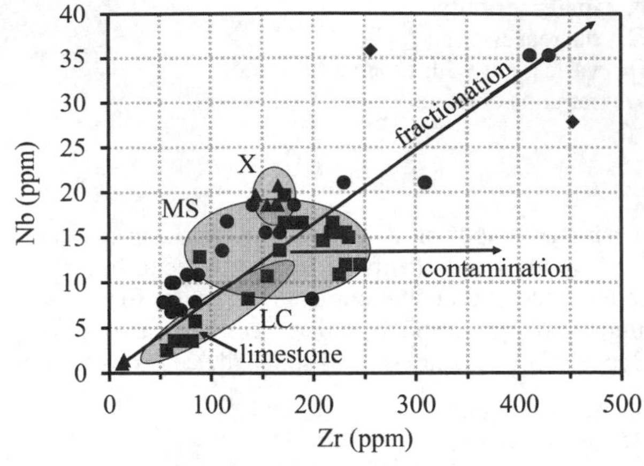

Figure 2

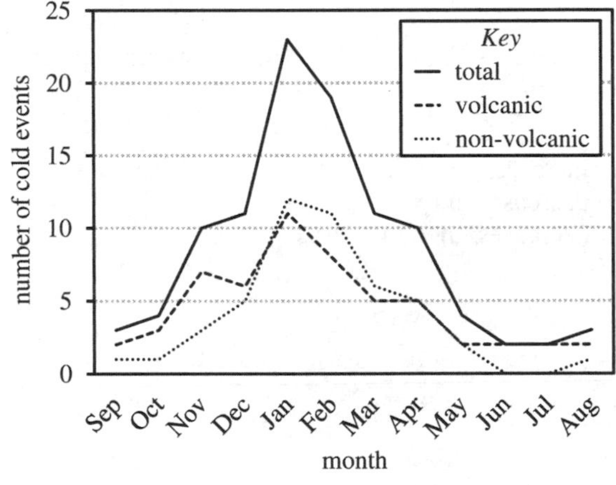

Figure 3

 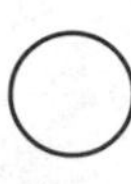   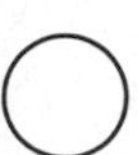  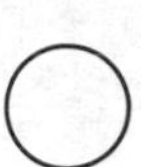 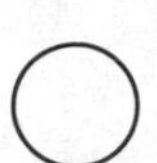  4

11. According to the information in Figure 1, as the cross-sectional altitude of trachyandesite increases from Site 5 to Site 6, the amount of andesite:

    A. increases.
    B. remains the same.
    C. increases, then decreases.
    D. decreases.

12. According to Figure 3, as the number of volcanic events increases from 4 to 12, the overall number of cold events:

    F. increases only.
    G. decreases only.
    H. increases, then decreases.
    J. decreases, then increases.

13. According to the information in Figure 3, does the total number of cold events depend on volcanic activity?

    A. Yes, because as volcanic-activity-based cold events increase, the total number of cold events increase.
    B. Yes, because as volcanic-activity-based cold events increase, the total number of cold events remain constant.
    C. No, because as volcanic-activity-based cold events increase, the total number of cold events increase.
    D. No, because as volcanic-activity-based cold events increase, the total number of cold events remain constant.

14. According to Figure 1, as the cross-sectional altitude of basalt decreases from Site 1 to Site 3, does the cross-sectional altitude of rhyolite and andesite increase or decrease?

    F. Rhyolite increases; andesite increases.
    G. Rhyolite increases; andesite decreases.
    H. Rhyolite decreases; andesite increases.
    J. Rhyolite decreases, andesite decreases.

15. According to Figure 2, the relationship between Nb content and Zr content is best represented by:

    A. $\text{Nb} = 3.0 \times \text{Zr}$
    B. $\text{Nb} = \dfrac{\text{Zr}}{3.0}$
    C. $\text{Nb} = \dfrac{\text{Zr}}{12.2}$
    D. $\text{Nb} = 12.2 \times \text{Zr}$

END OF SET THREE

STOP! DO NOT GO ON TO THE NEXT PAGE UNTIL TOLD TO DO SO.

Sum It Up

Variables and Mathematical Relationships

Bar Graph
A graph that relays information using bars of varying sizes to denote value

---

Line Graph
A graph that relays information through individual points that are connected to each other on a line

---

Table
A non-graphical way to relay information about a system, in which columns or rows are used to display data

Tips and Techniques

Keep Your Pencil Moving: Remember to mark the key information on the figures in the passage, such as units, variables, and patterns.

Plug It In: If you are working with an equation, try to plug data from the figures into the passage.

Lesson 6

Interpolation and Extrapolation

CAPTION:

6.1 Entrance Ticket

Write a paragraph responding to the following prompt.

A basic weather forecast gives predictions of the weather for the next ten days. These are not empty guesses made without evidence. Write a paragraph explaining how meteorologists might use weather patterns and scientific data to predict the weather and other climate changes in the near future.

6.2 Learning Targets

1. Recognize trends in data and predict the results of an additional trial or measurement in an experiment

2. Gather information from multiple areas of a science passage and draw conclusions based on the combination of these pieces of data

Self-Assessment

Circle the number that corresponds to your confidence level in your knowledge of this subject before beginning the lesson. A score of 1 means you are completely lost, and a score of 4 means you have mastered the skills. After you finish the lesson, return to the bottom of this page and circle your new confidence level to show your improvement.

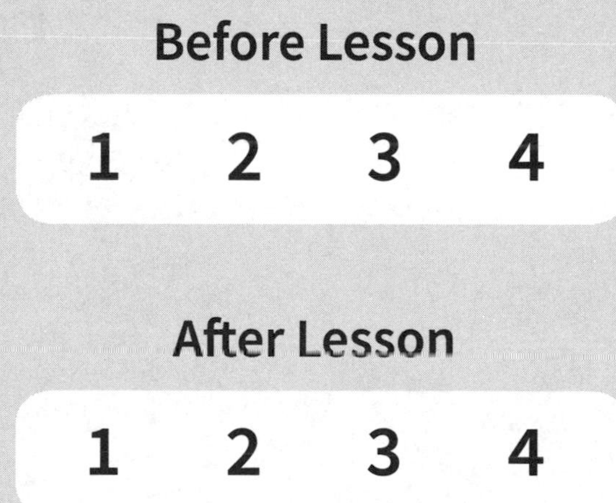

Before Lesson
1 2 3 4
After Lesson
1 2 3 4

6.3.1 Trends in Data

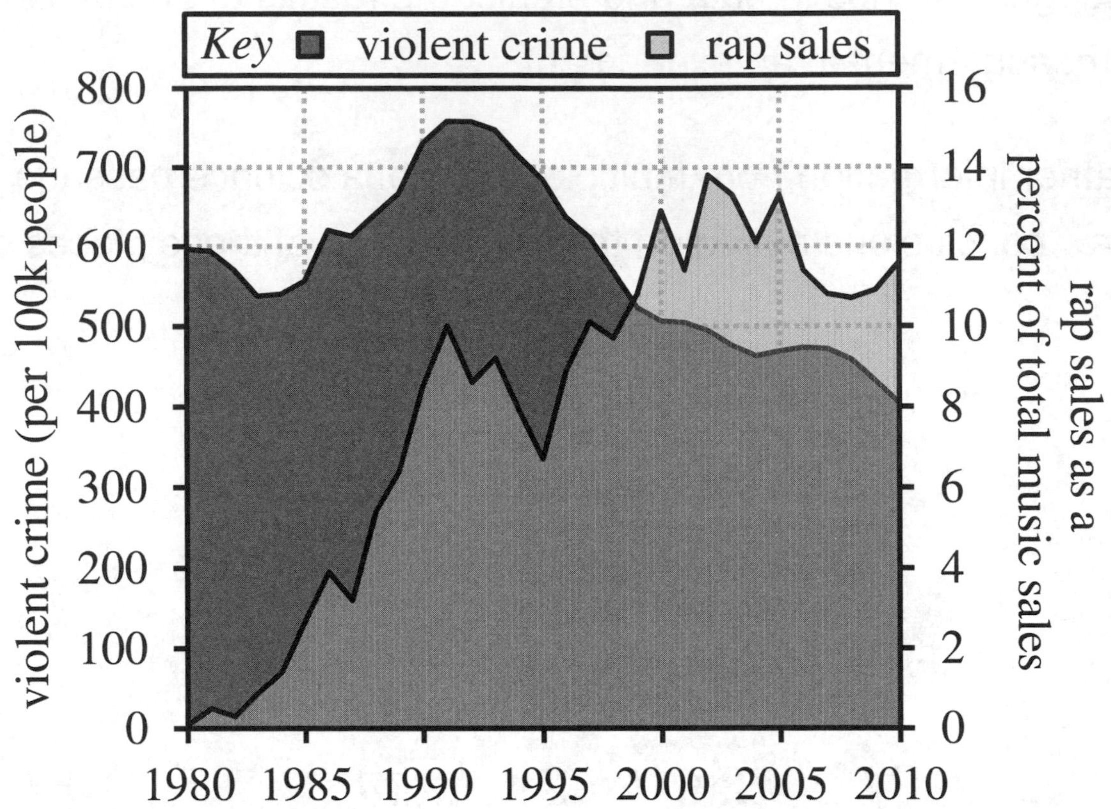

6.3.1 Trends in Data

Table 1			
Pressure altitude (ft)	GPH	Knots true airspeed (KTAS)	
		Standard temperature	20°C above standard temperature
4,000	8.1	114	113
6,000	7.8	113	112
8,000	7.4	112	111
10,000	7.1	111	109

6.3.2 Puzzle Pieces

Using the circuit shown in Figure 1, students studied the variables that affect capacitance and capacitive reactance. The capacitor was constructed as shown in Figure 2.

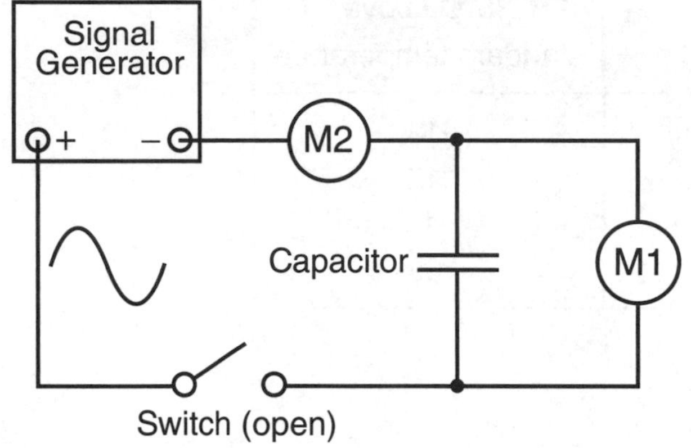

Figure 1

The students used the following procedure to find *C* (capacitance) and X_C (capacitive reactance). Two brass plates measuring 100 mm × 100 mm were sandwiched between clamped wood, with a dielectric material between the plates. A metric ruler was used to determine the overlapping area of the plates. A digital multimeter (M1) was used to measure capacitance. Reactance was calculated using the formula:

$$X_C = \frac{1}{2\pi fC}$$

M1 was set to measure AC voltage, M2 was set to measure AC current, and the switch was closed. Voltage and current measurements were used at different signal generator frequencies to prove the capacitive reactance formula.

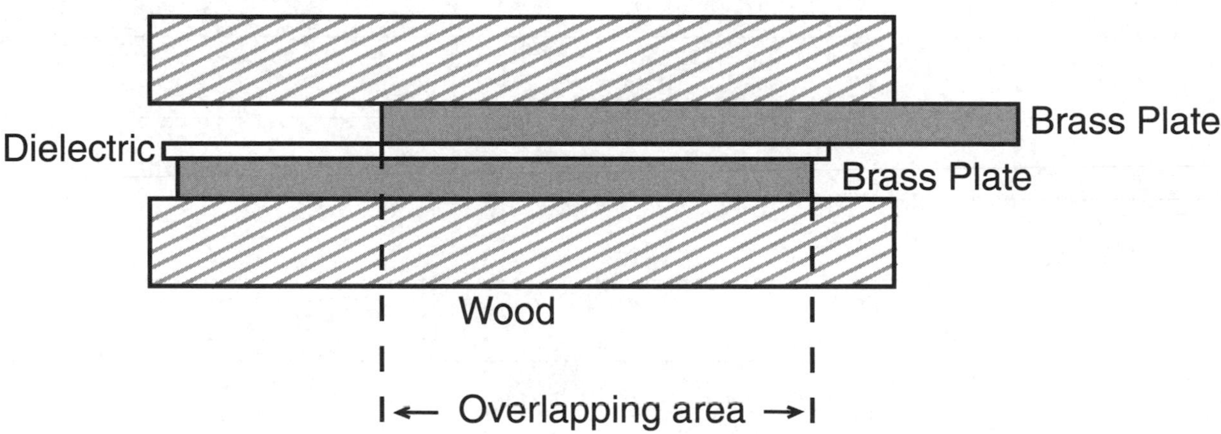

Figure 2

6.3.2 Puzzle Pieces

Study 1

The students found capacitance for each of four dielectric materials. Each capacitor was constructed of two brass plates with an overlapping area of 200 mm^2 and was separated by a 1 mm thickness of the dielectric material. Reactance was calculated at a frequency of 500 kHz.

Table 1		
Material	Capacitance	Reactance
Teflon	3.72 pF	85.5 kΩ
Polyethylene	4.0 pF	79.6 kΩ
Paper	6.2 pF	51.3 kΩ
Rubber	12.4 pF	25.6 kΩ

Study 2

The students found capacitance with four different overlapping areas of the capacitor's plates. In each test the plates were separated by a 1 mm thickness of paper dielectric. Reactance was calculated at a frequency of 500 kHz.

Table 2		
Overlapping area	Capacitance	Reactance
100 mm^2	3.1 pF	102.6 kΩ
200 mm^2	6.2 pF	51.3 kΩ
300 mm^2	9.3 pF	34.2 kΩ
400 mm^2	12.4 pF	25.7 kΩ

Study 3

The students found capacitance with four different thicknesses of paper dielectric. In each test the plates overlapped by 200 mm^2. Reactance was calculated at a frequency of 500 kHz.

Table 3		
Thickness	Capacitance	Reactance
0.5 mm	12.4 pF	25.6 kΩ
1.0 mm	6.2 pF	51.3 kΩ
1.5 mm	4.1 pF	77.0 kΩ
2.0 mm	3.1 pF	102.6 kΩ

Study 4

The students found reactance at four different signal frequencies. In each test the plates overlapped by 200 mm^2 and were separated by a 1 mm thickness of paper dielectric. Reactance was calculated by dividing voltage by current (capacitance is not affected by frequency).

Table 4		
Frequency	Capacitance	Reactance
100 kHz	6.2 pF	256.7 kΩ
250 kHz	6.2 pF	102.6 kΩ
500 kHz	6.2 pF	51.3 kΩ
1000 kHz	6.2 pF	25.7 kΩ

6.3.2 Puzzle Pieces

1. Suppose the overlapping area of the plates in Study 3 had been 600 mm^2 instead of 200 mm^2. Based on the results in Study 2, when the dielectric thickness was 1 mm, capacitance would most likely have been closest to which of the following?
   A. 2.1 pF
   B. 12.4 pF
   C. 18.6 pF
   D. 24.8 pF

2. Suppose the dielectric thickness in Study 4 had been 2 mm instead of 1 mm. Based on the results in Study 3, when the signal generator frequency was set to 500 kHz, reactance would most likely have been closest to which of the following?
   F. 25.7 kΩ
   G. 102.6 kΩ
   H. 256.2 kΩ
   J. 513.4 kΩ

Science Tip

Road Signs: If the question mentions multiple experiments, studies, terms, or line numbers, be sure to consider all of them before determining your answer.

This page is intentionally left blank.

6.4.1 Set One

Passage I

Freezing point depression occurs when a substance (solute) is added to a solvent, decreasing the solvent's freezing point. The process can be monitored over a short range (depending on the solute) by using a hydrometer, which floats in the solution at varying depths as an indication of the mixed solution's specific gravity. Freezing point is the temperature at which the solution becomes a solid, at normal atmospheric pressure.

Three experiments were performed using distilled water, mixed with precise amounts of ethylene glycol ($C_2H_6O_2$), propylene glycol ($C_3H_8O_2$), or methanol (CH_4O), in concentrations varying from 10–90% by weight. All solutions were aqueous, with a starting temperature of 25°C. A hydrometer was used to indicate the relative change in specific gravity as the solute percentage was increased.

Table 1 shows the density for each of the three solutes.

Table 1

Solute	Density
ethylene glycol	1,110.00 kg/m^3
propylene glycol	1,040.00 kg/m^3
methanol	791.30 kg/m^3

Experiment 1

Distilled water was mixed with precise concentrations of ethylene glycol in various concentrations by weight. For each concentration, a hydrometer was used to measure specific gravity at 25°C, and the freezing point was determined using a precision thermometer. Figure 1 shows results through 50% concentration.

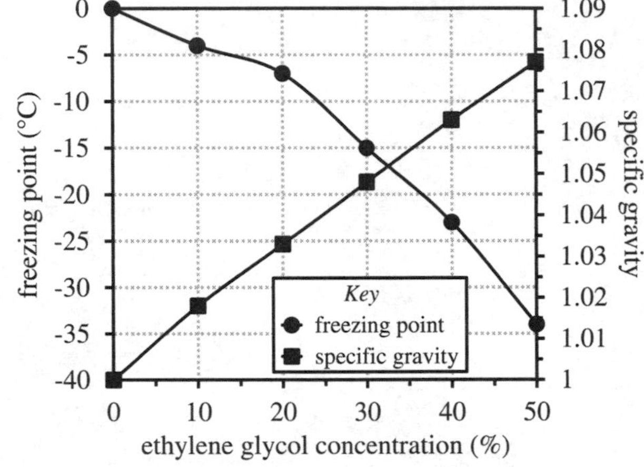

Figure 1

Experiment 2

Experiment 1 was repeated, except propylene glycol was used instead of ethylene glycol. Figure 2 shows results through 50% concentration.

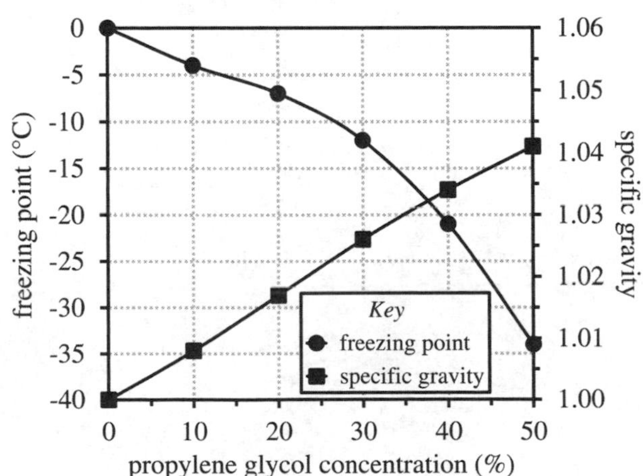

Figure 2

Experiment 3

Experiment 1 was repeated, except methanol was used instead of ethylene glycol, and specific gravity was not recorded because of methanol's low evaporation point. Figure 3 shows results for all concentrations of the three solutes.

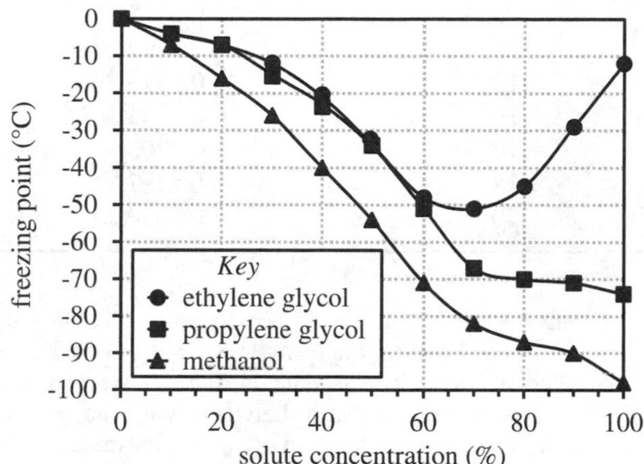

Figure 3

1. In Experiment 1, if 60% ethylene glycol had been added to the sample, the freezing point would most likely have been:

   A. greater than –15°C.
   B. between –15°C and –25°C.
   C. between –25°C and –35°C.
   D. less than –35 °C.

2. Consider two of the solutes, temporarily named Solute A and Solute B. At increasing concentrations, both solutes initially provided similar levels of freeze protection. At 70% concentration, however, Solute B began to lose effectiveness, while Solute A continued to provide an increasing level of freeze protection as concentration increased. What are the actual names for Solutes A and B?

	Solute A	Solute B
F.	ethylene glycol	propylene glycol
G.	propylene glycol	methanol
H.	methanol	ethylene glycol
J.	propylene glycol	ethylene glycol

3. Suppose another concentration of propylene glycol had been tested in the same way described in Experiment 2. The specific gravity for a 60% propylene glycol solution would most likely have been: :

   A. greater than 1.04.
   B. between 1.02 and 1.04.
   C. between 1.01 and 1.02.
   D. less than 1.01.

4. Based on Table 1, the mass of 0.5 m^3 of propylene glycol would be closest to which of the following values?

   F. 395.65 kg
   G. 520.00 kg
   H. 555.00 kg
   J. 791.30 kg

5. Based on the results of the three experiments, which of the following combinations of solute, solute weight, and solution weight will provide the lowest possible freezing point?

	Solute Weight	Solution Weight	Solute
A.	80 lbs	200 lbs	methanol
B.	70 lbs	280 lbs	ethylene glycol
C.	90 lbs	150 lbs	ethylene glycol
D.	90 lbs	180 lbs	propylene glycol

END OF SET ONE

STOP! DO NOT GO ON TO THE NEXT PAGE UNTIL TOLD TO DO SO.

6.4.2 Set Two

Passage II

A conductor is a material that, because of loosely-bound outer electrons, helps the flow of electrical current through the material. Students found the relative resistivity of different conductors by measuring the amount of voltage each consumed along a precise length and cross-sectional area. Measurements were taken using a digital voltmeter, with all materials at ambient room temperature.

Study 1

The students constructed an electrical circuit consisting of a battery, a potentiometer, an ammeter, a precision voltmeter, and ten-foot lengths of different gauges or diameters of solid copper wire, denoted as AWG.

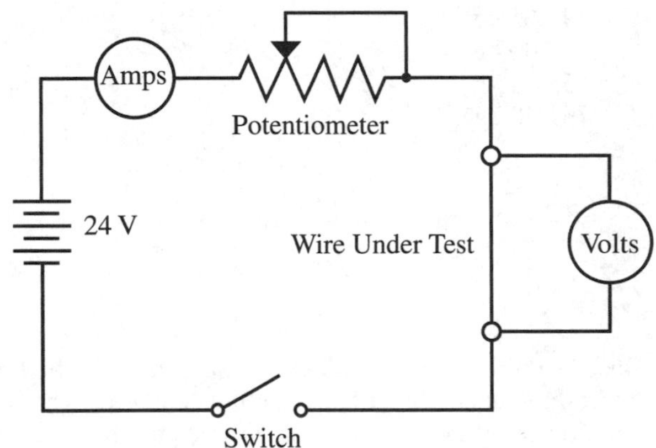

Figure 1

For each test, a 10-foot length of solid copper wire was connected as shown in Figure 1. The switch was closed, and the potentiometer was adjusted for a current (I) of 2.0 amps. The voltage drop (V) across the copper wire was measured and recorded.

Table 1

AWG	Voltage drop (V)
4	0.0049
6	0.0079
8	0.0125
10	0.0199
12	0.0317
14	0.0505
16	0.0803
18	0.1277
20	0.2030

Using the data in Table 1, the students calculated the wire's resistance (R) using the formula $R = V/I$ and the results are recorded in Table 2. The data in Table 2 were plotted to investigate the relationship between wire gauge and resistance as shown in Figure 2. In addition, the students also determined that resistance is directly related to the length of the wire being tested.

Table 2

AWG	Diameter (in)	Resistance (Ω)
4	0.2043	0.00248
6	0.1620	0.00395
8	0.1284	0.00628
10	0.1018	0.00998
12	0.0808	0.01588
14	0.0640	0.02525
16	0.0508	0.04016
18	0.0403	0.06385
20	0.0319	0.10150

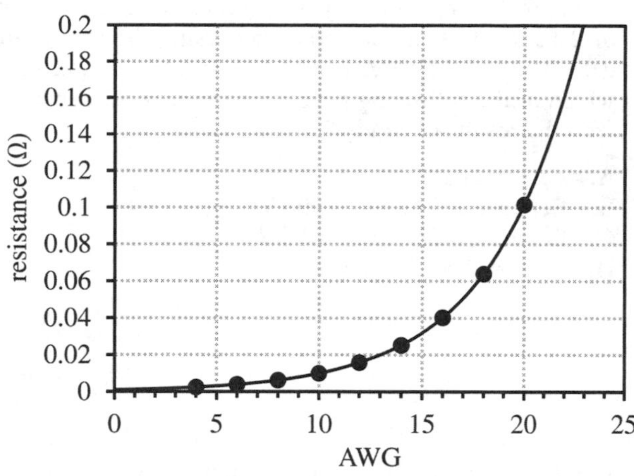

Figure 2

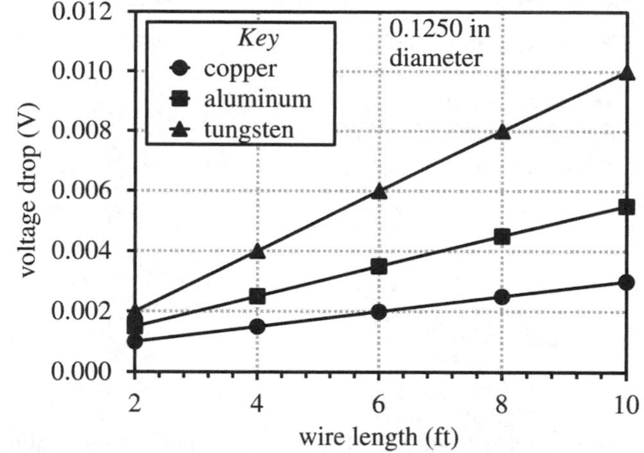

Figure 4

Study 2

Using the circuit constructed in Study 1, the students found the voltage drop for various lengths of silver, copper, and aluminum wire in both 0.0625 in and 0.1250 in diameters. The results of this study are shown in Figures 3 and 4. The resistivities of the three analyzed metals were calculated and are summarized in Table 3.

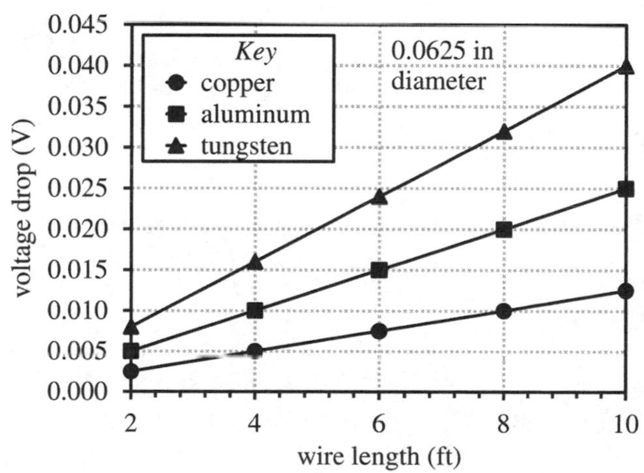

Figure 3

Table 3

Conductor	Resistivity (Ω/m)	Density (kg/m³)
copper	1.74×10^{-8}	8,940
aluminum	2.65×10^{-8}	2,720
tungsten	5.65×10^{-8}	19,600

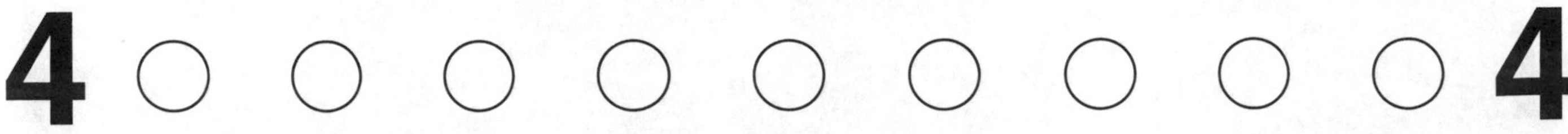

6. Based on Table 1, it is most likely that a wire of what gauge would measure a voltage drop of 0.0258 V?

   F. Less than 8 AWG
   G. Between 8 and 10 AWG
   H. Between 10 and 12 AWG
   J. Greater than 12 AWG

7. Based on a Figure 3, if a 13-foot length of aluminum with a 0.0625 in diameter had been used in the circuit, the voltage drop would have been:

   A. less than 0.015 V.
   B. between 0.015 and 0.028 V.
   C. between 0.028 and 0.040 V.
   D. greater than 0.040 V.

8. Based on Table 2, the resistance of 50 feet of 12 AWG solid copper wire would be closest to which of the following?

   F. 0.01588 Ω
   G. 0.03140 Ω
   H. 0.07940 Ω
   J. 0.12625 Ω

9. A fourth conductor with a 0.1250 in diameter and 10 feet in length, having a density of 5,490 kg/m^3 and resistivity of 2.12×10^{-8} Ω/m, was analyzed using the procedures described in Study 2. A voltage drop for that conductor in which of the following ranges would be most consistent with the results of Study 2?

   A. Less than 0.003 V
   B. Between 0.003 and 0.006 V
   C. Between 0.006 and 0.010 V
   D. Greater than 0.011 V

10. Based on the results of the studies, a conductor with which of the following combinations of diameter, length, and material will exhibit the smallest voltage drop?

	Diameter (in)	Length (ft)	Material
F.	0.0625	8	copper
G.	0.1250	4	aluminum
H.	0.1250	10	copper
J.	0.0625	2	tungsten

END OF SET TWO

STOP! DO NOT GO ON TO THE NEXT PAGE UNTIL TOLD TO DO SO.

This page is intentionally left blank.

6.4.3 Set Three

Passage III

Capacitors charge to full circuit voltage in a time that is determined by the circuit capacitance (*C*) and resistance (*R*). The circuit's *RC* time constant ($T = RC$) is the amount of time it takes for a capacitor to charge to 63% of the applied voltage.

Given a steady DC (direct current) input, a capacitor will reach 50% of its full charge in seven-tenths of a time constant. The transient period is the time required for the capacitor to reach 99% of its full charge. After four time constants, the capacitor reaches a steady state period. Once the input voltage is removed, the capacitor will discharge at the same rate it charged up. Figure 1 shows a characteristic charging curve for a capacitor.

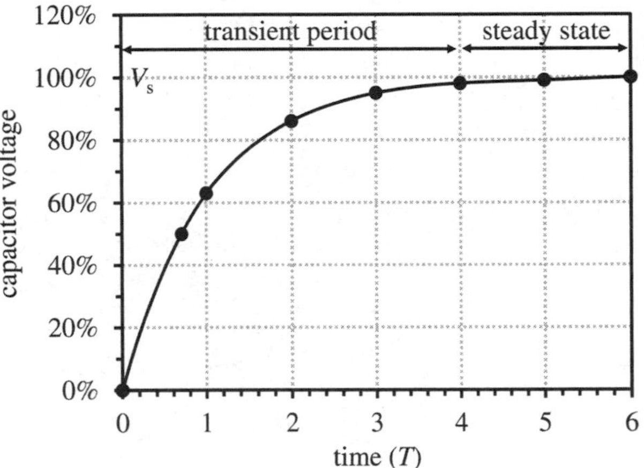

Figure 1

Variations in the input voltage (common in AC circuits and digital or RF signals) may limit the amount of charge the capacitor is able to reach. A square wave signal (Figure 2) with a pulse length greater than the capacitor's charge time ($5T$) will allow the capacitor to reach a full charge during each cycle. However, if the pulse duration is less than the charging time, the capacitor will begin discharging before it can store the full input voltage level (Figure 3).

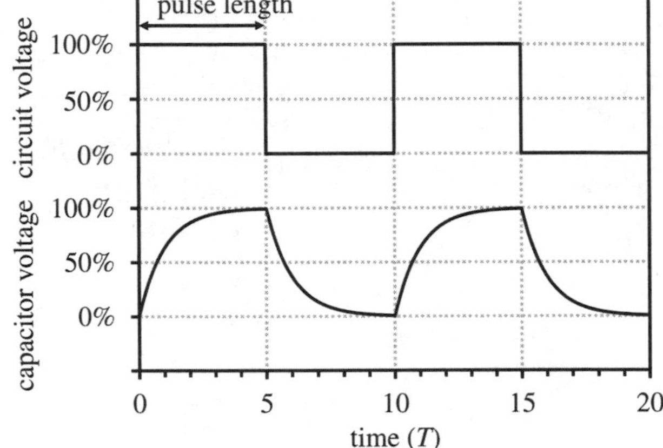

Figure 2

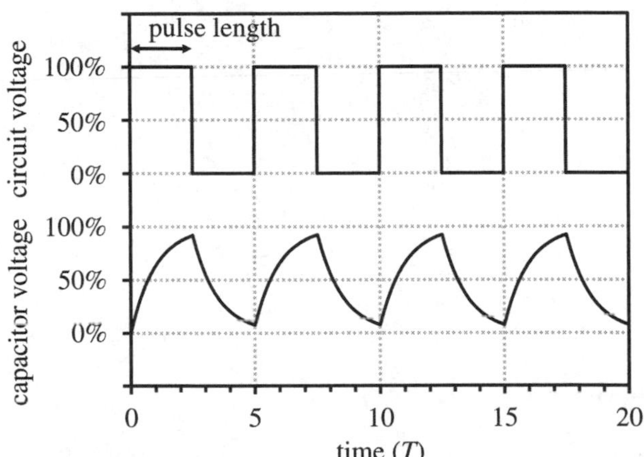

Figure 3

Experiment 1

Using the equation $T = RC$, the time constants for the resistance and capacitance values noted in Tables 1–3 were calculated. A simple RC circuit (Figure 4) was constructed using each of the RC combinations listed in the tables. The switch was closed, and the waveform on the oscilloscope display was used to validate the equation.

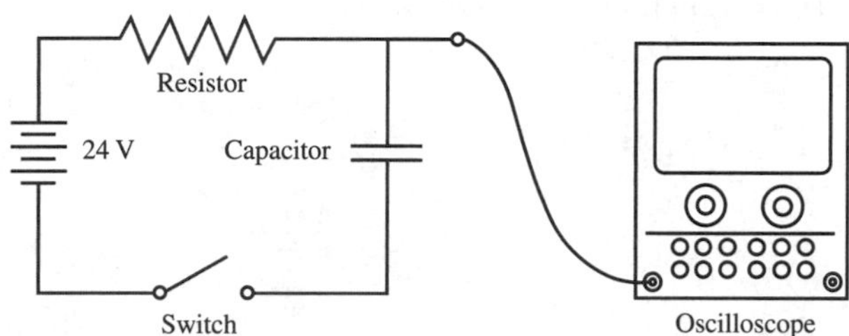

Figure 4

Table 1	
Resistance = 7.5 kΩ	
Capacitance (μF)	Time constant (*RC*)
1.5	11.25 ms
2.5	18.75 ms
6.0	45.00 ms
10.0	75.00 ms
12.5	93.75 ms

Table 2	
Resistance = 5.0 kΩ	
Capacitance (μF)	Time constant (*RC*)
0.05	0.250 ms
0.10	0.500 ms
0.20	1.00 ms
0.25	1.25 ms
0.50	2.50 ms

Table 3	
Capacitance = 25 μF	
Resistance (kΩ)	Time constant (*RC*)
1.0	25.0 ms
1.5	37.5 ms
3.0	75.0 ms
5.0	125.0 ms
7.5	187.5 ms

11. Based on the data in Table 1, if a capacitor having a value of 3 μF is in series with a resistor having a value of 7.5 kΩ, the time required for the capacitor to reach 63% of its full charge will be:

A. less than 11.25 ms.
B. between 11.25 ms and 18.75 ms.
C. between 18.75 ms and 45.00 ms.
D. greater than 45.00 ms.

12. If a square wave with a pulse duration of $2T$ is applied and V_s is equal to 5.0 volts, the maximum charge on the capacitor will most likely be closest to which of the following?

F. 3.2 volts
G. 4.1 volts
H. 5.0 volts
J. 5.2 volts

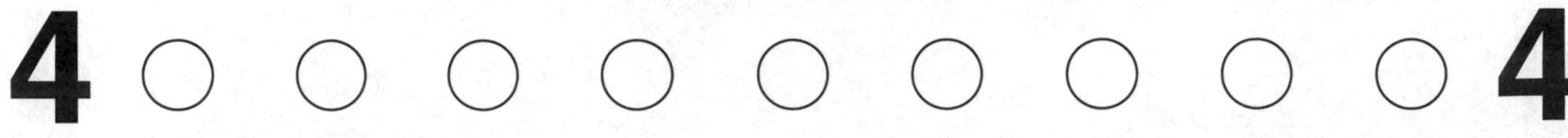

13. Suppose a sixth capacitor had been added to the data in Table 2, and its capacitance was 1.00 μF. The time to charge the capacitor to 63% of its full charge, as observed on the oscilloscope, would most likely have been closest to which of the following?

A. 3.00 ms
B. 3.50 ms
C. 4.25 ms
D. 5.00 ms

14. If, in Table 3, an additional trial had been conducted with a 12-volt battery, a resistance of 5.0 kΩ and a capacitance of 25 μF, the voltage observed 125 ms after the switch was closed would most likely have been:

F. less than 4.0 volts.
G. between 4.0 and 7.0 volts.
H. between 7.0 and 11.5 volts.
J. greater than 11.5 volts.

15. If, in Experiment 1, an additional trial had been conducted with 15.1 volts observed on the oscilloscope with a time constant of 50.0 ms, the values for resistance and capacitance could have been which of the following?

	Resistance	Capacitance
A.	2.0 kΩ	25 μF
B.	3.0 kΩ	50 μF
C.	5.0 kΩ	2 μF
D.	7.5 kΩ	3 μF

END OF SET THREE
STOP! DO NOT GO ON TO THE NEXT PAGE
UNTIL TOLD TO DO SO.

Sum It Up

Interpolation and Extrapolation

Direct Trend
An upward sloping line, or a line sloping toward the direction in which the units are increasing

---

Inverse Trend
A downward sloping line, or a line sloping toward the direction in which the units are decreasing

---

Neutral or Uncorrelated
A straight, non-sloping line

Extrapolate
To extend (a graph, curve, or range of values) by inferring unknown values from trends in the known data

Tips and Techniques

Road Signs: If the question mentions multiple experiments, studies, terms, or line numbers, be sure to consider all of them before determining your answer.

Lesson 7

New Information and Predictions on Models

CAPTION:

7.1 Entrance Ticket

Describe a time in your life when you "predicted the future." For instance you may have looked at dark clouds in the sky and predicted it would rain soon, or you may have realized that a certain action would get you in trouble, so you avoided repeating it. How did your prediction of the future alter your behavior?

7.2 Learning Targets

1. Use new information to make a prediction based on a model

2. Determine the implications of new information based on the previous findings of a scientist or experiment

Self-Assessment

Circle the number that corresponds to your confidence level in your knowledge of this subject before beginning the lesson. A score of 1 means you are completely lost, and a score of 4 means you have mastered the skills. After you finish the lesson, return to the bottom of this page and circle your new confidence level to show your improvement.

Before Lesson

1 2 3 4

After Lesson

1 2 3 4

7.3.1 Making Predictions

Two scientists are studying the effects of organic food on health.

Scientist A is studying how eating organic food affects ______________________________

____,

while Scientist B is studying how eating organic food affects __________________________

____.

Scientist A hypothesizes that eating more organic food will ___________________________

____,

while Scientist B hypothesizes that eating more organic food will ______________________

____.

Suppose studies show that increased consumption of organic foods decreases the risk of disease. How would Scientist A explain this result?

____

____

____

Suppose studies show that increased consumption of organic foods helps people lose weight. How would Scientist B explain this result?

____

____

____

7.3.1 Making Predictions

Scientist 1

When an external net force does work on an object, the object's velocity is changed. When work is done on the object over a distance, the kinetic energy of the object is changed proportionally to the amount of work done. Since kinetic energy is related to the object's mass and velocity and the object's mass is not changing as work is done on it, the object's velocity either increases or decreases. The change in the object's kinetic energy is proportional to the change in the object's velocity.

1. Suppose studies show that doing more work on an object can increase the amount that the object's velocity changes. Scientist 1 would most likely explain this result by arguing that doing more work on an object:

A. increases the amount that the object's kinetic energy changes and thus increases the change in the object's velocity.

B. increases the amount that the object's kinetic energy changes and thus decreases the change in the object's velocity.

C. decreases the amount that the object's kinetic energy changes and thus increases the change in the object's velocity.

D. decreases the amount that the object's kinetic energy changes and thus decreases the change in the object's velocity.

Science Tip

Process of Elimination: If an answer choice contains information mentioned in the passage that is not related to the scientist or experiment mentioned in the question, it is not the right answer. Eliminate it and choose from the remaining choices.

7.3.1 Making Predictions

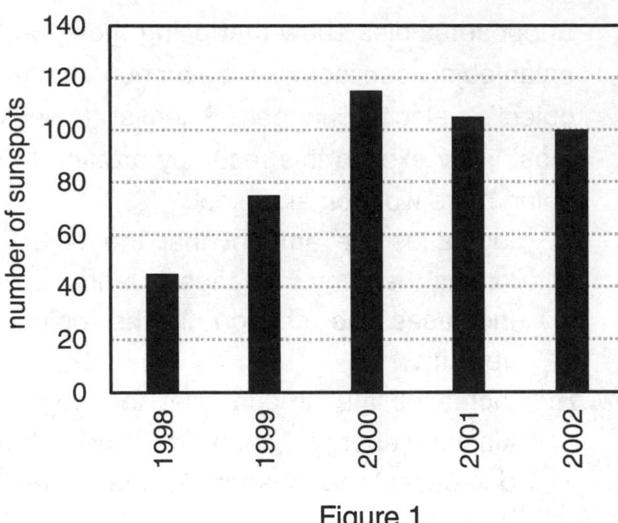

Figure 1

2. A scientist hypothesized that sunspots peak every 11 years. If this hypothesis is correct, Figure 1 indicates that the next peak in sunspots most likely occurred in:
   F. 2009.
   G. 2010.
   H. 2011.
   J. 2012.

7.3.2 Locating Necessary Information

Tip #1: When answering questions on the ACT, it is important to ______________________________ .

Tip #2: In order to ________________ , you must know ________________ to find important ________________ .

1. A given volume of gasoline has an energy density roughly 4 times higher than that of liquid hydrogen. Given this information and Scientist 1's viewpoint, the current amount of liquid hydrogen that would be necessary to replace gasoline as an energy source in the U.S. for a single day would be:

A. 188 million gallons.
B. 375 million gallons.
C. 750 million gallons.
D. 1,500 million gallons.

New information: ____

Reference: ____

2. Silver (Ag) has the lowest resistivity of all the metals. Based on Tables 1 and 2, the resistance, in ohms, of a 10 cm long, 0.1 cm diameter silver wire at 20°C would most likely be:

F. less than 0.001.
G. between 0.001 and 0.003.
H. between 0.003 and 0.005.
J. greater than 0.005.

New information: ____

Reference: ____

7.3.2 Locating Necessary Information

3. Many different elements are formed inside stars over the course of their lives. Based on Student 1's model, a star exploding in a supernova would most likely cause:

A. water to separate into hydrogen and oxygen.
B. silver and germanium to combine to form gold.
C. heavier elements to be destroyed in the explosion.
D. elements to be dispersed across space.

New information: ______________________________

Reference: ______________________________

4. The results of an astronomical survey suggest that light that has become more redshifted has been traveling for a longer time period than light that is less redshifted. How would Scientist 2 explain this result? Scientist 2 would most likely argue that the higher redshift indicates that:

F. the light has been traveling longer, allowing more time for the space it travels through to expand.
G. the light was emitted from a source already traveling away from Earth; the expansion of space is not related.
H. the light has been traveling less time, allowing less time for the space it travels through to expand.
J. the path that the light took was highly distorted due to gravitational phenomena not related to the source's motion or expansion of space.

New information: ______________________________

Reference: ______________________________

Science Tip

Follow the Road Signs: If a question tells you which figure, table, graph, or part of the passage to use to answer the question, go straight there. You do not need to use most of the passage to answer any one question.

This page is intentionally blank.

7.4.1 Set One

Passage I

Scientists are developing a new universal lubricant designed to reduce the coefficient of friction between a wide variety of materials. Their research studies the lubricant's effect on reducing the coefficient of static friction, making it easier for two objects to begin sliding relative to one another.

The frictional forces between two materials can be modeled using the formula $F_F = \mu_S F_N$ where μ_S is the coefficient of static friction for the materials interacting, and F_N is the normal force between them. Researchers used this formula and a series of experiments to gather the following data.

Table 1

Materials	Coefficient of static friction
Car tire/asphalt	0.72
Cast iron/wood	0.49
Carbon/steel	0.14
Brick/wood	0.60
Car tire/grass	0.35

Table 2

Materials	Coefficient of static friction	Normal force (N)	Frictional force (N)
Car tire/asphalt	0.72	49 98 147 196 245	35.28 70.56 105.84 141.12 176.40
Brick/wood	0.60	49 98 147 196 245	29.4 58.8 88.2 117.6 147.0
Car tire/grass	0.35	49 98 147 196 245	17.15 34.30 51.45 68.60 85.75

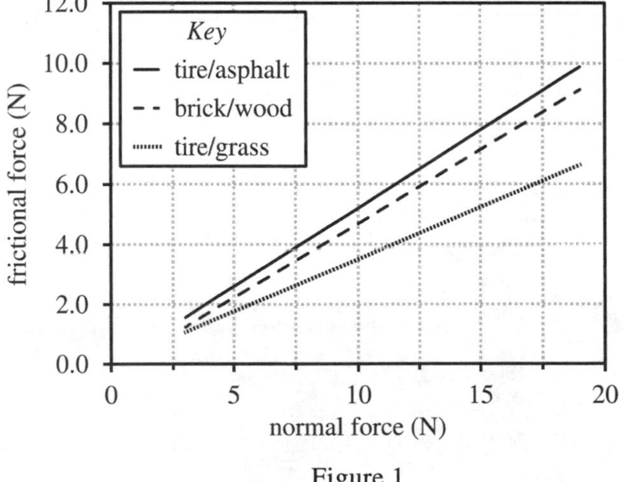

Figure 1

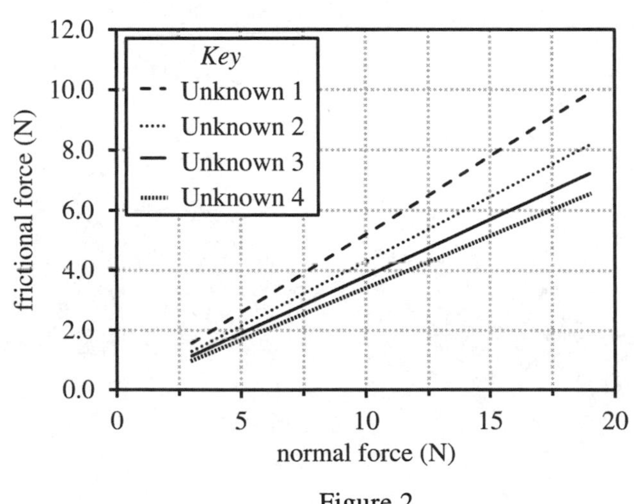

Figure 2

1. Lead and cast iron have a coefficient of static friction of 0.43. Based on the results in Table 2, if Figure 1 included the results of the same experiment performed using lead and cast iron, the line formed from the results of the experiment would most likely fall:

   A. above tire/asphalt.
   B. between brick/wood and tire/asphalt
   C. between tire/asphalt and tire/grass.
   D. below tire/grass.

2. For situations in which the normal forces between surfaces are equal, materials that have a lower coefficient of friction will experience smaller frictional forces between one another compared to materials with a higher coefficient of friction. Based on this information and the results of the experiment presented in Figure 2, which unknown material will experience the smallest frictional force?

   F. Unknown 1
   G. Unknown 2
   H. Unknown 3
   J. Unknown 4

3. Suppose further research shows that the use of a particular lubricant allows materials to begin sliding relative to one another with only half the frictional force required without any lubrication. How would the researchers explain this result? The researchers would most likely argue that using the lubricant:

   A. decreases the coefficient of friction between the materials, decreasing the frictional force between them.
   B. decreases the normal force between the materials, decreasing the frictional force between them.
   C. increases the coefficient of friction between the materials, increasing the frictional force between them.
   D. increases the normal force between the materials, increasing the frictional force between them.

4. Suppose research had been conducted to find the coefficient of friction between another set of materials, horseshoes and rubber. Based on Tables 1 and 2, if the frictional force between the horseshoe and rubber is 32.8 N when the normal force between them is 49 N, and the frictional force is 95 N when the normal force between them is 147 N, the coefficient of friction between the horseshoe and rubber is most likely:

   F. greater than 0.72.
   G. between 0.72 and 0.60.
   H. between 0.60 and 0.35.
   J. less than 0.35.

5. When chromium is in contact with itself, it has a coefficient of friction about three times as large as the coefficient of friction between carbon and steel. Given this information, the frictional force that two pieces of chromium would feel when they are in contact with one another with a 50 N normal force between them would be approximately:

   A. 21 N.
   B. 14 N.
   C. 7 N.
   D. 2 N.

END OF SET ONE

STOP! DO NOT GO ON TO THE NEXT PAGE UNTIL TOLD TO DO SO.

7.4.2 Set Two

Passage II

Two scientists propose different models attempting to explain frictional forces, and the results of their experiments are presented below.

Scientist 1

The frictional force (F_F) between an object and a surface can be modeled mathematically using two different values. The first value, the coefficient of friction μ_F, is dependent on the two types of materials that are in contact with one another. The second value A_S is the surface area over which the object is in contact. This model can be formulated as:

Equation 1: $F_F = \mu_F A_S$

Scientist 2

The frictional force between an object and a surface can be mathematically modeled using three different values. The first value is the coefficient of static friction, μ_S, which depends on the identity of the materials in contact and is unchanging until the moment they begin sliding. For a wet tire driving on a wet road, μ_S is about 0.2. The second value, called the coefficient of kinetic friction, μ_K, also depends on the materials that are in contact with one another; it takes the place of the coefficient of static friction once the object begins sliding. The third value is the normal force (F_N), which is perpendicular to the surface and remains unchanged as the objects slide against each other. These models of static friction (F_S) and kinetic friction (F_K) can be formulated as:

Equation 2: $F_S = \mu_S F_N$

Equation 3: $F_K = \mu_K F_N$

Table 1

Material 1	Material 2	Static friction	Kinetic friction
Concrete	rubber	1	0.75
Brass	steel	0.5	0.44
Glass	glass	0.9	0.4
Steel	steel	0.75	0.55

Table 2

Material 1	Material 2	Normal force (N)	Frictional force (N)
Concrete	rubber	5	5.0
Brass	steel	8	4.0
Glass	glass	7	6.3
Steel	steel	6	4.5

6. Suppose studies suggest that the frictional force between two objects drops as they begin to slide. How would Scientist 2 explain this result? Scientist 2 would most likely argue that:

   F. as the object begins to slide, the coefficient of kinetic friction takes over, which is lower than the coefficient of static friction.
   G. as the object begins to slide, the normal force between the object and surface decreases.
   H. as the object begins to slide, the coefficient of kinetic friction takes over, which is higher than the coefficient of static friction.
   J. as the object begins to slide, the normal force between the object and surface increases.

7. Suppose the experiment is performed again for steel in contact with glass, and it is determined that for a situation in which the objects experience a 5 N normal force, a frictional force of 4 N is measured just before the objects begin to slide. Based on Equation 2, the coefficient of static friction between steel and glass is most likely to be:

   A. less than 0.5.
   B. between 0.5 and 0.7.
   C. between 0.7 and 0.9.
   D. greater than 0.9.

8. Scientists are able to determine that the coefficient of static friction between wood and concrete is 3 times higher than friction between a wet road and tire. Given this information, as well as Scientist 2's viewpoint, the coefficient of static friction between wood and concrete is approximately:

   F. 0.2
   G. 0.4
   H. 0.6
   J. 0.8

9. When two diamonds are rubbed together, the frictional force just before they begin to slide is about one tenth the normal force between them, and once they begin sliding, the frictional force drops to about half that. Based on Equation 2, which of the following are the most likely coefficients of friction for diamond-diamond contact?

	μ_S	μ_K
A.	0.6	0.3
B.	0.5	0.25
C.	0.25	0.125
D.	0.1	0.05

10. Suppose the experiment is run twice, once using a combination of wood against wood and again using a combination of wood against ice. The normal and frictional forces for each combination are given in the table below.

Table 1

Material 1	Material 2	Normal force (N)	Frictional force (N)
Wood	wood	8	2.4
Wood	ice	10	0.5

Based on Equation 2 and Scientist 2's statement, which combination of materials has the lowest coefficient of static friction?

   F. Wood/wood, because it has the smallest ratio of frictional force to normal force.
   G. Wood/wood, because it has the smallest ratio of normal force to frictional force.
   H. Wood/ice, because it has the smallest ratio of frictional force to normal force.
   J. Wood/ice, because it has the smallest ratio of normal force to frictional force.

END OF SET TWO

STOP! DO NOT GO ON TO THE NEXT PAGE UNTIL TOLD TO DO SO.

7.4.3 Set Three

Passage III

Students in a high school physics class are conducting experiments using springs of varying stiffness and carts of different masses on a track with one side of the cart attached to a spring, as in Figure 1. A spring always wants to be at equilibrium. When a spring is either stretched or compressed in one direction, it begins exerting a force in the opposite direction in an attempt to restore itself to its equilibrium position. During this process, kinetic energy is converted into potential energy. Figure 2 shows the exchange of energy over time in a spring.

Definition 1: The force exerted by a spring is $F = kx$ where k is a constant related to the stiffness of the spring and x is the amount the spring is stretched or compressed.

Definition 2: The potential energy stored in a spring is $U = \frac{1}{2}kx^2$.

Definition 3: The kinetic energy of an object attached to the spring is $K = \frac{1}{2}mv^2$ where m is the mass of the object and v is its velocity.

Definition 4: The total energy of the particle-spring system is given by $E = K + U$.

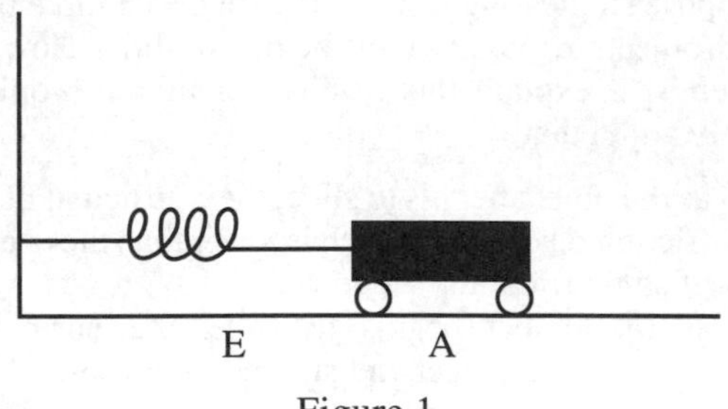

Figure 1

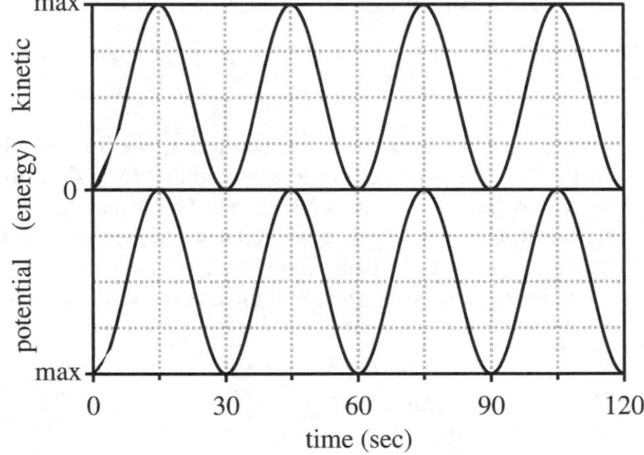

Figure 2

11. When a spring is stretched or contracted, the amount of energy exerted to stretch or compress it is stored in the spring as potential energy which can be used to do work. Based on Definition 2, in order to increase the amount of work that a particular spring is able to do, one must:

A. increase the mass of the spring.
B. decrease the mass of the spring.
C. increase the amount that the spring is stretched or compressed.
D. decrease the amount that the spring is stretched or compressed.

12. Suppose a spring with a stiffness constant of 5 is used in an experiment. Based on Definition 1, how would the force exerted by this new spring when stretched a distance of 10 cm compare to a standard spring with a stiffness constant of 2 stretched the same distance?

F. The force exerted would be greater since x is the same and k is larger in the new spring.
G. The force exerted would be less since x is the same and k is smaller in the new spring.
H. The force exerted would be greater since x is larger and k is the same in the new spring.
J. The force exerted would be smaller since x is smaller and k is the same in the new spring.

13. Suppose that the spring is not expanded or compressed at all when attached to the cart on the track. Based on the information provided, the cart will:

A. cause the spring to be stretched or compressed to a new equilibrium position.
B. be pulled from its current position to a new position as the spring returns to its equilibrium position.
C. increase the potential energy stored in the spring.
D. remain at rest since the spring is not exerting any forces on it.

14. Suppose that the spring pictured in Figure 1 is stretched to a new position before the cart is attached, such that the cart begins at Point P on the track to the right of Point A. Based on Definition 1, compared to the force in the spring pictured at equilibrium in Figure 1, the force in this spring would be:

F. Less, because the distance the spring is stretched has increased.
G. Less, because the distance the spring is stretched has decreased.
H. Greater, because the distance the spring is stretched has increased.
J. Greater, because the distance the spring is stretched has decreased.

15. A student hypothesized that every 15 seconds, beginning when the spring is released, the spring would alternate between having all of its potential energy converted to kinetic energy and, in the following 15 seconds, having all of its kinetic energy converted back into potential energy. If this hypothesis is correct, Figure 2 indicates that after 60 seconds have elapsed, the spring would have had all of its potential energy converted to kinetic energy how many times?

A. 2
B. 3
C. 4
D. 6

END OF SET THREE

STOP! DO NOT GO ON TO THE NEXT PAGE UNTIL TOLD TO DO SO.

Sum It Up

Tips and Techniques

Process of Elimination: If an answer choice contains information mentioned in the passage that is not related to the scientist or experiment mentioned in the question, it is not the right answer. Eliminate it and choose from the remaining choices.

Follow the Road Signs: If a question tells you which figure, table, graph, or part of the passage to use to answer the question, go straight there. You do not need to use most of the passage to answer any one question.

Lesson 8

Creating Figures

8.1 Entrance Ticket

Think about the last four years and recall the number of books you have read each year. Create a table, a bar graph, and a line graph depicting the number of books you read each year.

8.2 Learning Targets

1. Create graphs and figures from scientific descriptions

2. Create graphs and figures from tables of data

3. Combine select information from multiple graphs into a single graph

Self-Assessment

Circle the number that corresponds to your confidence level in your knowledge of this subject before beginning the lesson. A score of 1 means you are completely lost, and a score of 4 means you have mastered the skills. After you finish the lesson, return to the bottom of this page and circle your new confidence level to show your improvement.

Before Lesson

1 2 3 4

After Lesson

1 2 3 4

8.3.1 Creating Figures

Round 1

A

Time	Speed (mph)
1	10
2	10
3	10
4	10
5	10
6	0
7	0
8	15
9	15
10	15
11	15
12	15

B

Time	Speed (mph)
1	10
2	10
3	15
4	15
5	15
6	10
7	5
8	5
9	10
10	10
11	15
12	15

C

Time	Speed (mph)
1	20
2	20
3	20
4	20
5	15
6	15
7	15
8	10
9	10
10	10
11	5
12	5

D

Time	Speed (mph)
1	0
2	0
3	0
4	0
5	5
6	5
7	10
8	10
9	15
10	15
11	10
12	5

8.3.1 Creating Figures

Round 2

A

Time	pH
1	2
5	3
10	5
15	7
20	8

B

Time	pH
1	8
5	3
10	7
15	4
20	5

C

Time	pH
1	7
5	6
10	5
15	4
20	3

D

Time	pH
1	8
5	3
10	1
15	4
20	5

8.3.1 Creating Figures

Round 3

A

Site	NaOH (%)
A	8
B	10
C	6

B

Site	NaOH (%)
A	6
B	8
C	10

C

Site	NaOH (%)
A	10
B	6
C	8

D

Site	NaOH (%)
A	8
B	6
C	10

8.3.1 Creating Figures

Round 4

A

Year	ppm
2010	250
2011	275
2012	280
2013	300

B

Year	ppm
2010	250
2011	280
2012	275
2013	295

C

Year	ppm
2010	260
2011	250
2012	260
2013	280

D

Year	ppm
2010	260
2011	260
2012	280
2013	300

8.3.1 Creating Figures

Round 5

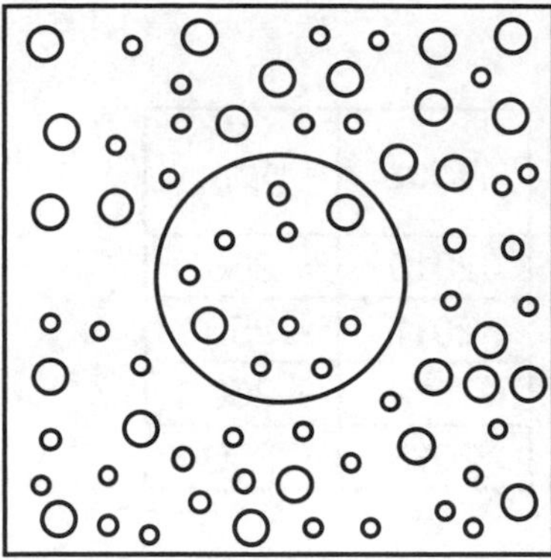

In an isotonic solution, there is little to no osmosis, or movement of water, between the cell and the solution. The cell remains stable.

A

In a *hypertonic solution*, there is a higher concentration of solute outside the cell than inside, which causes water to move out of the cell and can result in a shriveled appearance.

B

In a *hypotonic solution*, the concentration of solute is higher inside the cell than outside, which causes water to move into the cell and can cause the cell to burst.

8.3.1 Creating Figures

Round 6

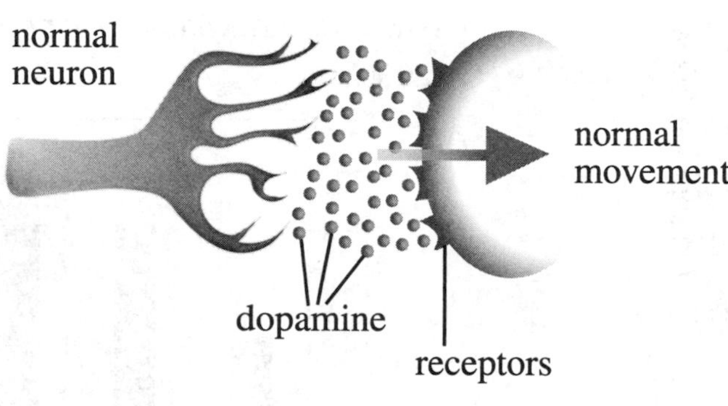

A functioning neural synapse will produce an appropriate amount of dopamine resulting in normal signal movement between neurons.

A

B

Schizophrenia is a disorder in which an individual interprets reality abnormally. It is theorized that an overabundance of dopamine is associated with its occurrence.

Parkinson's disease is a disorder in which the dopamine producing neurons in the brain are attacked by acetylcholine. This results in neurons which are not able to produce the required dopamine.

8.3.2 Flower Picking

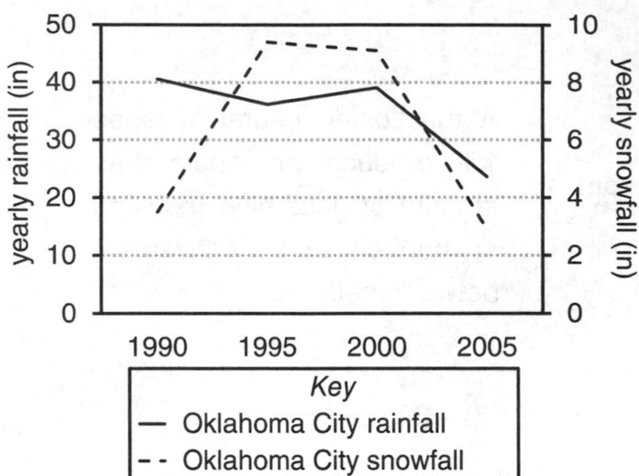

Figure 1

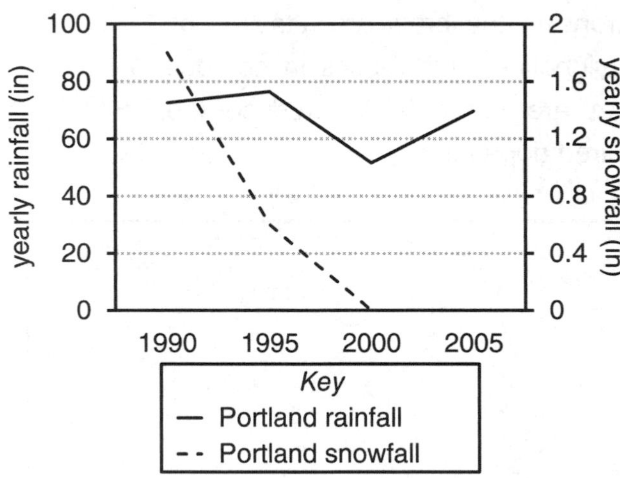

Figure 2

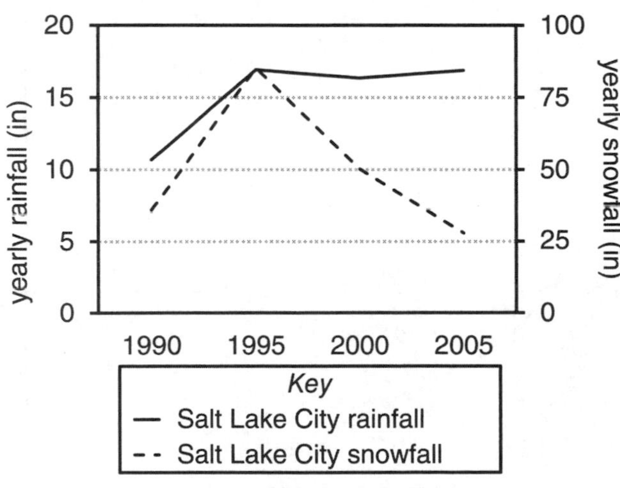

Figure 3

1. Which of the following figures best represents the average snowfall level for each of the cities in 2000?

A.

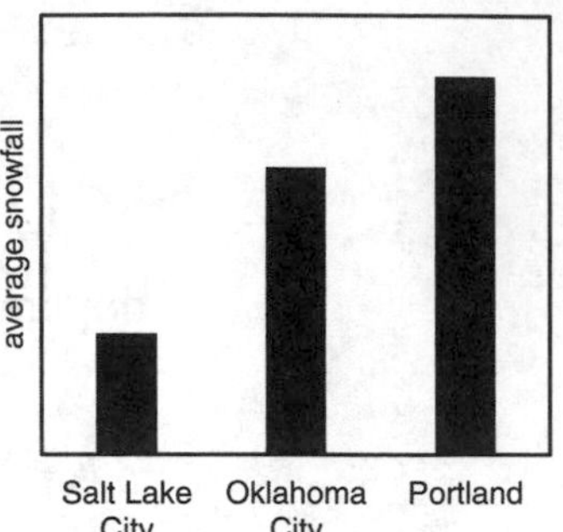

B.

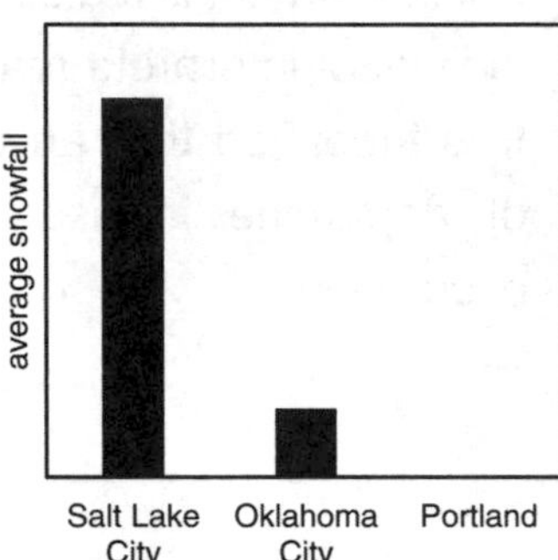

C.

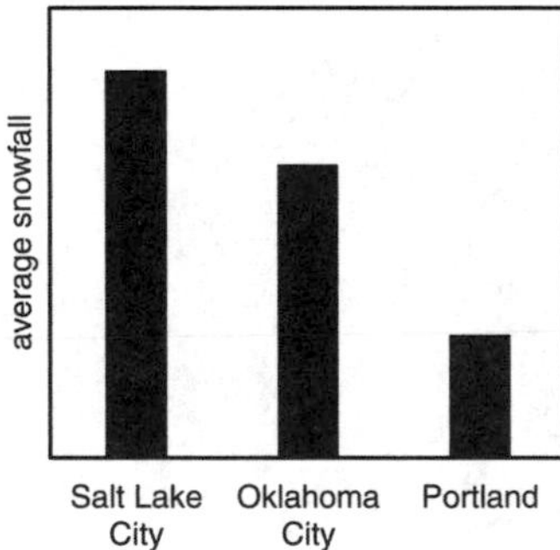

D.

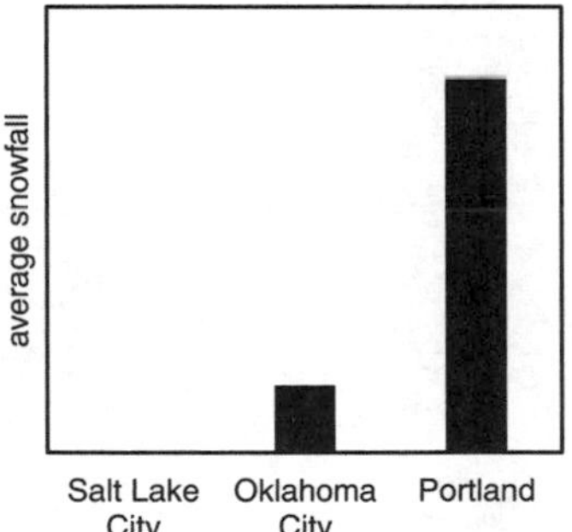

8.3.2 Flower Picking

2. Which of the following graphs best represents the information in Figures 1–3 for average rainfall during the year 1995?

A.

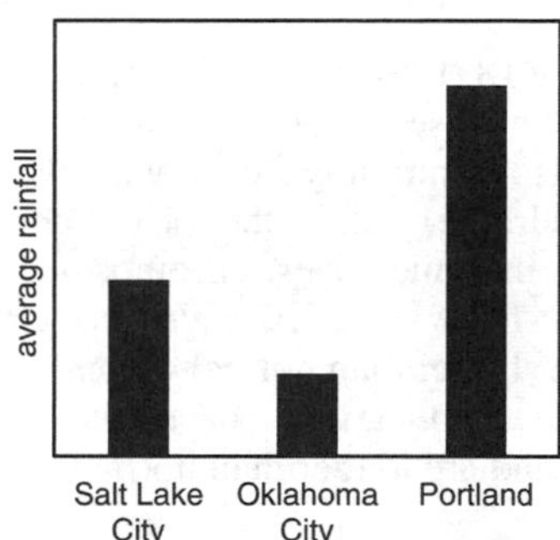

C.

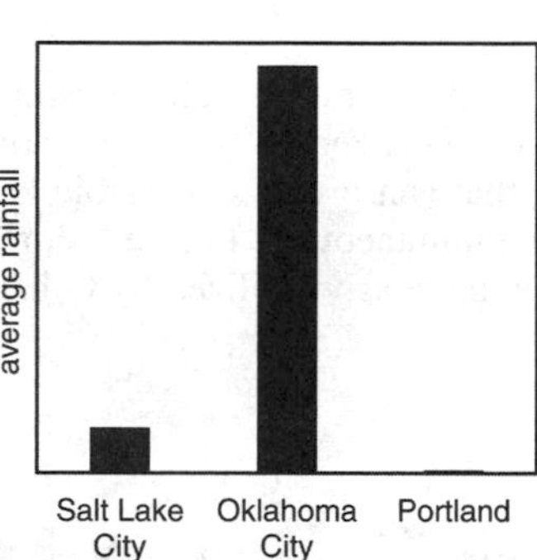

B.

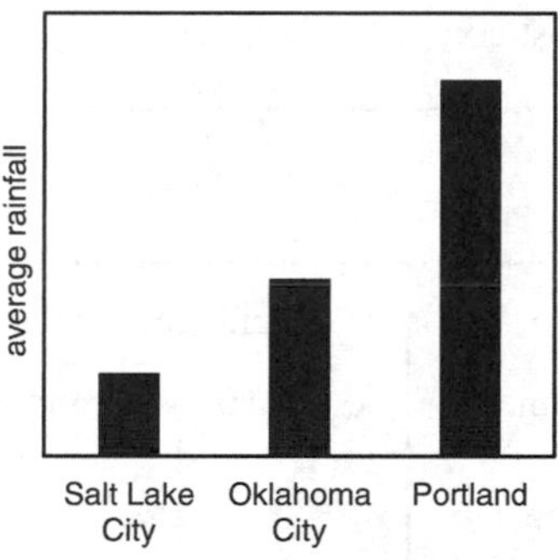

D.

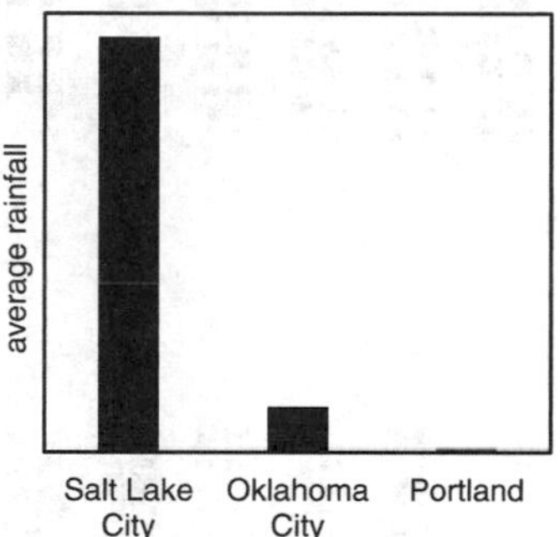

Science Tip

Data is Key: Most questions on the ACT science test do not require you to read the passage text. Any time you see a question with graphs or tables in the answer choices, try answering it without reading the passage. Just focus on the data.

8.4.1 Set One

Passage I

Humans have 23 pairs of chromosomes. These chromosomes can be visualized by genetic testing such as *G-banding*, staining that can produce a visible karyotype of all 23 chromosomes simultaneously. Figure 1 shows a normal karyotype of a human male as visualized by G-banding.

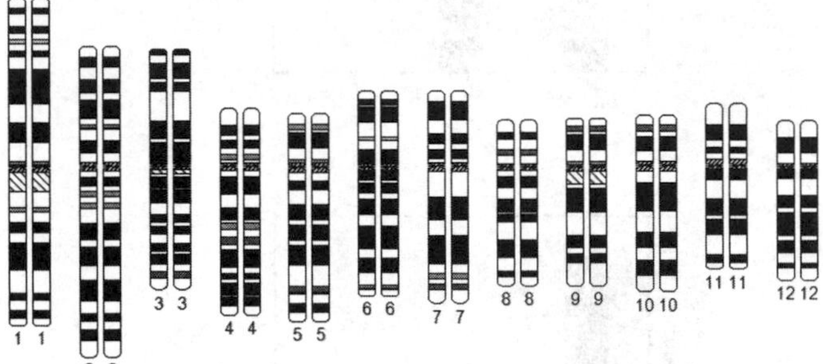

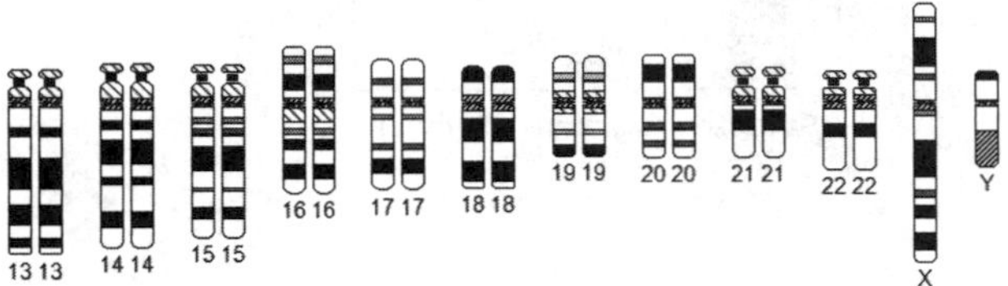

Figure 1

The banding on each chromosome can be used to rule out various conditions and identify common chromosomal issues such as deletions, duplications, and trisomies. Figure 2 shows an example of Trisomy 18 as visualized by G-banding.

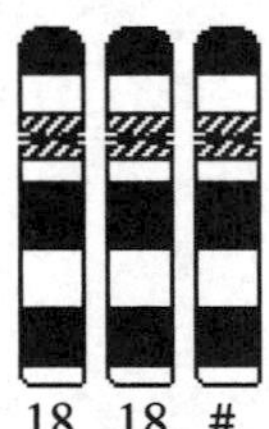

Figure 2

Trisomy 18 (Edwards syndrome), is a genetic condition caused by the presence of an additional 18th chromosome. Trisomies also commonly occur with the 21st chromosome (Down syndrome) and the 13th chromosome (Patau syndrome). In some cases, chromosomes may be missing information. This is called *deletion*. Chromosomes with deletions are shorter than normal chromosomes. Conversely, chromosomal duplications have an excess of genetic information and are longer than normal chromosomes.

Table 1 shows the incidence rates and survival rates of the three most common trisomies.

Table 1

Syndrome	Incidence rate (per 100,000 live births)	Survival rate
T13 (Patau)	15	5-10%
T18 (Edwards)	10	1%
T21 (Down)	125	70-75%

1. Based on the information from the passage, which of the following illustrations best represents an example of a chromosomal deletion?

A.

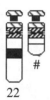

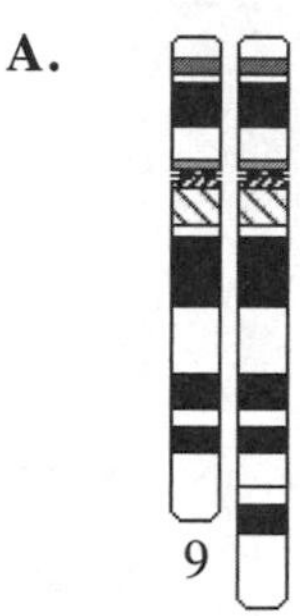

B.

#
22

C.

7

D.

8 8 #

2. Which of the following graphs best represents the survival rates of trisomies 13, 18, and 21?

F.

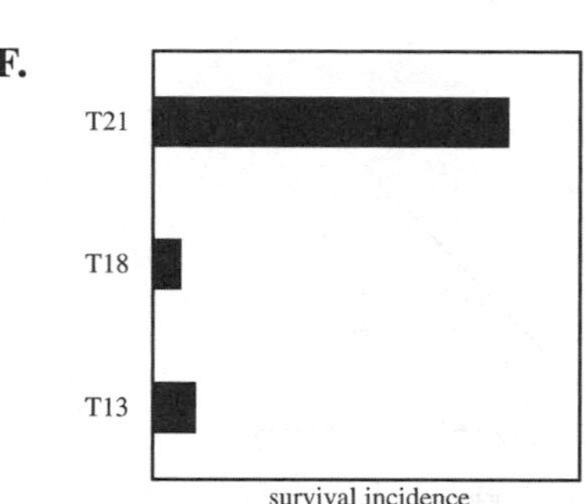

G.

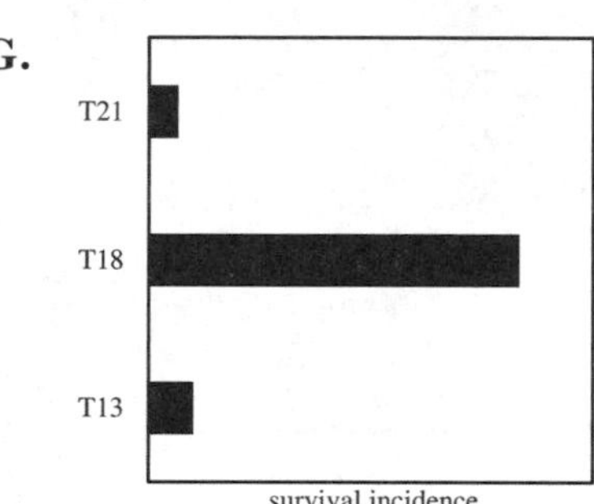

H.

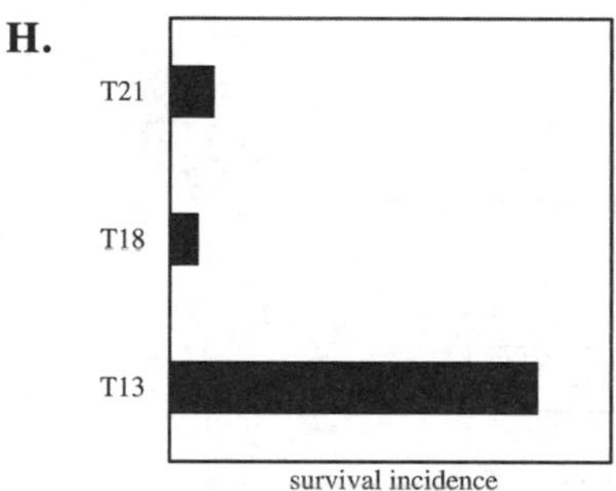

J.

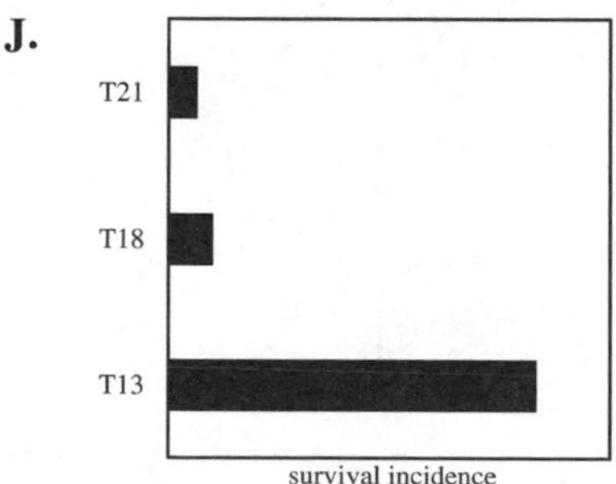

  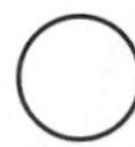      

3. Based on the information in Table 1, which of the following graphs best represents the relationship between incidence rate and survival rate?

A.
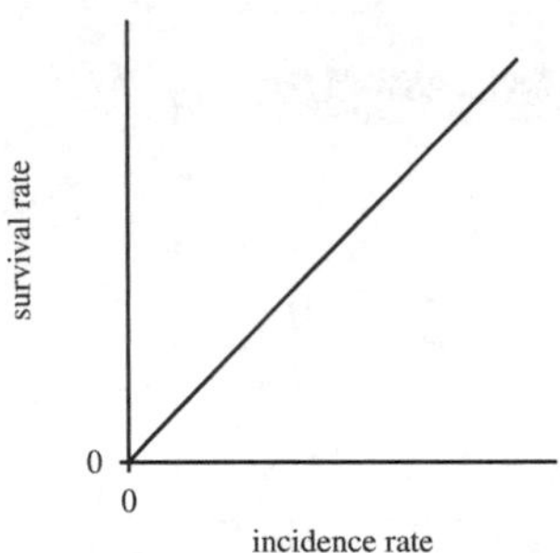

B.
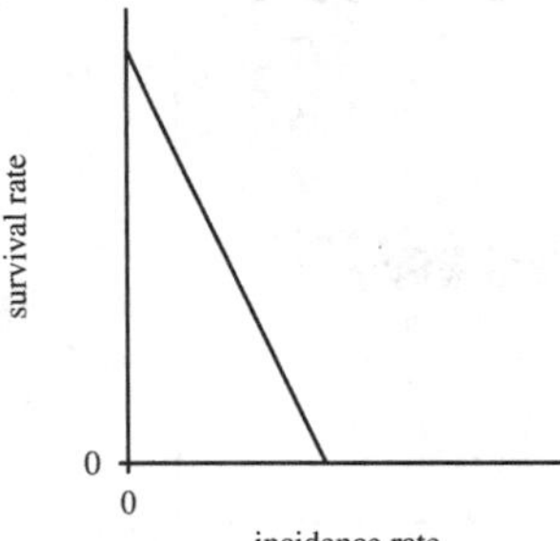

C.
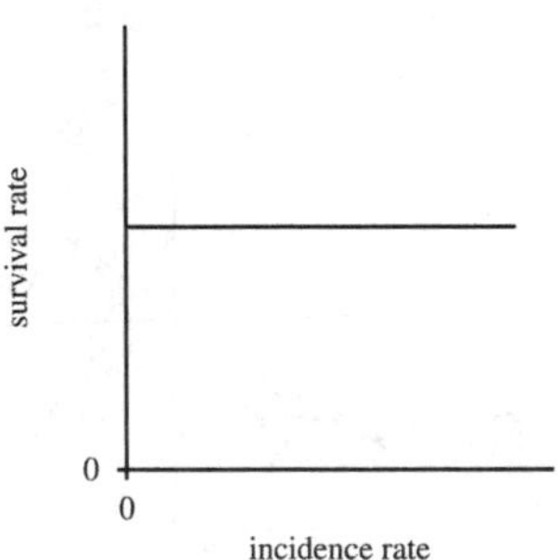

D.

4. According to the information from the passage, which of the following pictures best represents an example of a chromosomal duplication?

F.
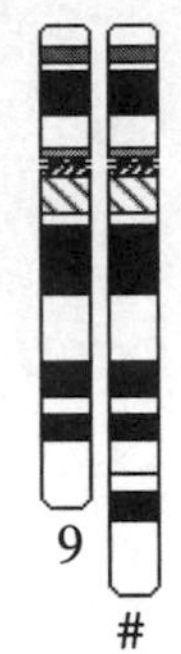

G.

H.

J.
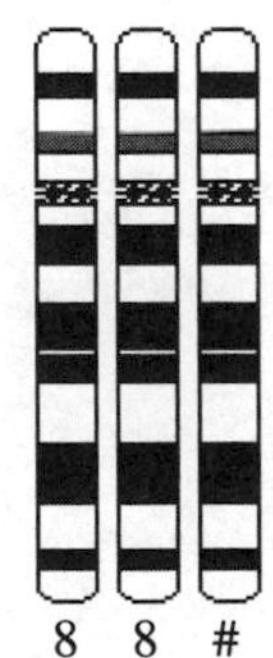

5. According to Table 1, which of the following graphs best shows the survival rates of each of the three trisomies listed in Table 1?

A.

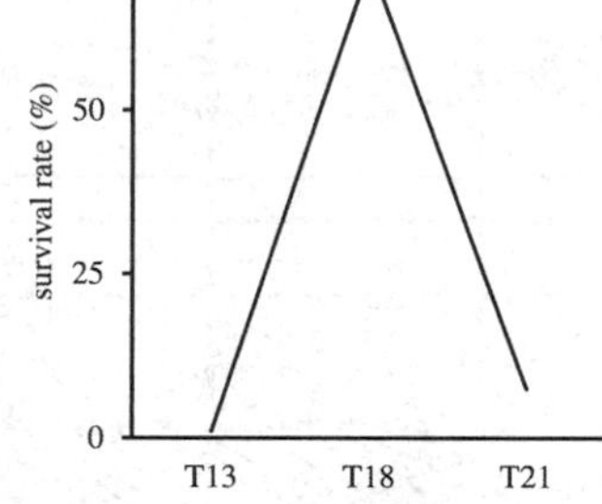

B.

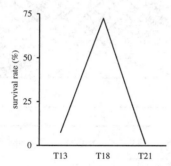

75
50
25
0
survival rate (%)
T13
T18
T21

C.

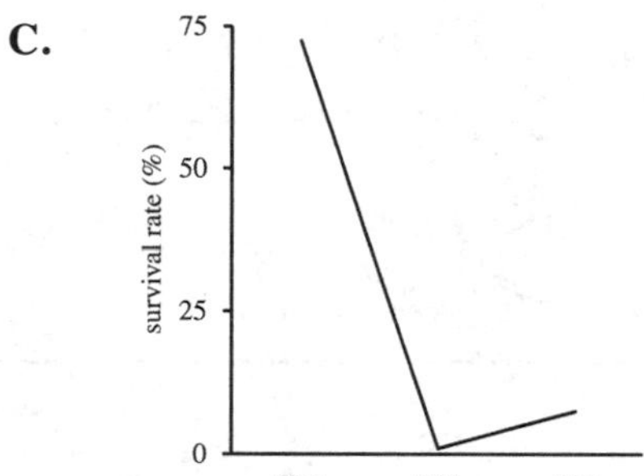

D.

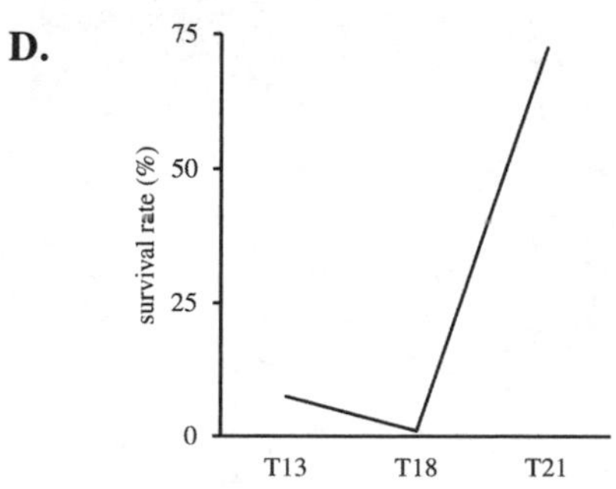

END OF SET ONE
STOP! DO NOT GO ON TO THE NEXT PAGE UNTIL TOLD TO DO SO.

8.4.2 Set Two

Passage II

Scientists evaluated the composition of a cliff face by identifying the rock formations at three different sites. They recorded the thickness of each unique cross-sectional layer at all three sites from core samples (Figure 1). They then reported the range of elevations above sea level for 2–3 types of rocks from the main three categories of rocks—igneous, sedimentary, and metamorphic—in Tables 1–3.

Table 1

	Igneous rocks	
Elevation range (m above sea level)	diorite	basalt
Lower limit Upper limit	1,600 1,710	1,930 1,960

Table 2

	Sedimentary rocks		
Elevation range (m above sea level)	sandstone	dolostone	conglomerate
Lower limit Upper limit	1,900 1,970	1,850 1,900	1,800 1,850

Table 3

	Metamorphic Rocks		
Elevation range (m above sea level)	schist	gneiss	marble
Lower limit Upper limit	1,720 1,800	1,640 1,730	1,680 1,780

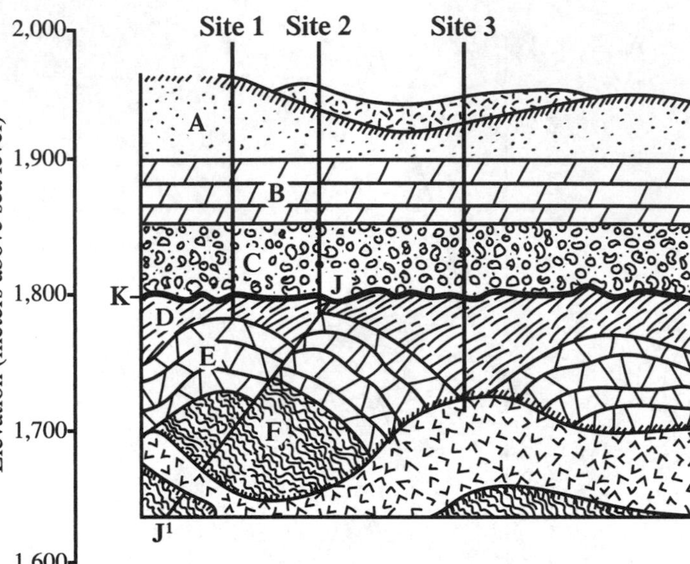

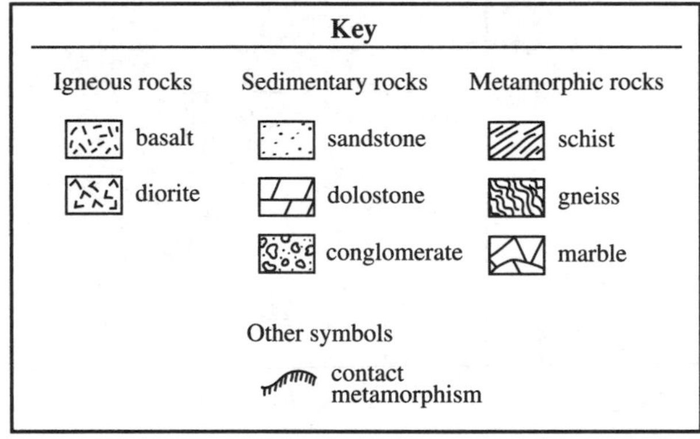

Figure 1

6. According to Figure 1, which of the graphs best represents the elevations (in meters above sea level) of the bottom of the schist layer at each of the three sites?

F.

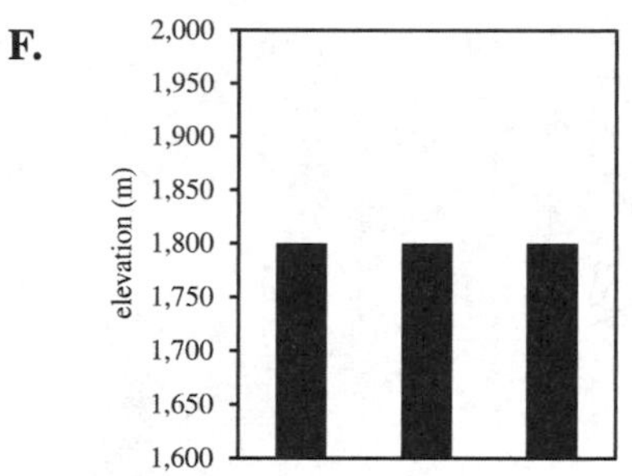

G.

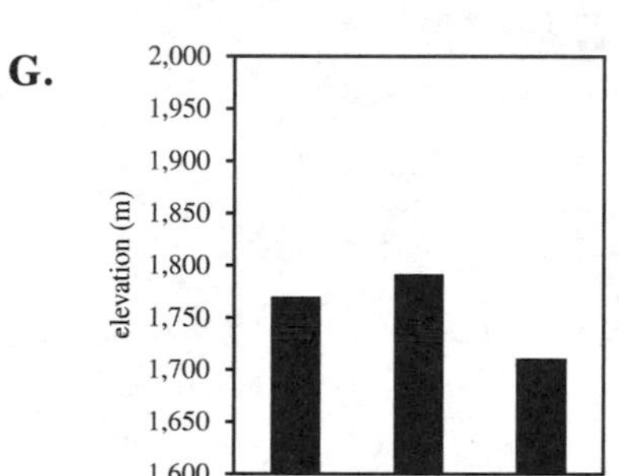

H.

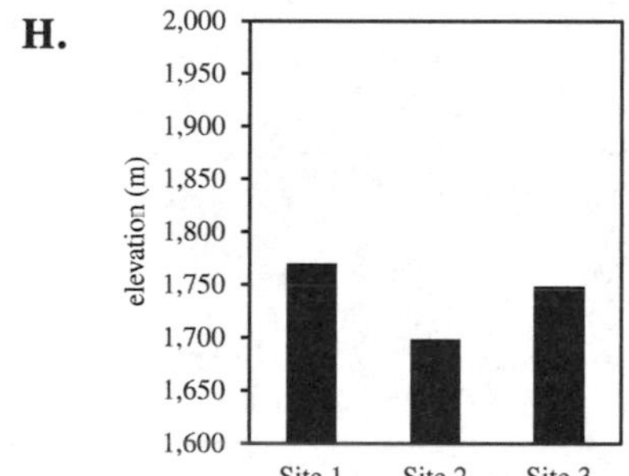

J.

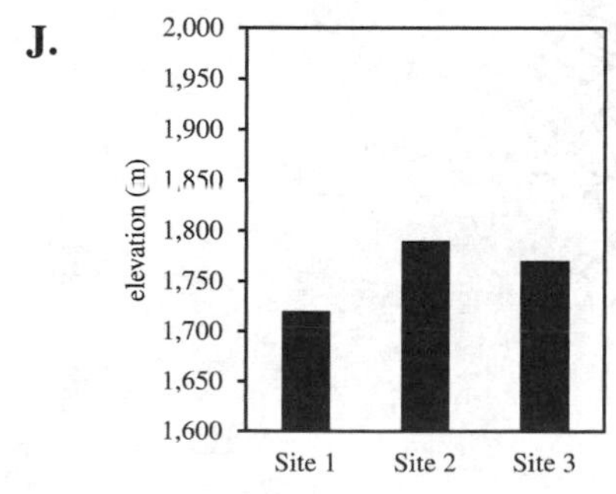

7. According to the information in Figure 1, which illustration best represents the most likely rock configuration from a site with similar geologic history?

A.

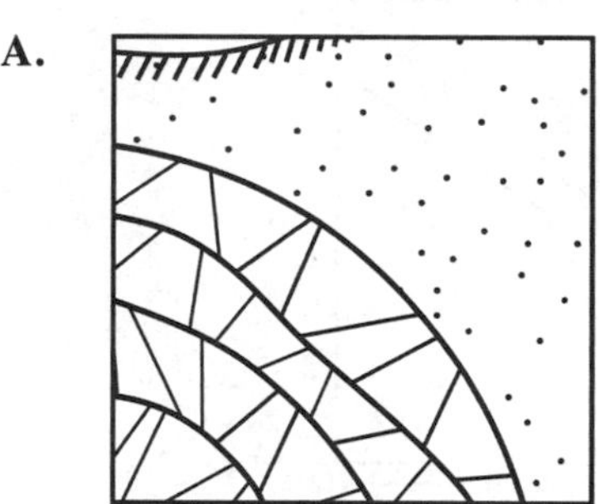

B.

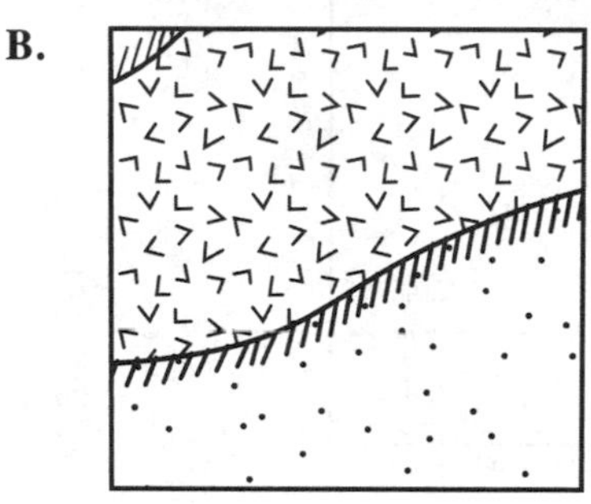

C.

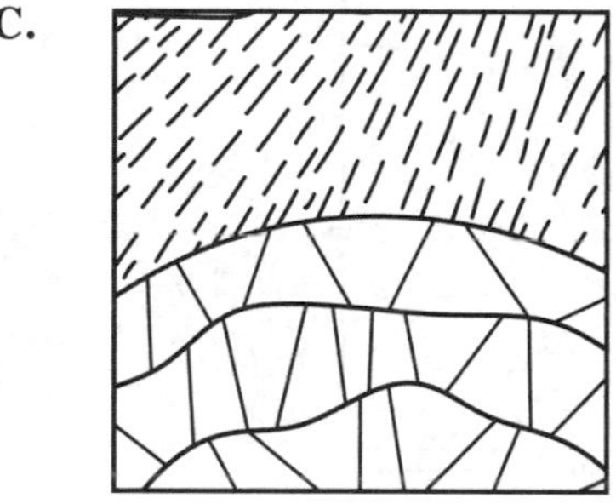

D.

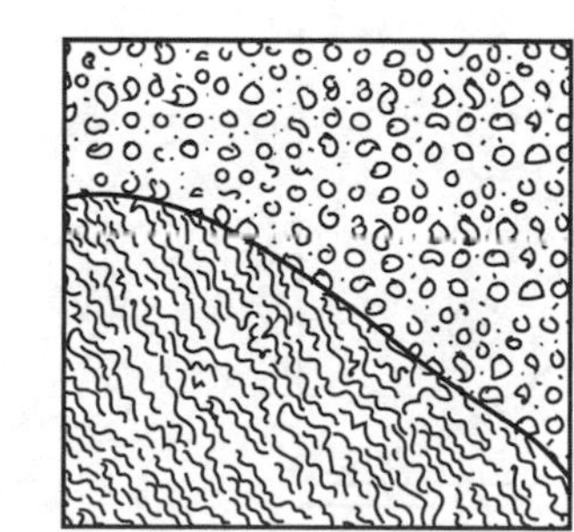

8. The relationship between the upper limit and lower limit of elevation measurements in Table 2 is best represented by which of the following graphs?

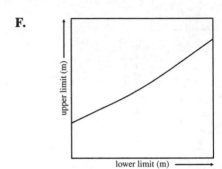

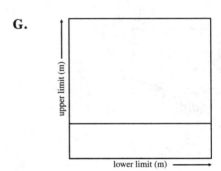

F. upper limit (m) / lower limit (m)

G. upper limit (m) / lower limit (m)

H. upper limit (m) / lower limit (m)

J. upper limit (m) / lower limit (m)

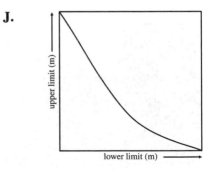

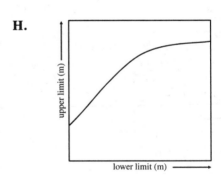

9. Based on Figure 1 and Table 3, which of the following illustrations best represents the elevation range for the marble layer between Sites 2 and 3?

A.
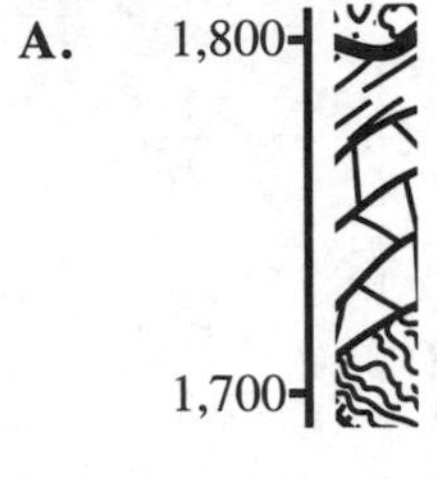

B.
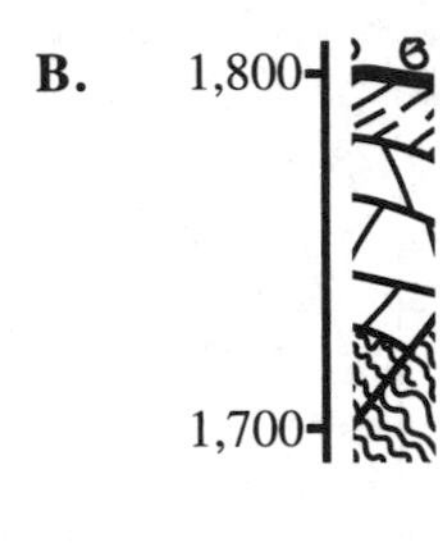

C.
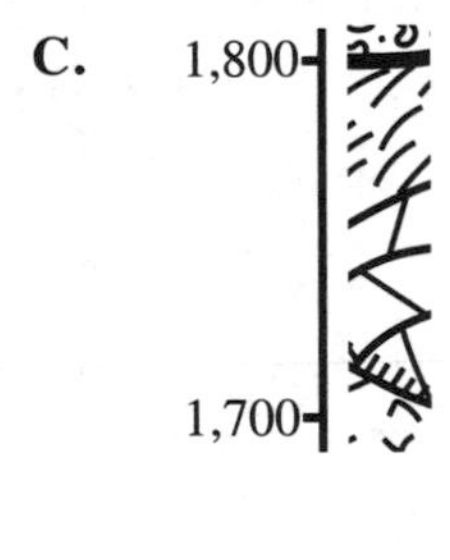

D.
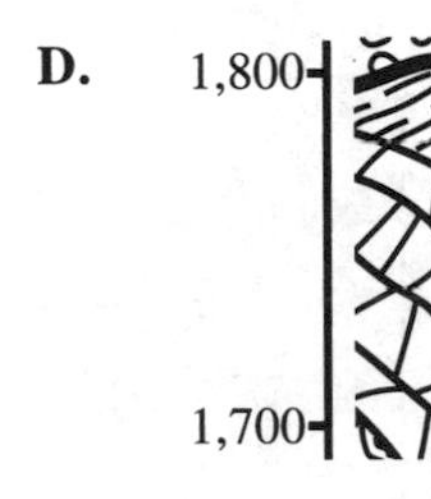

10. Which of the following graphs best represents the information from Tables 1–3 for the upper limit of elevation for igneous, sedimentary, and metamorphic rocks?

F.

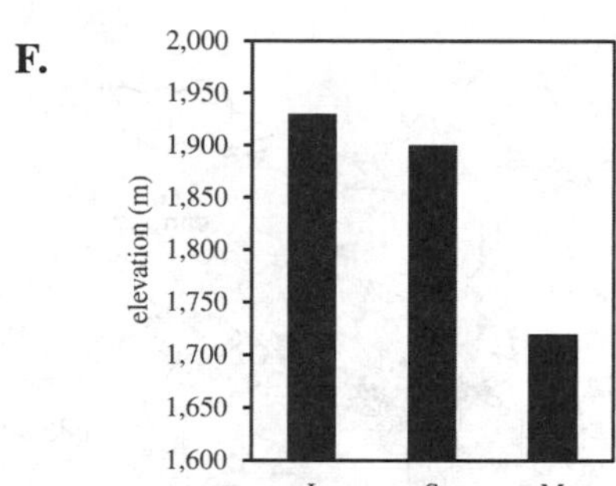

G.

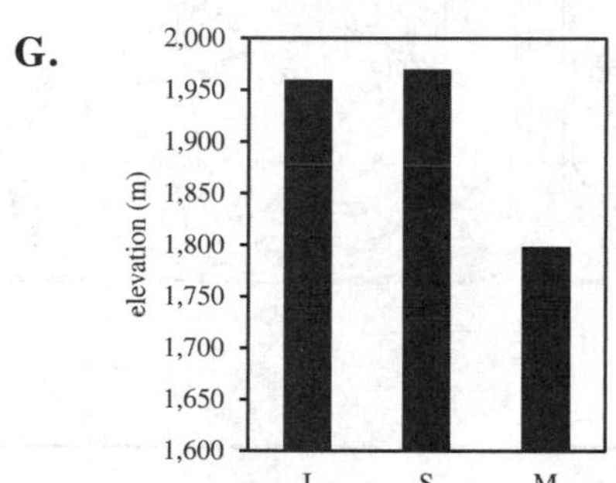

H.

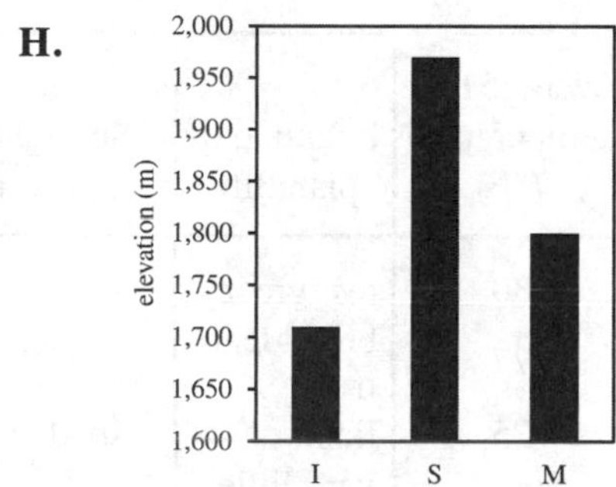

J.

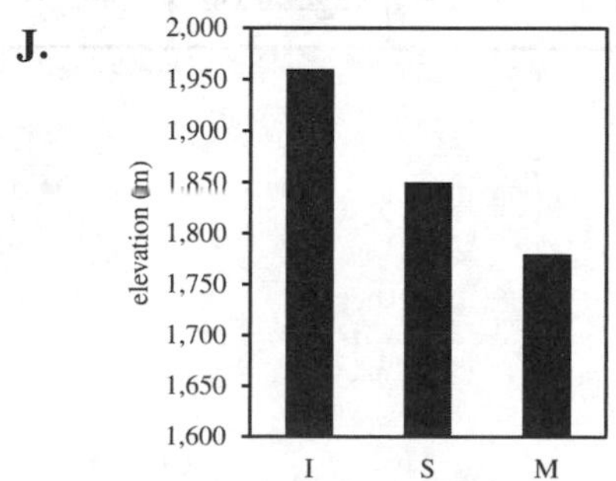

END OF SET TWO

STOP! DO NOT GO ON TO THE NEXT PAGE UNTIL TOLD TO DO SO.

8.4.3 Set Three

Passage III

A *rainforest* is a biome, or ecosystem, that can be found in many regions on Earth, especially along the Equator. Rainforests have four distinct layers: emergent, canopy, understory, and shrub. An illustration of these layers is shown in Figure 1.

Each layer has unique features contributing to the water and nutrient cycle that allow rainforests to thrive. The dark, humid shrub layer allows fallen leaves and debris to decompose much more quickly than they do in other environments. This quick decomposition results in rapid absorption of nutrients across all layers of the rainforest. The canopy levels collect much of the rainwater; this prevents flooding in the shrub level which would disrupt decomposition. Statistics for each layer are shown in Table 1.

The rain collection at the canopy level also aids the convectional rainfall cycle. The canopy provides a source of water for evaporation to fuel the next day's rain event as the humidity and heat begin to rise in the understory and shrub layers. Shallow roots absorb water from the shrub level and transport it to the upper emergent layers.

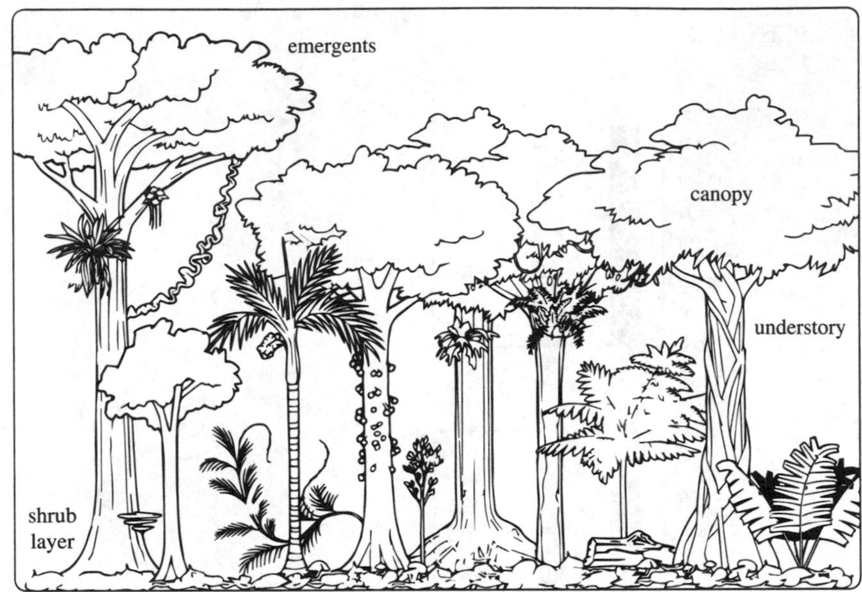

Figure 1

Table 1

Rain forest layer	Highest vegetation (ft)	Humidity	Average high temperature (°F)	Example of plant life	Sunlight exposure
Emergent	200	low	80	evergreen	full
Canopy	130	mid	77	broad leaf trees	partial
Understory	12	very high	75	liana	shaded
Shrub	3	high	74	very little vegetation	minimal

11. Based on Table 1, which of the following graphs best represents the relationship between humidity and temperature in the rainforest ecosystem?

A.

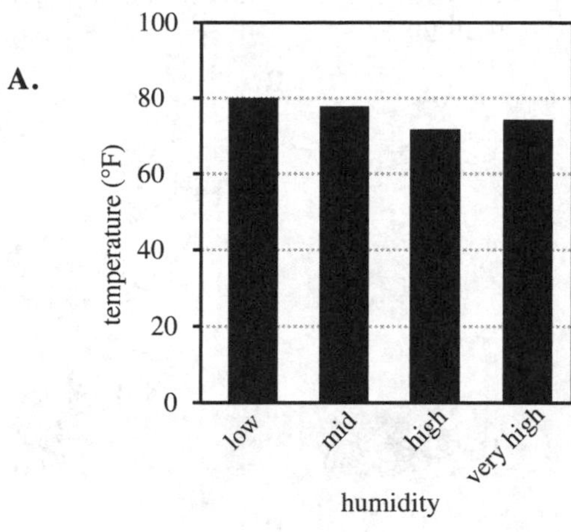

B.

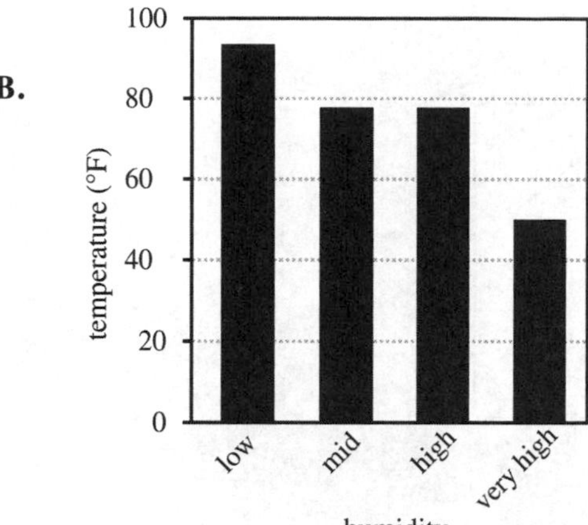

C.

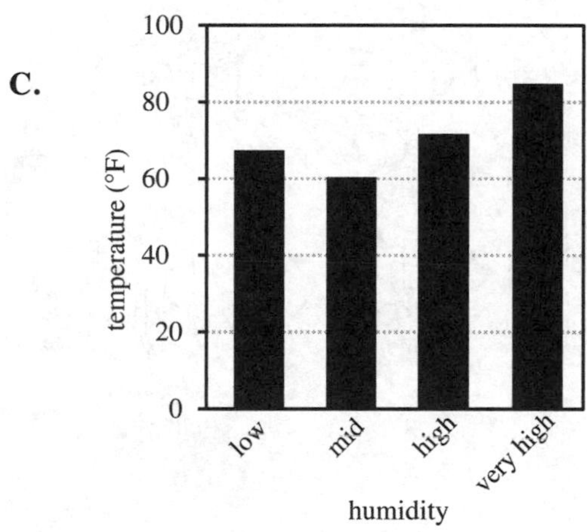

D.

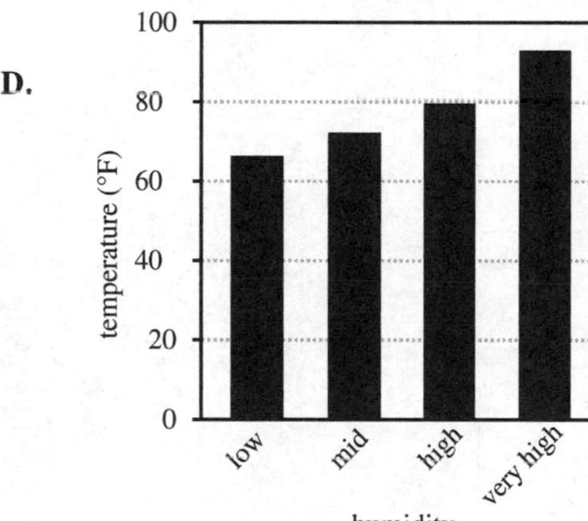

12. According to Table 1, which of the following graphs best shows the changes in humidity across the four rainforest levels?

F.

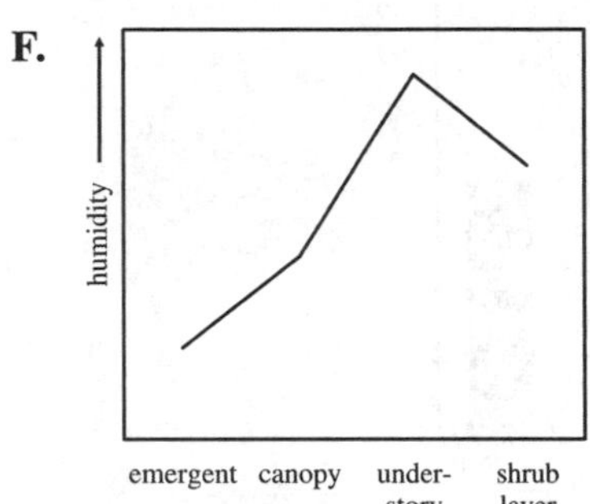

G.

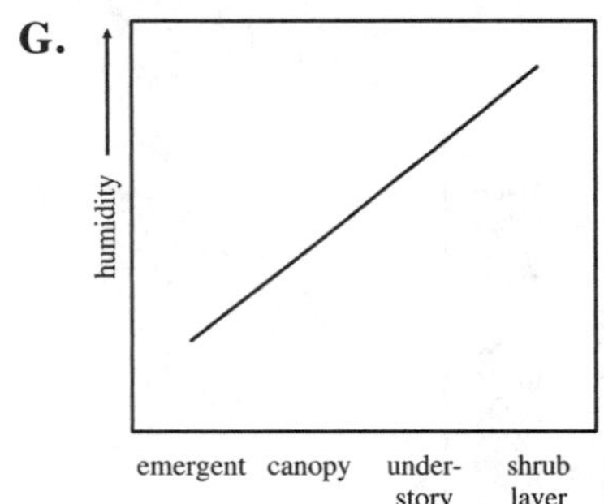

H.

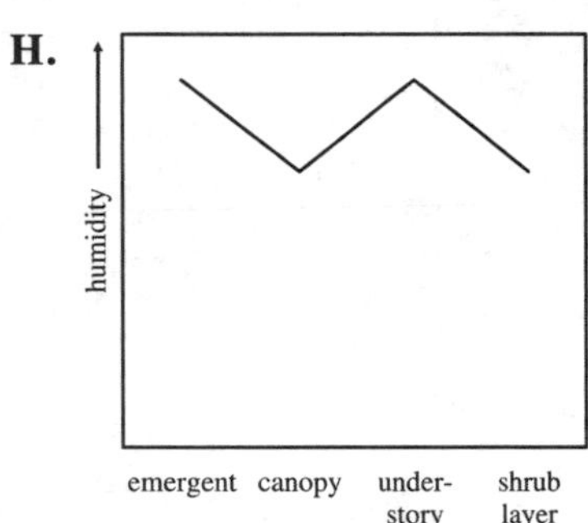

J.

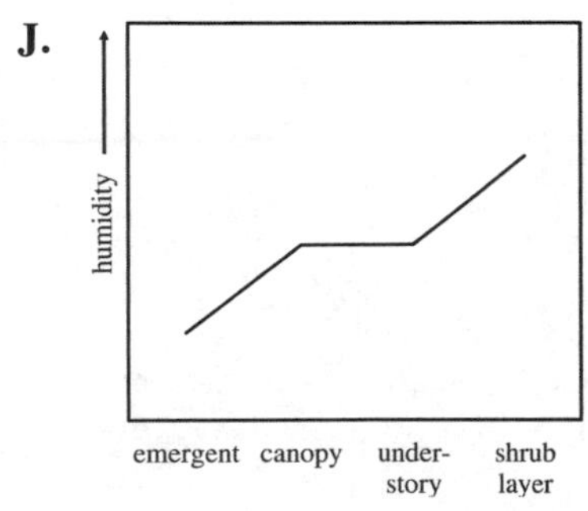

13. It is common for lianas (woody tree vines) to climb from the shrub layer into the understory layer to obtain more sunlight. Which of the following diagrams best illustrates the location of the growth of the lianas plant?

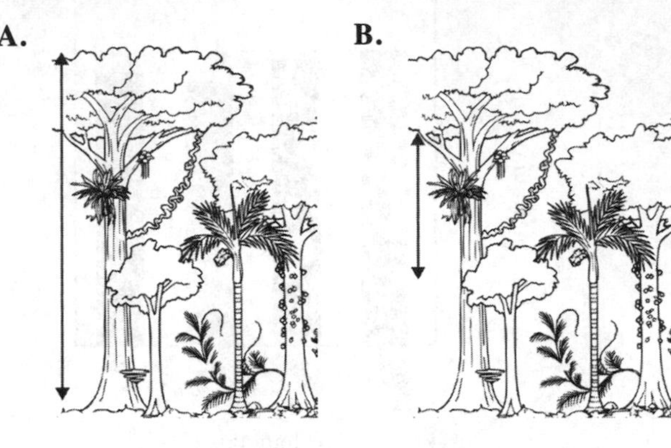

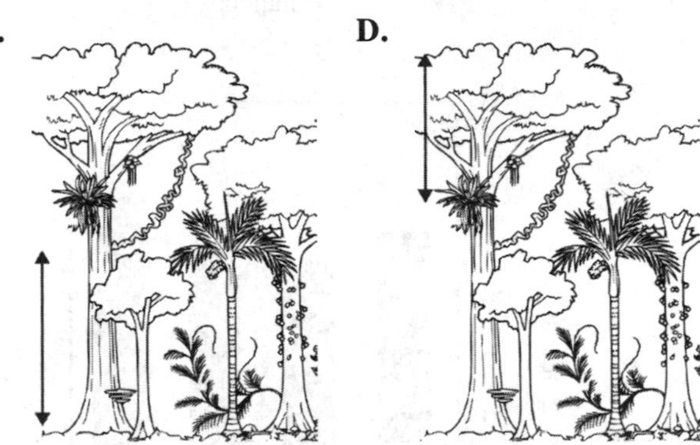

14. Which of the following graphs represents the top tree height for the emergent, canopy, and understory rainforest layers?

F.

height (ft): 0, 50, 100, 150, 200, 250
emergent, canopy, understory

G.

height (ft): 0, 50, 100, 150, 200, 250
emergent, canopy, understory

H.

height (ft): 0, 50, 100, 150, 200, 250
emergent, canopy, understory

J.

height (ft): 0, 50, 100, 150, 200, 250
emergent, canopy, understory

15. According to the information in Table 1, the high temperature at each layer is best represented by which graph?

A.

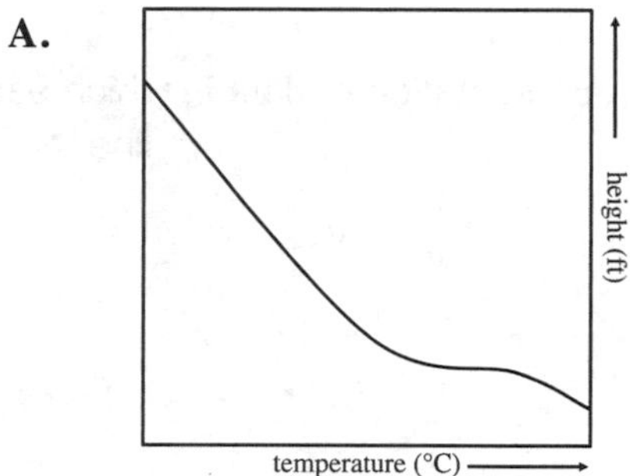

B.

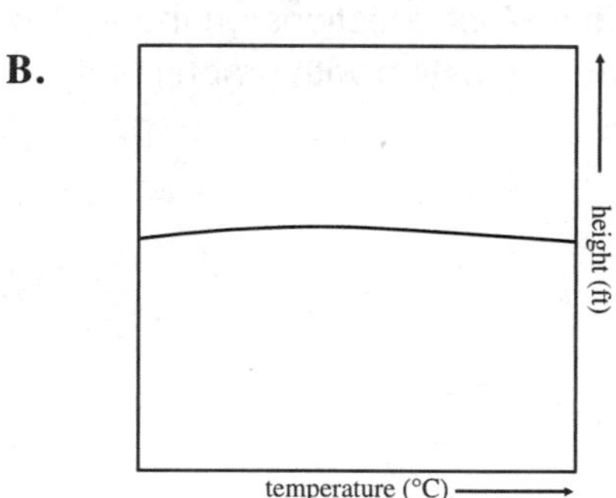

C.

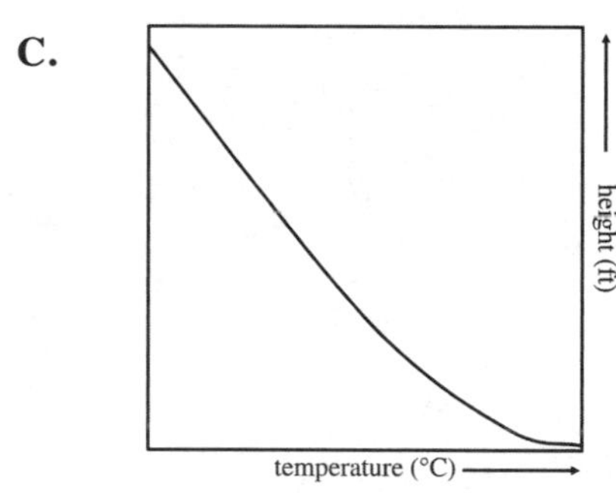

D.

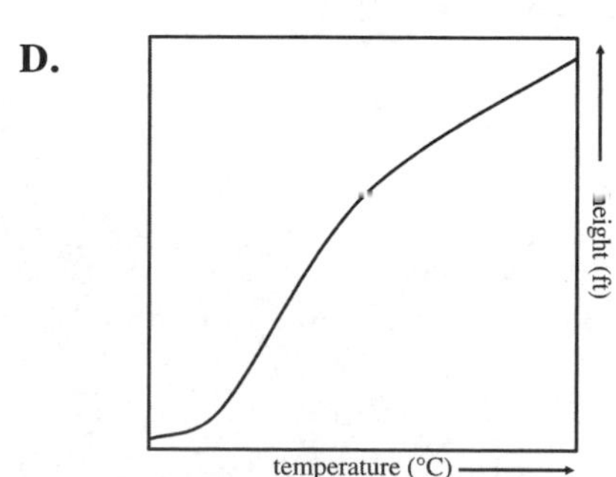

Sum It Up

Creating Figures

Bar graph
A graphical representation that uses either vertical or horizontal bars to display data

---

Line graph
A graphical representation of data in which each data point is connected to the rest of the data points with a line that runs from point to point

Tips and Techniques

Data Is Key: Most questions on the ACT science test do not require you to read the passage text. Any time you see a question with graphs or figures in the answer choices, try answering it without reading the passage. Just focus on the data.

Lesson 9

Understanding Design

CAPTION:

9.1 Entrance Ticket

Complete the activity below.

The melanic moth's dark coloring is passed to its progeny and thus is an inheritable trait. Researchers have studied the melanic peppered moth in both Britain and the United States from the late 1950s to the mid-1990s.

Study 1

Researchers calculated the percentage of melanic moths at sites with a high general moth population in both Britain and the United States and tabulated this data over a course of more than 30 years. The measurements were taken in June and July each year.

Study 2

After analyzing the results from Study 1, the researchers then looked at the pollution levels in both the United States and Britain moth population sites. They also measured the lifespan and reproduction rates of melanic moths in a lab environment with no pollutant exposure.

1. In Study 1, why were the measurements taken in the same months every year? What effect would changing the time of measurement each year have on the results?

____

____

____

____

2. In Study 2, why did scientists study the melanic moths in the lab environment? How does this information affect their conclusions?

____

____

____

____

9.2 Learning Targets

1. Identify elements of experimental design

2. Infer how and why aspects of experimental design were implemented

Self-Assessment

Circle the number that corresponds to your confidence level in your knowledge of this subject before beginning the lesson. A score of 1 means you are completely lost, and a score of 4 means you have mastered the skills. After you finish the lesson, return to the bottom of this page and circle your new confidence level to show your improvement.

Before Lesson

1 2 3 4

After Lesson

1 2 3 4

9.3.1 Method and Purpose

In anoles (genus *Anolis*), hindlimb length (see Figure 1) is a *heritable* trait (it is inherited by offspring from parents).

Figure 1

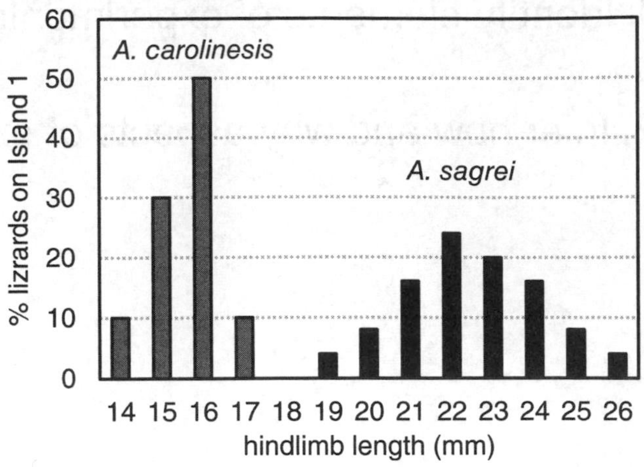

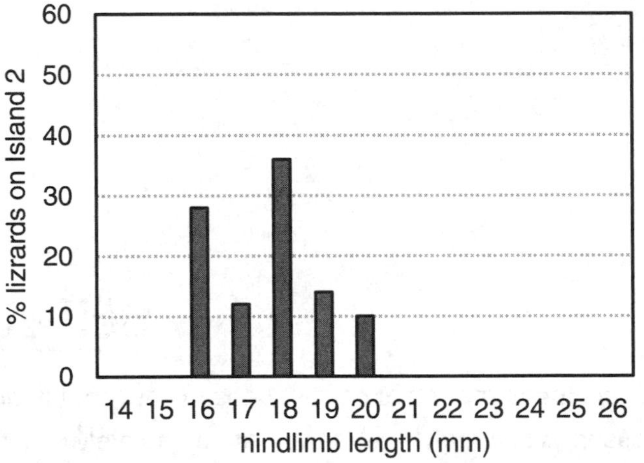

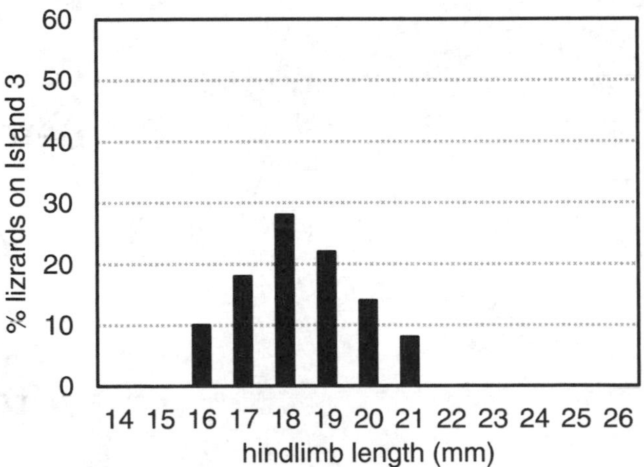

Figure 2

Biologists examined the hindlimb length of two species of lizards, *Anolis carolinesis* and *Anolis sagrei*, in a group of neighboring islands. Both species inhabit Island 1, only *Anolis carolinesis* inhabits Island 2, and only *Anolis sagrei* inhabits Island 3. Trees provide the primary habitat for both species. Lizards with shorter hindlimbs can only perch in trees with thin branches. Lizards with longer hindlimbs can perch in trees with both thick and thin branches, but are more frequently found in trees with thicker branches.

Study 1

Biologists caught 20 *Anolis carolinesis* and 20 *Anolis sagrei* on Island 1. They measured the hindlimb length of each lizard, then tagged and released all lizards. They then calculated the percent of lizards with each of the hindlimb lengths that they had measured. The biologists repeated these procedures with 20 *Anolis carolinesis* from Island 2 and 20 *Anolis sagrei* from Island 3. The results the biologists obtained are shown in Figure 2.

9.3.1 Method and Purpose

Study 2

After having completed Study 1, the biologists returned to Island 2 once per year over the next 8 years, from 2002 to 2009. In each visit, the biologists caught a minimum of 20 *Anolis carolinesis* and measured their hindlimb lengths. The biologists then calculated the average hindlimb length for each of the 8 years. The biologists observed that, during the 8-year study period, 3 years had exceptionally violent hurricane seasons, and 1 year was exceptionally rainy. During rainy years, smaller branches are abundant. After hurricane events, both small and large branches are less available, and the remaining branches have a larger average size.

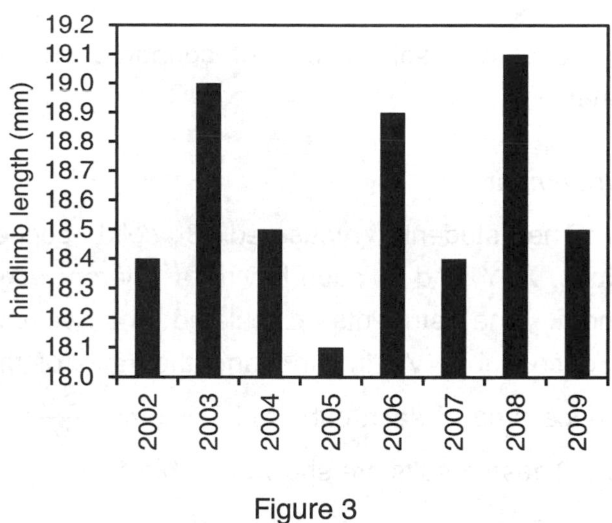

Figure 3

1. What were the experimenters trying to accomplish through this study?

____

____

2. How did the experimenters conduct the experiment?

____

____

3. What made the studies referenced in the passage different from one another?

____

____

9.3.1 Method and Purpose

Students investigated the rates at which individual hot, solid cubes of copper cooled in water.

Experiment 1

The students measured 3 solid copper cubes, X, Y, and Z, each having a different edge length. The students calculated the volume of each cube (*V*), in cm³, and the ratio of the surface area of each cube to its volume ($\frac{SA}{V}$), in cm⁻¹. These results are shown in Table 1.

Table 1		
Cube	*V* (cm³)	$\frac{SA}{V}$ (cm⁻¹)
X	5.8	3.3
Y	47	1.7
Z	512	0.75

A small cylindrical hole was drilled into the center of each cube, and a thermistor probe was inserted into each cube to measure the cube's *core temperature* (the temperature at the center of the cube). The three cubes were then heated. Once the core temperature of each cube had reached 120°C, the 3 cubes were immediately placed at $t = 0$ in individual closed containers filled with equal volumes of water at 18°C (see Figure 1).

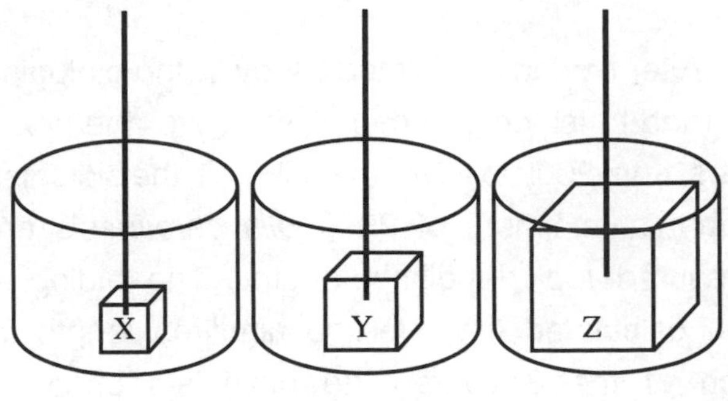

Figure 1

Over the next 10 minutes, the cubes were allowed to cool while the temperature of the water was held constant at 18°C. A plot of each cube's core temperature versus time for the 10-minute period is shown in Figure 2. For each cube, the slope of the line at a certain time equals the cube's *instantaneous cooling rate*.

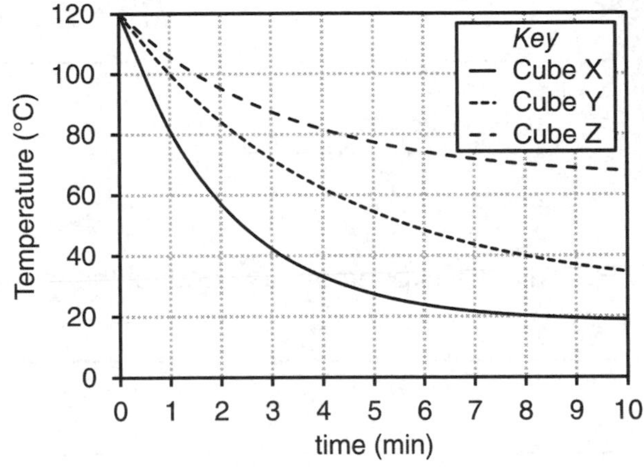

Figure 2

9.3.1 Method and Purpose

Experiment 2

The students then tested two solid copper cubes, A and B, of identical size. The students covered Cube A with Material 1 and Cube B with Material 2. As in Experiment 1, a thermistor probe was inserted into each cube, and both cubes were heated. When the core temperature of each cube had reached 150°C, both cubes were immediately placed at $t = 0$ in individual closed containers filled with equal volumes of water at 18°C. Over the next 20 minutes, the cubes were allowed to cool while the temperature of the water was held constant at 18°C. Figure 3 shows a plot of the core temperature of each cube over the 20-minute period.

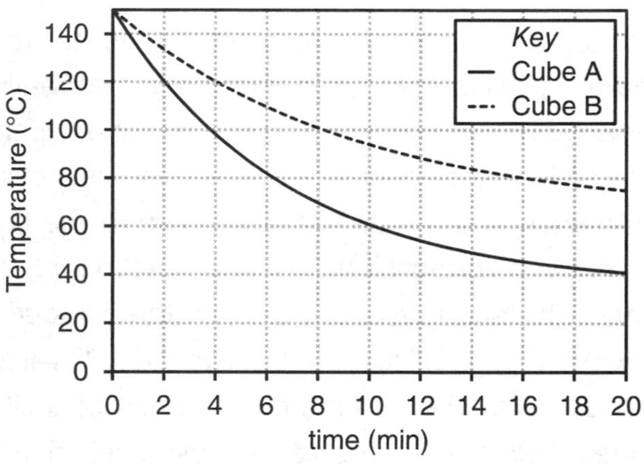

Figure 2

1. What were the experimenters trying to accomplish through this study?

2. How did the experimenters conduct the experiment?

3. What made the experiments referenced in the passage different from one another?

Science Tip

Road Signs: Check to see what the question is asking. Is it asking you to **analyze part of one** experiment or to **compare two** different experiments?

9.3.2 Embrace Your Inner 5-Year-Old

Terrapin Lake was formed over 12,000 years ago on James Ross Island in Antarctica (see Figure 1). This lake was formed as retreating glaciers created a depression in the land, which collected melting snow. Lakebed sediments provide information about Antarctic vegetation at the time of sediment deposition. A cross section of the sediments (sand, silt, and clay) in the lakebed is shown in Figure 2. Figure 3 displays the $\delta^{13}C$ values of sediments taken from the top 60 cm of 3 sites of the lakebed along the same cross section. $\delta^{13}C$ is calculated as the ratio of two carbon isotopes (^{12}C and ^{13}C) in the sediment. Higher $\delta^{13}C$ values indicate higher amounts of vegetation.

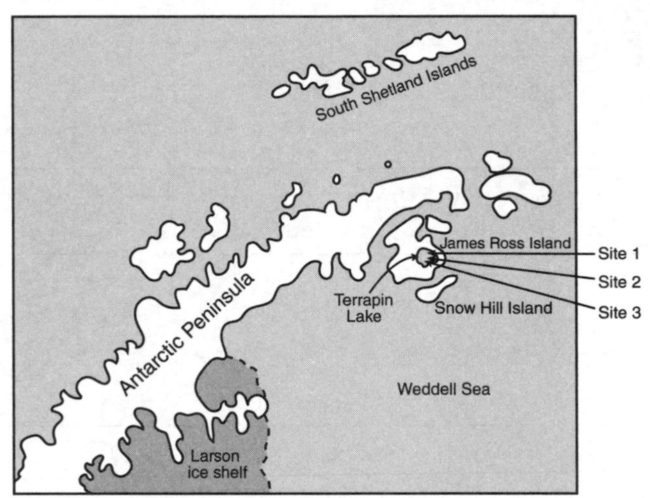

Figure 1

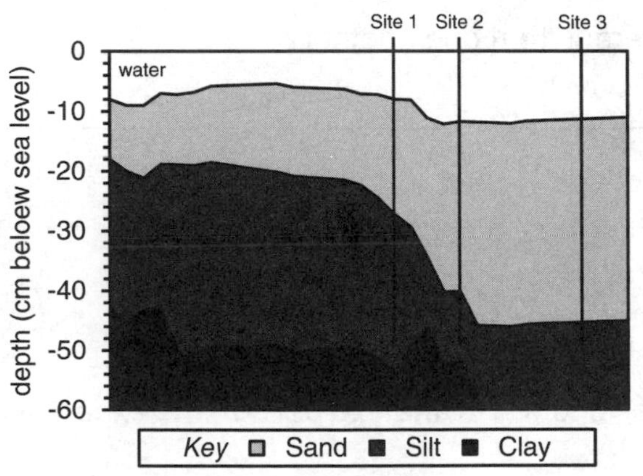

Figure 2

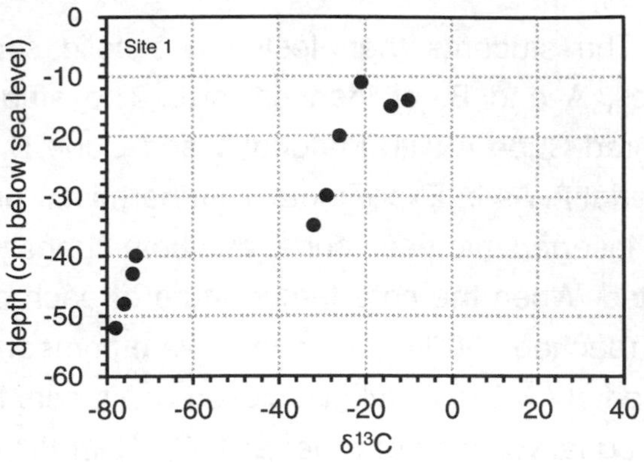

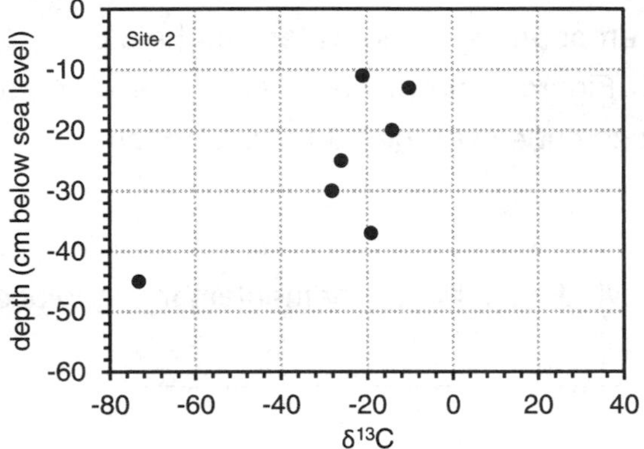

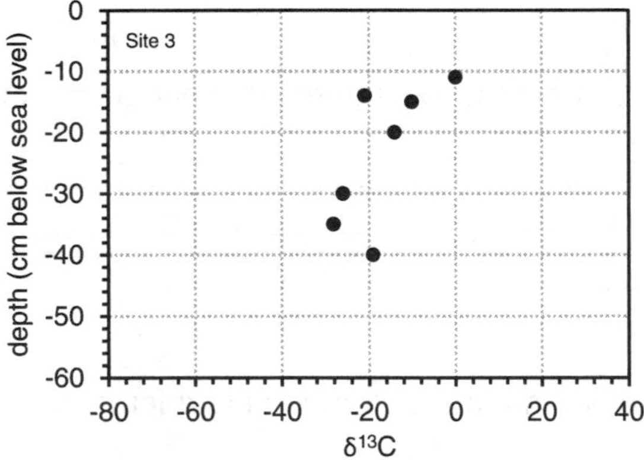

Figure 3

Note: $\delta^{13}C = \left(\dfrac{^{13}C\ /\ ^{12}C\ \text{sediment}}{^{13}C\ /\ ^{12}C\ \text{standard}} - 1\right) \times 1000$

9.3.2 Embrace Your Inner 5-Year-Old

1. Sediments were taken from 3 different sites of the lakebed.

Why? ____________________

Why? ____________________

Why? ____________________

Why? ____________________

2. The ^{13}C value was calculated for each of the sites.

Why? ____________________

Why? ____________________

Why? ____________________

Why? ____________________

Science Tip

Embrace Your Inner 5-Year-Old: When the ACT asks you a question about the design of an experiment, remember to keep asking yourself, "But why?" until you can determine the root answer.

9.4.1 Set One

Passage I

In agricultural regions, drainage runoff from farms can contain high levels of *ammonium* (NH_4^+), a substance that damages aquatic ecosystems. NH_4^+ can be removed from the water via uptake by growing plants, storage within roots of plants, or deposition onto the soil. Three studies were completed to study NH_4^+ removal in manmade marshes.

Study 1

Researchers constructed 5 open-surface circular marshes (Marshes 1–5), each 6 m in diameter, in a tropical climate in May 1999. Upon construction, 4 of the marshes were planted with the same density of 1 or 2 species of freshwater plants. From May 1999 to July 1999, wastewater containing an average NH_4^+ concentration of 30 mg/L was continuously pumped into each marsh at a flow rate of 64 gallons/day by an inflow pipe at the center of the marsh. The average *retention time* (*RT*), the length of time a certain volume of water remains in the marsh, was determined for each marsh (see Table 1).

Table 1

Marsh	Plant species in marsh	Average *RT* (days)
1	papyrus	4
2	none	3
3	violet grass	6
4	common reed	7
5	papyrus and violet grass	8

Study 2

Every week from May 1999 to July 1999, the researchers took samples from the streams emptying marshes 1–5, and then analyzed the samples for NH_4^+. The average NH_4^+ concentration of each stream was determined for each month (see Figure 1).

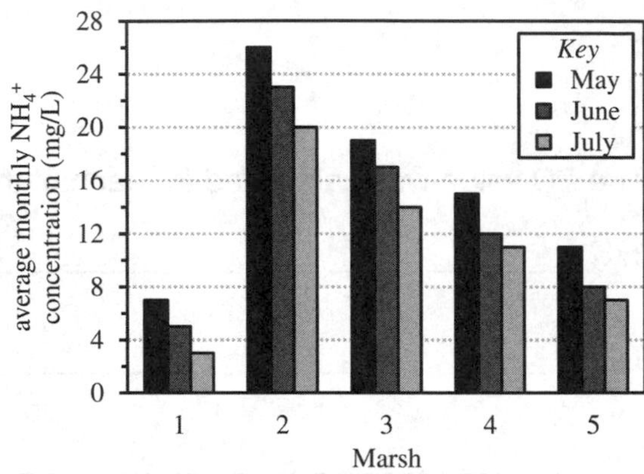

Figure 1

Study 3

In August 1999, the researchers collected samples of each of the following materials from multiple locations within each marsh: marsh soil (the top 5 cm of sediment), roots, and leaves. Each sample was analyzed for NH_4^+ concentration, and their average NH_4^+ concentrations, in milligrams per kilogram (mg/kg), were determined (see Figure 2).

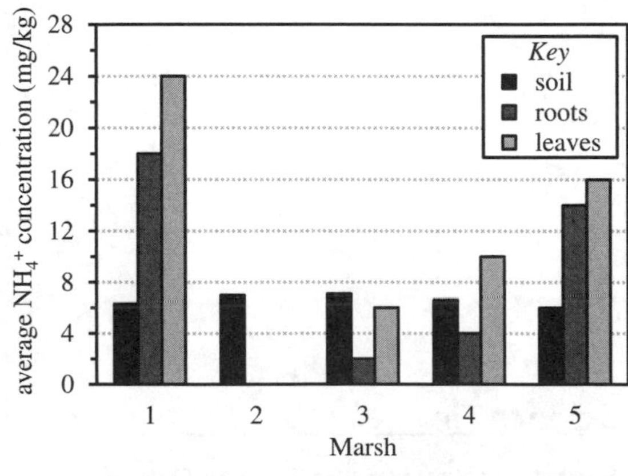

Figure 2

1. How did the unit of measurement of NH_4^+ concentration differ between Studies 2 and 3? In Study 2, the NH_4^+ concentration:

   A. was determined for several different solids, while in Study 3 the NH_4^+ concentration of a liquid was determined.
   B. was determined for a liquid, while in Study 3 the NH_4^+ concentration of several different solids was determined.
   C. was determined for a single solid, while in Study 3 the NH_4^+ concentration was determined for several different solids.
   D. was determined for a certain liquid, while in Study 3 the NH_4^+ concentration was determined for a different liquid.

2. The researchers most likely included Marsh 2 to:

   F. determine the effect of NH_4^+ uptake on plant growth.
   G. calculate the average rate of NH_4^+ uptake.
   H. determine the amount of NH_4^+ removed from the water in a normal marsh environment.
   J. determine the amount of NH_4^+ removed from the water in the absence of plants.

3. To determine NH_4^+ concentration in sediment samples from each marsh, the researchers most likely collected samples from sites that were:

   A. at least 6 m away from the inflow pipe in each marsh.
   B. between 1 to 3 m away from the inflow pipe in each marsh.
   C. 1 m away from the inflow pipe in Marsh 2, and 3 m away from the inflow pipe in Marshes 1, 3, 4, and 5.
   D. 3 m away from the inflow pipe in Marsh 2, and 1 m away from the inflow pipe in Marshes 1, 3, 4, and 5.

4. Through which of the following changes to Study 3 could the researchers obtain the most information about the total amount of NH_4^+ uptake in marsh plants?

   F. Sampling stems from living adult plants
   G. Removing the root samples
   H. Increasing the size of the constructed marsh
   J. Decreasing the size of the constructed marsh

5. In Studies 2 and 3, was NH_4^+ concentration an independent or dependent variable?

   A. Independent, because NH_4^+ concentrations are already established for certain plants.
   B. Independent, because NH_4^+ concentrations were measured by the researchers.
   C. Dependent, because NH_4^+ concentrations are already established for certain plants.
   D. Dependent, because NH_4^+ concentrations were measured by the researchers.

END OF SET ONE

STOP! DO NOT GO ON TO THE NEXT PAGE UNTIL TOLD TO DO SO.

9.4.2 Set Two

Passage II

For over 3,500 years, Lake Punta Laguna has existed in the Mayan lowlands of the Yucatán Peninsula (see Figure 1). These lowlands are covered with multiple lakes, each formed from the collection of rainwater and runoff. The fossilized calcium carbonate ($CaCO_3$) shells of aquatic invertebrates embedded in the sediment underneath these lakes provide information about the temperature of the water at the time the shells were formed. Figure 2 shows a cross-section of the sedimentation in several lakebeds of the Mayan lowlands. Figure 3 shows the $\delta^{18}O$ values of the shells of two different invertebrate species (*Cytheridella ilosvayi* and *Pyrgophorus coronatus*) taken from the top 6 m of the Lake Punta Laguna lakebed as well as the results of a separate study that determined $\delta^{18}O$ values of the shells of a single aquatic invertebrate species in a separate Mayan lowland lake (Lake Chichancanab). $\delta^{18}O$ values are calculated as the ratio of two isotopes of oxygen, ^{18}O and ^{16}O. Higher $\delta^{18}O$ values indicate colder water temperatures at the time the shell was formed.

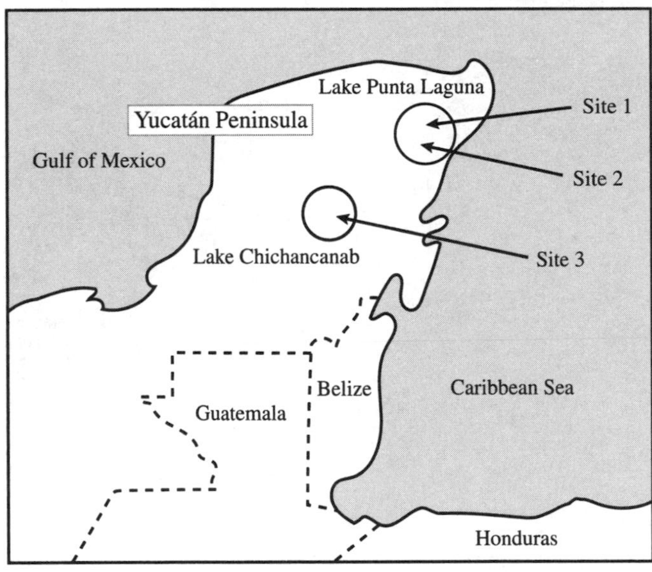

Figure 1

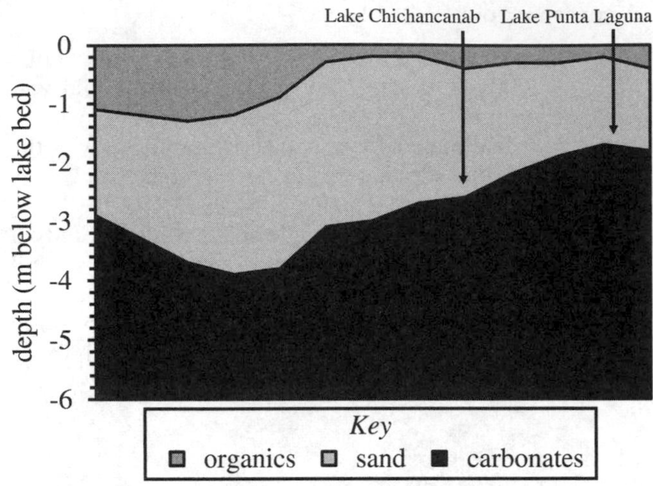

Figure 2

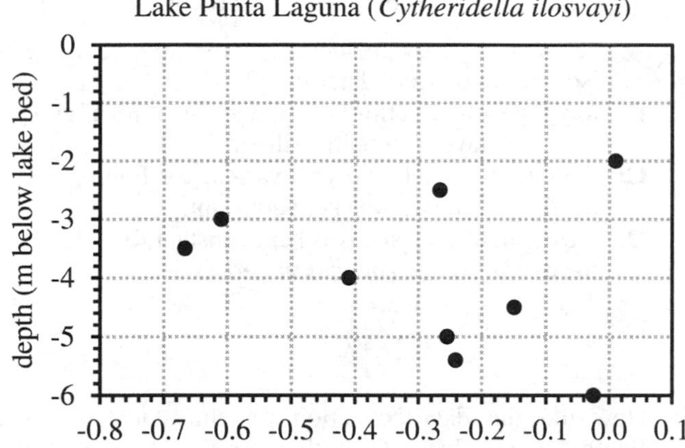

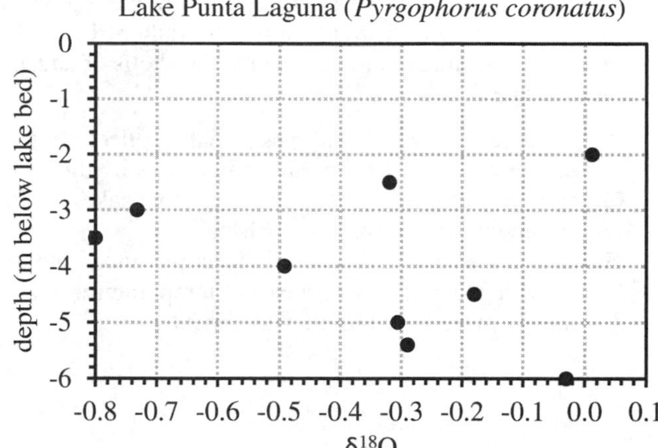

Lake Chichancanab (*Pyrgophorus coronatus*)

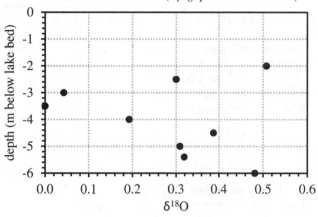

depth (m below lake bed)

0
-1
-2
-3
-4
-5
-6

0.0 0.1 0.2 0.3 0.4 0.5 0.6

$\delta^{18}O$

Figure 3

$$\text{Note: } \delta^{18}O = \left(\frac{{}^{18}O / {}^{16}O \text{ sample}}{{}^{18}O / {}^{16}O \text{ standard}} - 1 \right) \times 1000$$

6. In determining the temperature history of Lake Punta Laguna, what is the most likely reason the shells of aquatic invertebrates were sampled, rather than lake sediments? Compared to sediments, the shells of aquatic invertebrates:

   F. contain oxygen isotopes that reflect water temperatures at the time the animal was living.
   G. require little effort to catch in the lake, while sediment samples require drilling.
   H. vary in size based on water temperature, and so provide a direct way to measure temperature.
   J. are far more abundant than sediments.

7. The $\delta^{18}O$ values from the study in Lake Punta Laguna were most likely compared to those from the study in Lake Chichancanab to:

   A. demonstrate that *Cytheridella ilosvayi* is not a reliable source of $\delta^{18}O$ values.
   B. provide a point of comparison to help calibrate the results found in Lake Punta Laguna.
   C. examine the effect of the abundance of aquatic invertebrates on the $\delta^{18}O$ values of each lake.
   D. increase the sample size of the Lake Punta Laguna study only.

8. Before the $\delta^{18}O$ values of the fossilized aquatic invertebrates were measured, the invertebrates were most likely collected by:

   F. drilling through only the top 2 m of sediment in the lakebed.
   G. sampling water at different locations in the lake.
   H. drilling through at least the top 6 m of sediment in the lakebed.
   J. netting aquatic invertebrates from the lake water.

9. In which of the following ways did the collection of data for Figure 2 differ from that for Figure 3? For Figure 2:

   A. sediment layers were identified; for Figure 3, oxygen isotope ratios were determined.
   B. oxygen isotope ratios were determined; for Figure 3, sediment layers were identified.
   C. the depth at each site was varied; for Figure 3, the depth at each site was kept constant.
   D. the depth at each site was kept constant; for Figure 3, the depth at each site was varied.

10. How did the data collection for the study in Lake Punta Laguna differ from that for the study in Lake Chichancanab? In Lake Punta Laguna:

   F. one invertebrate species was sampled; in Lake Chichancanab two invertebrate species were sampled.
   G. two invertebrate species were sampled; in Lake Chichancanab one invertebrate species was sampled.
   H. both ^{16}O and ^{18}O were measured; in Lake Chichancanab only ^{18}O was measured.
   J. only ^{18}O was measured; in Lake Chichancanab both ^{16}O and ^{18}O were measured.

END OF SET TWO
STOP! DO NOT GO ON TO THE NEXT PAGE
UNTIL TOLD TO DO SO.

This page is intentionally left blank.

9.4.3 Set Three

Passage III

In certain regions, wastewater from coal production facilities contains cobalt (Co), a heavy metal that can be toxic to aquatic organisms. Cobalt can be removed from the water by uptake and storage in the roots of aquatic plants, uptake into plant leaves and stems, or deposition into the soil. Three studies were completed to evaluate Co removal and storage in manmade wetlands.

Study 1

In May 1996, an open-surface rectangular wetland was constructed and subdivided into 5 rectangular cells (Cells A–E), each 36 m × 9 m and isolated from the other cells. Four of these cells were planted with an equal density of 1 or 2 types of wetland plants. From May 1996 to May 1998, coal wastewater containing an average Co concentration of 0.02 mg/L was separately pumped into each cell at a flow rate of 200 m^3/day. The average *removal time* (*RT*), the duration a certain volume of water remains in an area before flushing, was determined for each cell (see Table 1).

Table 1

Cell	Plant species in wetland	Average *RT* (hours)
A	none	2
B	cattail	3
C	common reed	6
D	cattail and common reed	8
E	bur-reed	4

Study 2

Every month from May 1996 to May 1998, the water released through the outflows of Cells A–E was sampled and analyzed for Co. The average Co concentration for each outflow was then determined for each year (see Figure 1).

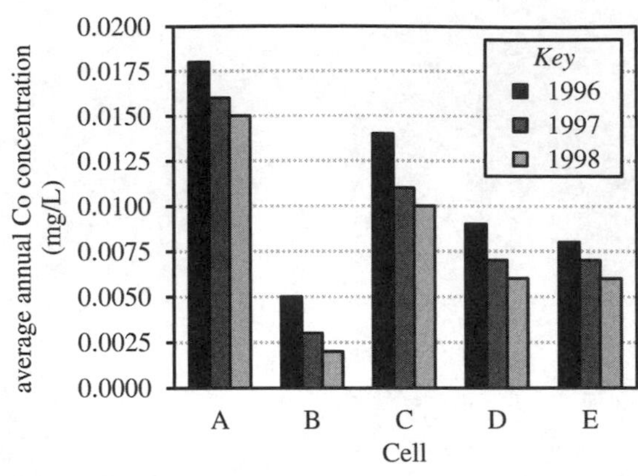

Figure 1

Study 3

In May 1998, samples of each of the following materials were collected from multiple locations within each cell: *rhizomes* (submerged rootstalks), fallen plant litter (dead stems and leaves), and the top 15 cm of soil. The samples of each material were analyzed for Co concentration, and the average Co concentration, in mg/kg, was determined for each material from each cell (see Figure 2). Each cell's Co *removal efficacy* was then calculated as the ratio of the concentration of Co in the rhizomes (mg/kg) to the concentration of Co in the outflow in 1998 (in mg/L):

$$\text{Removal efficacy} = \frac{\text{Co in rhizomes}\left(\frac{\text{mg}}{\text{kg}}\right)}{\text{Co in outflow}\left(\frac{\text{mg}}{\text{L}}\right)}$$

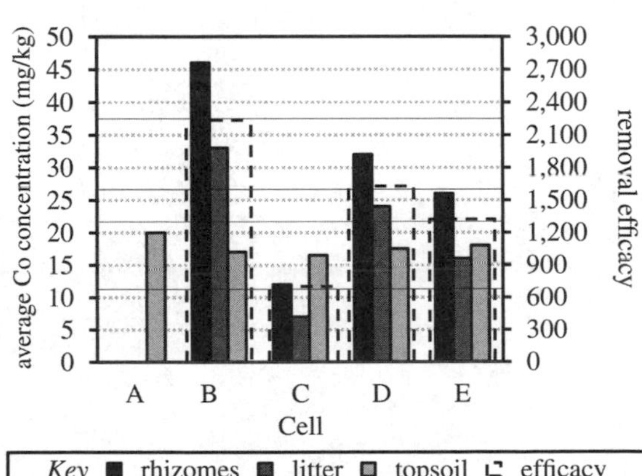

Figure 2

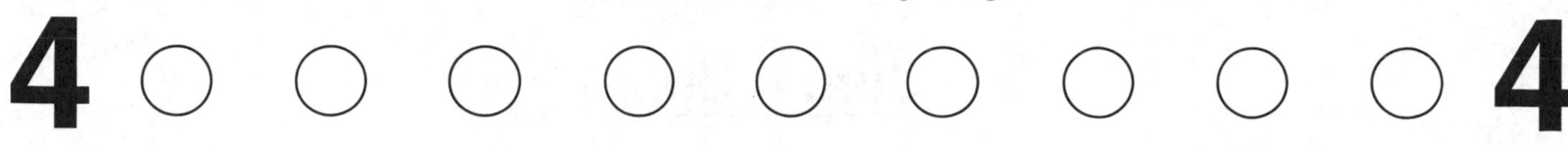

11. By planting each cell with the same density of plants as part of the procedure for constructing the wetland cells, which of the following outcomes were the researchers attempting to avoid?

   F. Having a higher volume of plant material in a certain cell, artificially increasing the cell's removal efficacy
   G. Having a higher volume of plant material in a certain cell, which would have no effect on the cell's removal efficacy
   H. Having identical volumes of plant material in all cells, artificially decreasing the removal efficacy in certain cells
   J. Having identical volumes of plant material in all cells, artificially increasing the removal efficacy in certain cells

12. In Study 1, to subdivide the original wetland into five smaller cells, the researchers most likely constructed barriers made out of:

   A. plastic fencing with 5 cm × 5 cm divisions.
   B. pond netting.
   C. impermeable plastic sheets.
   D. rope.

13. Why did the unit of measurement of Co concentration differ between Studies 2 and 3? In Study 2, the Co concentration of:

   A. multiple solids was determined, while in Study 3, the Co concentration of a liquid was determined.
   B. a solid was determined, while in Study 3, the Co concentration of a different solid was determined.
   C. a liquid was determined, while in Study 3, the Co concentrations of multiple solids were determined.
   D. a liquid was determined, while in Study 3, the Co concentration of a different liquid was determined.

14. Based on Figures 1 and 2 and the description of Study 3, the removal efficacy of Cell B was most likely calculated using which of the following expressions?

   F. 0.02 mg/kg ÷ 46 mg/L
   G. 0.02 mg/L ÷ 46 mg/kg
   H. 46 mg/kg ÷ 0.02 mg/L
   J. 46 mg/L ÷ 0.02 mg/kg

15. Which of the changes to the methods of Study 1 given below would have allowed the researchers to obtain the most information about the effect of increasing Co concentration on the cell's Co removal efficacy?

   A. Using wastewater with a Co concentration of 0.05 mg/L
   B. Using wastewater with a Co concentration of 0.005 mg/L
   C. Increasing the number of cells with no plants
   D. Decreasing the number of cells with no plants

END OF SET THREE
STOP! DO NOT GO ON TO THE NEXT PAGE
UNTIL TOLD TO DO SO.

Sum It Up

Understanding Design

Scientific Method
A method of research used to approach a scientific question by defining a problem, creating an experiment, and analyzing results to draw a conclusion

---

Independent Variable
The condition changed in an experiment in order to examine its effects (what is changed)

Dependent Variable
The condition that may occur as a result of the changes in the independent variable (what is observed and measured)

Tips and Techniques

Road Signs: Check to see what the question is asking. Is it asking you to **analyze part of one** experiment or to **compare two** different experiments?

Embrace Your Inner 5-Year-Old: When the ACT asks you a question about the design of an experiment, remember to keep asking yourself, "But *why*?" until you can determine the root answer.

Lesson 10

Controls

CAPTION:

10.1 Entrance Ticket

Solve the questions below.

For his school's science fair, Preston decides to do an experiment to test if water causes bread to grow mold. On one slice of bread, Preston sprinkles a teaspoon of water. On another slice of bread, he pours a tablespoon of water. He puts each slice of bread in a resealable plastic bag. He then puts a third slice of bread, this one without added water, in a resealable plastic bag and leaves all three bags on a tray near a window in his kitchen. Every three days, he inspects the bread and writes down the coloring and number of mold spots. At the end of two weeks, he writes his final observation. The bread slice with no added water has a small spot of mold, the slice with a teaspoon of water has twenty mold spots, and the slice with a tablespoon of water is completely black.

1. What is being tested in the experiment?

____

____

2. List at least three variables that stayed constant throughout the experiment.

i.
ii.
iii.

3. What is changing in the experiment?

____

____

4. What conclusion can Preston draw?

____

____

10.2 Learning Targets

1. Understand what an experiment is testing

2. Identify controls and variables in an experiment

Self-Assessment

Circle the number that corresponds to your confidence level in your knowledge of this subject before beginning the lesson. A score of 1 means you are completely lost, and a score of 4 means you have mastered the skills. After you finish the lesson, return to the bottom of this page and circle your new confidence level to show your improvement.

Before Lesson

1 2 3 4

After Lesson

1 2 3 4

10.3.1 Variables and Controls

1. You want to know whether boys or girls are better at throwing a paper ball into a trash can.

   Test: ____

   Variable: ____

   Constants: ____

2. You want to know if exposure to sunlight affects plant growth.

   Test: ____

   Variable: ____

   Constants: ____

3. You want to know if the year a car was made affects its crash test results.

   Test: ____

   Variable: ____

   Constants: ____

4. You want to know if amount of time spent studying affects how well a student performs on a test.

   Test: ____

   Variable: ____

   Constants: ____

10.3.1 Variables and Controls

Constant: Something that ______________________________ throughout an experiment.

Variable: Element or factor that can ________________ or ________________.

Control: The standard against which the experimenter ______________________________ results; the group or test subject that does not have the ____________________________ act on it.

Science Tip

Eliminate Changing Variables: When a question asks what is controlled or held constant in an experiment, look for what is *not* changing from experiment to experiment. If Experiment 2 or 3 says "Experiment 1 was repeated except that," you can eliminate the answer choice containing the given difference, since it is the changing variable.

10.3.2 Correcting Experiments

1. A teacher wants to test the effectiveness of her calculus lessons. She gives students a test at the start of the week. After teaching the material, she then gives her students another test at the end of the week. Some classes were taught for 15 minutes per class, while others were taught for the full 90-minute class period. Some students were given multiple-choice tests, while others were given open-ended essay questions. Some students were allowed to use a calculator, while others were not.

   Problem: ____

   ____

   Correction: ____

   ____

   Control: ____

   ____

2. A gardener wants to test how the frequency of watering her plants affects their growth. She waters some plants every day for a week and others only once that week. She waters one orchid, one cilantro plant, and one cactus. She determines that whichever one is the tallest at the end of the week will have had the most growth from watering.

   Problem: ____

   ____

   Correction: ____

   ____

   Control: ____

   ____

10.3.2 Correcting Experiments

3. A runner wants to know if not getting enough sleep at night affects how fast she can run. She varies her hours of sleep and observes her runs. Some days she does sprint workouts; some days she does long runs; some days she runs on hills; some days she runs on the track.

Problem: ____________________

____

Correction: ____________________

____

Control: ____________________

____

10.4.1 Set One

Passage I

Three experiments were conducted using the solvents water, acetic acid, and ethanol to examine how addition of a solute (NaCl) affects a liquid's boiling point.

For each solvent:

1. Two uncovered 1-L beakers (Beaker A and Beaker B) were filled to 0.5 L with the solvent, and a thermometer was immersed in each liquid.
2. Each beaker was placed on a balance, and the mass of each was recorded.
3. NaCl was added to the liquid in Beaker A, and the solution was stirred until the solute dissolved completely.
4. The new mass of Beaker A was recorded.
5. Both beakers were placed on a hot plate and heated, and the temperature at which the solutions boiled was recorded.
6. Steps 1–5 were repeated multiple times.

The experiments were then repeated, except that the beakers were filled to 0.25 L with the solvent. The results are shown in Figures 1 and 2.

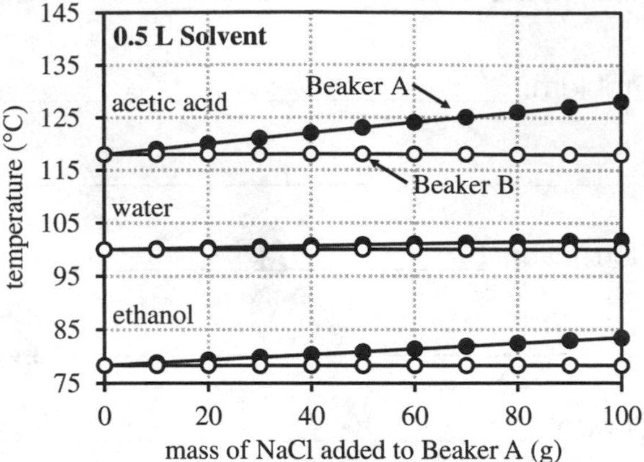

Figure 1

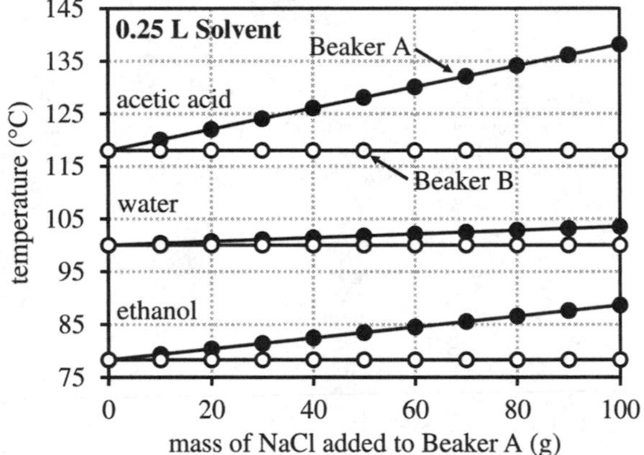

Figure 2

1. Which of the following served as a control for the acetic acid (Beaker A) measurements shown in Figure 1?
   - **A.** The beaker containing 0.5 L of water only
   - **B.** The beaker containing 0.5 L of water and NaCl
   - **C.** The beaker containing 0.5 L of acetic acid only
   - **D.** The beaker containing 0.25 L of water only

2. Which of the variables listed below was held constant in the experiment shown in Figure 2?
   - **F.** Type of solvent
   - **G.** Mass of NaCl added
   - **H.** Volume of solvent
   - **J.** Boiling point

3. In the experiment shown in Figure 2, what property of the ethanol solutions was varied?
   - **A.** Mass of NaCl
   - **B.** Volume of ethanol
   - **C.** Chemical composition of ethanol
   - **D.** Mass of ethanol

END OF SET ONE

STOP! DO NOT GO ON TO THE NEXT PAGE
UNTIL TOLD TO DO SO.

10.4.2 Set Two

Passage II

In the 1990s, researchers believed that *ribosomes*, located in the cell cytoplasm, were the sites of protein synthesis and were responsible for creating new proteins by combining individual *amino acids* (the subunits of proteins; see Figure 1).

Ribosomes are composed of two types of molecules: proteins and ribonucleic acid (RNA). A ribosome acts as a *catalyst*, meaning it increases the rate of the protein synthesis reaction without going through any change itself. The ribosome holds two amino acids in its *active site* (the site where the reaction will take place) and initiates bond formation between the two amino acids. Biological catalysts made out of proteins are called *enzymes*, while biological catalysts made out of RNA are called *ribozymes*.

Two scientists in the 1990s debated whether the protein or the RNA of the ribosome is responsible for the ribosome's catalytic activity.

Scientist 1: Enzyme Hypothesis

The proteins of a ribosome are responsible for the ribosome's catalytic activity. In almost all biological reactions studied, proteins—not RNA—are the catalysts, and the ribosome is made up of at least 50% proteins. Proteins, composed of twenty different amino acids, have flexible structures: proteins can bind many substances and can change shape once bound, which brings substances into the close contact needed for a reaction to occur. Ribosomal proteins must hold the new amino acids in place to catalyze the formation of the protein bond.

By contrast, RNA does not have the conformational flexibility needed for a functioning enzyme. RNA, made up of only four nucleotides, lacks the complex structure of proteins, cannot undergo such shape changes, and thus is unable to bring molecules into close contact.

Scientist 2: Ribozyme Hypothesis

The RNA of the ribosome is responsible for the ribosome's catalytic activity. The active site of the ribosome contains RNA but no proteins. The proteins of the ribosome are found primarily on the outside of the structure and are most likely involved in stabilizing the ribosome.

Though the majority of enzymes are proteins, RNA also exhibits catalytic activity. In a recent study, researchers measured a ribosome's catalytic activity (rate of protein synthesis) while gradually removing the ribosomal proteins. Ribosomes with reduced or absent ribosomal proteins but normal amounts of RNA continued to catalyze protein bond formation at the same rate as intact ribosomes, which were measured in the same media at the same time. The ability of the ribosome to retain its function when no ribosomal proteins are present definitively shows that RNA is the catalytic component of the ribosome.

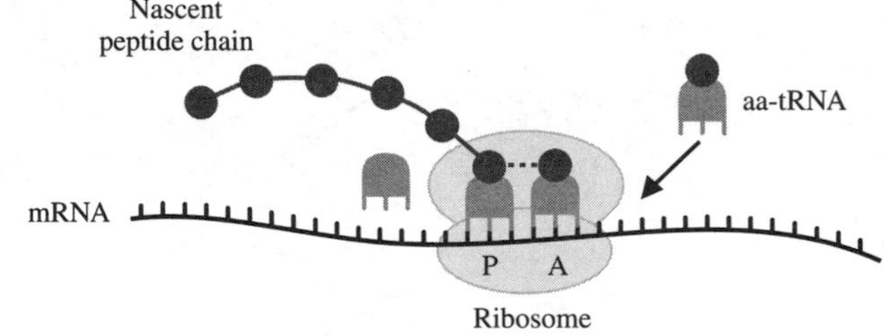

Figure 1

4. Scientist 2 references a study in which researchers measured the catalytic ability of the ribosome. Which of the following served as a control for this study?

   F. Ribosomes with all proteins removed
   G. Intact ribosomes (ribosomes with protein and RNA)
   H. Ribosomes lacking RNA
   J. Ribosomes with denatured RNA and denatured proteins

5. In the study described by Scientist 2, which of the following variables was held constant by the researchers?

   A. Amount of protein in the ribosome
   B. Amount of RNA in the ribosome
   C. Catalytic activity of the ribosomal protein
   D. Structure of the ribosomal protein

6. In the study described by Scientist 2, the researchers varied which of the following properties of the ribosome?

   F. Amount of RNA in the ribosome
   G. Catalytic activity of the RNA
   H. Amount of protein in the ribosome
   J. Amount of peptide synthesis

END OF SET TWO

STOP! DO NOT GO ON TO THE NEXT PAGE
UNTIL TOLD TO DO SO.

10.4.3 Set Three

Passage III

Researchers performed the following experiments to compare the densities of pumice (a type of volcanic rock) obtained from several deposits around volcanic plateaus.

Experiment 1

A dry 400-mL volumetric flask was placed on a balance, and the balance was reset to 0 g. Hexane was added to the volumetric flask until a certain mass was reached. As much canola oil as needed to fill the flask to the 200 mL mark was then added, and the solution was stirred for several minutes. The density of the solution was calculated. This procedure was repeated with varying amounts of hexane and canola oil, and the results are displayed in Table 1.

Experiment 2

A certain mass of pure iodine (I_2) was dissolved in a measured mass of hexane. A dry 400-mL volumetric flask was placed on a balance, and the balance was reset to 0 g. The solution was added to the flask until the volume was 200 mL. The density of the liquid was then calculated. This procedure was repeated several times with varying amounts of I_2 and hexane, and the results are displayed in Table 2.

Experiment 3

A pumice sample was covered completely with a thin layer of impermeable silicone-based putty (the mass of which was assumed to be negligible) and then placed at the top of a small amount of each of the solutions A–M from Experiments 1 and 2. If the sample remained at the top of the solution, a value of "F" (float) was recorded in Table 3. If the sample sank, a value of "S" was recorded in Table 3. The procedure was repeated for the different pumice samples. Two pumice samples of known density were also covered completely in silicone-based putty and placed in the top of a sample of each solution A–M.

Table 1

Solution	Mass of hexane (g)	Mass of canola oil (g)	Total mass (g)	Density (g/mL)
A	130.96	0	130.96	0.6548
B	106.08	34.96	141.04	0.705
C	86.4336	62.56	148.9936	0.744968
D	75.302	78.2	153.502	0.76751
E	61.5512	97.52	159.0712	0.795356
F	47.1456	117.76	164.9056	0.824528
G	17.6796	159.16	176.8396	0.884198
H	0	184	184	0.92

Table 2

Solution	Mass of hexane in solution (g)	Mass of iodide (I_2) in solution (g)	Mass of solution in flask (g)	Density (g/mL)
I	195.1304	89.8696	285	1.425
J	193.166	109.534	305.7	1.5285
K	191.2016	143.8984	335.1	1.6755
L	183.9988	272.9012	456.9	2.2845
M	176.1412	455.0588	631.2	3.156

Table 3

Pumice sample	Solution A	B	C	D	E	F	G	H	I	J	K	L	M
Chalfant Quarry, CA	F	F	F	F	F	F	F	F	F	F	F	F	F
Mount St. Helens, WA	S	S	F	F	F	F	F	F	F	F	F	F	F
Chalfant Quarry S2, CA	S	S	S	F	F	F	F	F	F	F	F	F	F
Aeolian Buttes, CA	S	S	S	S	F	F	F	F	F	F	F	F	F
Chalfant Quarry S3, CA	S	S	S	S	S	F	F	F	F	F	F	F	F
Medicine Lake, CA	S	S	S	S	S	S	F	F	F	F	F	F	F
Chalfant Quarry S4, CA	S	S	S	S	S	S	S	F	F	F	F	F	F
Aeolian Buttes S2, CA	S	S	S	S	S	S	S	S	S	F	F	F	F
Aeolian Buttes S3, CA	S	S	S	S	S	S	S	S	S	S	S	F	F
Lassen, CA	S	S	S	S	S	S	S	S	S	S	S	S	F
Known samples													
MSH S2 (density 0.68 g/mL)	S	F	F	F	F	F	F	F	F	F	F	F	F
LAC S2 (density 0.94 g/mL)	S	S	S	S	S	S	S	S	F	F	F	F	F

7. In Experiment 3, what did the researchers use as a control for their density-measuring technique?

A. The pumice samples of known density
B. The solution labeled A
C. The empty volumetric flask
D. The sample from Lassen, CA

8. In Experiment 1, which experimental variable was held constant?

F. Mass of the solution
G. Density of the solution
H. Volume of the solution
J. Size of the pumice

9. In Experiment 2, the researchers varied which property of the solutions?

A. Type of solvent used to make the solution
B. Temperature of the solution
C. Mass of I_2 and hexane
D. Type of solute used to make the solution

END OF SET THREE
STOP! DO NOT GO ON TO THE NEXT PAGE
UNTIL TOLD TO DO SO.

10.4.4 Set Four

Passage IV

A *Redox titration* is a technique in which a precise volume of a *titrant* (an oxidizing agent) is added to a known volume of an *analyte* (a solution to be analyzed). This process can be monitored by adding a *starch indicator* (a substance that changes color in relation to the concentration of ions in solution) or by measuring the *electric potential* of the solution. Electric potential (measured in volts) is a measurement of the difference in electric charge between the solution and a reference point.

Students conducted two experiments to calculate the concentration of ascorbic acid (vitamin C) in a sample of orange juice. Experiments were completed at 22°C using a 0.050 M (moles/liter) iodine solution as the titrant and either a 0.010 M ascorbic acid solution or an orange juice solution of unknown ascorbic acid concentration as the analyte. Iodine reacts with ascorbic acid to form dehydroascorbic acid; when all ascorbic acid has been used, the excess iodine in the solution forms the triiodide ion (I_3^-). A starch indicator added to the solution should be colorless in the absence of triiodide but turns deep blue in the presence of I_3^-.

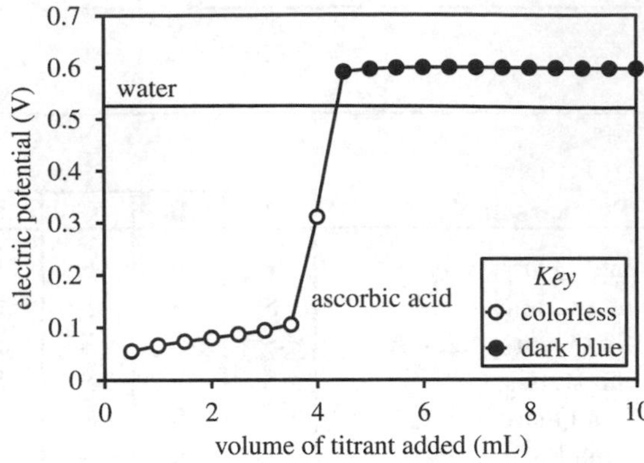

Figure 1

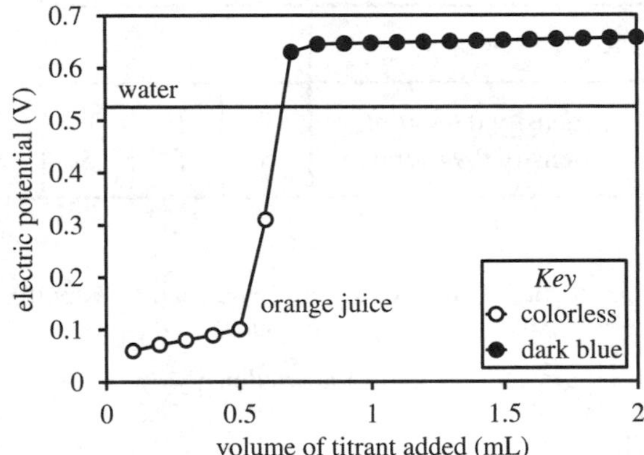

Figure 2

Experiment 1

A 1-mL aliquot of starch indicator was added to a volumetric flask containing 20 mL of the 0.010 M ascorbic acid solution. An electrode that measures electric potential was placed in each solution. The iodine solution was added to the ascorbic acid solution in 0.5-mL increments. Following each addition, the ascorbic acid solution was stirred and its electric potential and color were recorded. The same experiment was repeated using a volumetric flask containing 20 mL of distilled water in place of ascorbic acid. The results are shown in Figure 1.

Experiment 2

Experiment 1 was repeated, with the exception that 20 mL of orange juice solution of an unknown ascorbic acid concentration were used in place of the 0.010 M of ascorbic acid solution, and the titrant was added in 0.1-mL increments (see Figure 2).

10. What did the students use as a control in Experiment 1?

    F. The volumetric flask containing orange juice and starch indicator
    G. The volumetric flask containing distilled water and starch indicator
    H. The iodine solution
    J. The empty volumetric flask

11. In Experiment 1, which of the following variables did the students keep constant?

    A. Volume of iodine solution added per increment
    B. Electric potential of the analyte
    C. Color of the analyte
    D. Concentration of triiodide

12. In Experiment 2, which of the following properties of the analyte varies?

    F. Volume of starch indicator added to the analyte
    G. Total volume of analyte
    H. Concentration of ascorbic acid in the analyte
    J. Temperature of analyte

END OF SET FOUR

STOP! DO NOT GO ON TO THE NEXT PAGE UNTIL TOLD TO DO SO.

10.4.5 Set Five

Passage V

In fish, the number of gill rakers (see Figure 1) on each gill arch is a heritable trait and can be passed from parents to offspring.

Researchers studied the number of gill rakers in populations of the three-spined stickleback, *Gasterosteus aculeatus*. This species can be either benthic (bottom-dwelling) or limnetic (live in the upper water layer). Both benthic and limnetic *G. aculeatus* inhabit Lakes 1 and 2, and only benthic *G. aculeatus* inhabit Stream A. While benthic sticklebacks feed on both benthic invertebrates and plankton, limnetic stickleback feed only on plankton suspended in the water column. Sticklebacks with fewer gill rakers can capture only large pieces of plankton, while sticklebacks with more gill rakers can capture both small and large pieces of plankton.

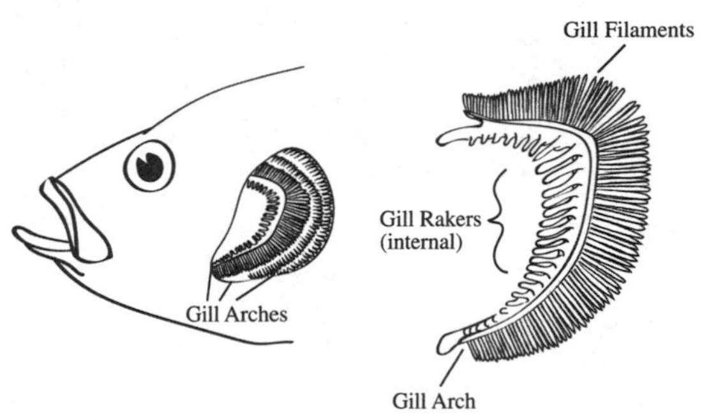

Figure 1

Study 1

Researchers collected fifty three-spined sticklebacks each from Lake 1 (a lake with no natural predators of sticklebacks), Lake 2 (a lake also inhabited by the rusty crayfish, *Orconectes rusticus*, a benthic predator of sticklebacks), and Stream A (a fast-moving inlet of Lake 2). The researchers obtained a sample of a gill arch from each fish and counted the number of gill rakers on each arch under a dissecting microscope. The researchers then calculated the percentage of fish from each body of water with the number of gill rakers they had measured. The results of this study are shown in Figures 2–4.

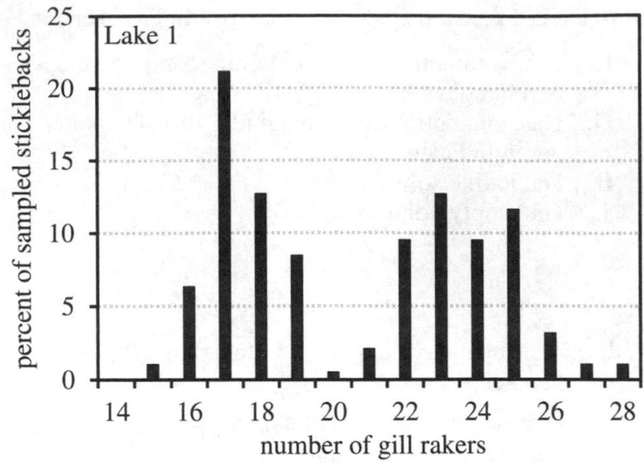

Figure 2

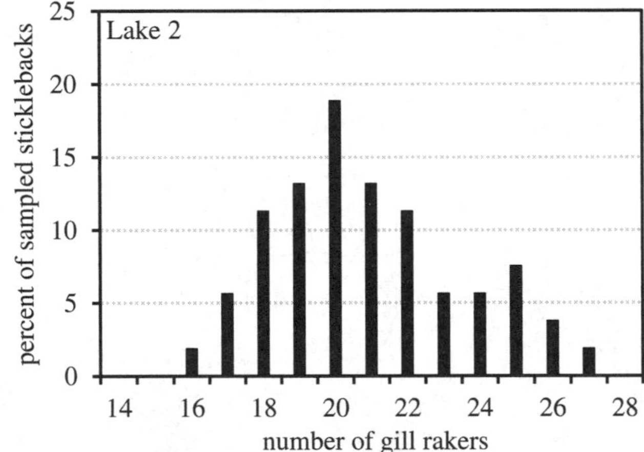

Figure 3

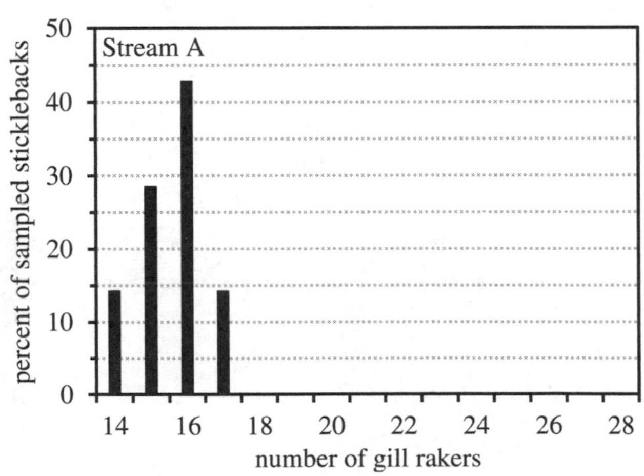

Figure 4

Study 2

After completing Study 1, the researchers transplanted a sample of 100 fish from Stream A to Lake 3 (a lake with no existing population of sticklebacks) to examine the influence of the lake habitat on the number of gill rakers. The researchers returned to both Stream A and Lake 3 once per year for the next twelve years (1994–2005). Every year, they captured twenty-five sticklebacks each from Stream A and Lake 3, obtained a gill sample from each fish, and counted the number of gill rakers in each sample. Then, they calculated the average number of gill rakers in the samples from each site for each year of the twelve-year period (Figure 5). The researchers noted that the rusty crayfish (*Orconectes rusticus*) moved into and colonized Lake 3 in 1996. In 2001, a wide-scale algae bloom in Lake 3 decreased the amount of plankton available in the water column.

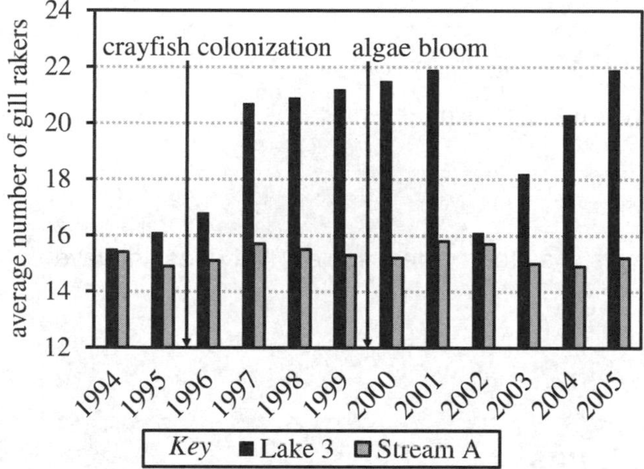

Figure 5

13. In Study 2, what did the researchers use as a control group?

A. Sticklebacks from Lake 3
B. Sticklebacks from Stream A
C. Benthic sticklebacks from Lake 1
D. Limnetic sticklebacks from Lake 3

14. In Study 1, which experimental variable did the researchers hold constant?

F. Number of sticklebacks sampled at each site
G. Number of gill rakers sampled per fish
H. Presence of predators in each lake
J. Amount of plankton at each sample site

15. In Study 2, the researchers varied which of the following?

A. Number of gill arches per stickleback
B. Average body size of limnetic sticklebacks
C. Environment of the sticklebacks
D. Dietary preferences of the sticklebacks

END OF SET FIVE

STOP! DO NOT GO ON TO THE NEXT PAGE UNTIL TOLD TO DO SO.

Sum It Up

Controls

Hypothesis
A proposed explanation based on evidence; a starting point for further investigation

Experiment
A scientific procedure to test a hypothesis

Results
The outcome of the experiment

Constant
Something that remains unchanged in an experiment

Variable
An element or factor that can change during an experiment

Control
The standard against which the experimenter compares results; the group or test subject that does not have a variable

Tips and Techniques

Eliminate Changing Variables: When a question asks what is controlled or held constant in an experiment, look for what is *not* changing from experiment to experiment. If Experiment 2 or 3 says "Experiment 1 was repeated except that," you can eliminate the answer choice containing the given difference, since it is the changing variable.

Terminology

CAPTION:

11.1 Entrance Ticket

Complete the activity below.

Prefixes		Root Words		Suffixes
re = again *ecto* = outside *omni* = all *ob* = against	*in* = into *inter* = between, among *per* = through	*nat* = birth, born *demo* = people *geo* = earth	*liter* = letter *radic* = root *polis* = city, community	*cracy* = government, rule *ics* = study of, science, skill, practice, knowledge

Use the information in the table above to fill in the blanks with the meaning of each word part.

1. Literate — liter ____________
2. Radical — radic ____________
3. Geopolitics — geo ____________ polit ____________ ics ____________
4. Reincarnation — re ____________ in ____________ nat ____________
5. Democracy — demo ____________ cracy ____________

Write each word from the list above next to its definition. Use the meaning of each word's roots to help determine the definition.

________________ the study of politics or international relations influenced by geographical factors

________________ a second or new birth

________________ a person who can read and write

________________ arising from or going to the root

________________ a group governed by the majority of its members

11.2 Learning Targets

1. Use word roots to answer questions with unfamiliar scientific terms

2. Use context to answer questions with unfamiliar scientific terms

Self-Assessment

Circle the number that corresponds to your confidence level in your knowledge of this subject before beginning the lesson. A score of 1 means you are completely lost, and a score of 4 means you have mastered the skills. After you finish the lesson, return to the bottom of this page and circle your new confidence level to show your improvement.

Before Lesson

1 2 3 4

After Lesson

1 2 3 4

11.3.1 Context Clues

A physics and astronomy class is given the following information about the formation of black holes.

1. Black holes can form in a number of ways: from a stellar collapse after a supernova explosion, from the merger of compact stellar remnants (such as two neutron stars), or gravitational collapse in the center of galaxies during their formation.

2. Gravitational collapse during the formation of galaxies is thought to produce supermassive black holes, which influence the evolution of galaxies and their structures. Scientists have yet to observe a primordial black hole in progress, though in the future it may be possible to observe them through the measurement of their thermodynamic effects.

3. The masses of primordial black holes vary, depending on the area of their formation and the related density contrast of the region.

4. Some scientists theorize about "quantum" black holes that may only exist in higher dimensions and that are not readily observable. They would be infinitesimally small, with a radius that approximates that of an atomic nucleus.

5. Black holes are categorized into two classes. Stellar black holes generally have a mass above 20 solar masses. Supermassive black holes can have solar masses in the billions.

Two students discuss the evolution of the NGC2276-3c black hole, which was discovered in a galaxy near Earth. This black hole has a mass of 50,000 times that of the Sun and is known as an "intermediate-mass black hole" (IMBH), which falls between a stellar black hole and a supermassive black hole. These types of black holes have masses that range from a few hundred to a hundred thousand solar masses.

Student 1

The NGC2276-3c black hole is most likely the result of the merger of compact stellar remnants. Its intermediate mass points to this origin; likely two neutron stars merged to produce the black hole.

Student 2

The NGC2276-3c black hole could have formed in a number of ways. It could be a primordial black hole, since these vary in size and only later develop into supermassive black holes. If that is the case, scientists could use this black hole to further their research about these types of elusive black holes. If the black hole is a primordial black hole, then it was formed during the gravitational collapse in the formation of its galaxy.

A. Quantum forces
B. Nuclear forces
C. Evolutionary forces
D. Gravitational forces

11.3.1 Context Clues

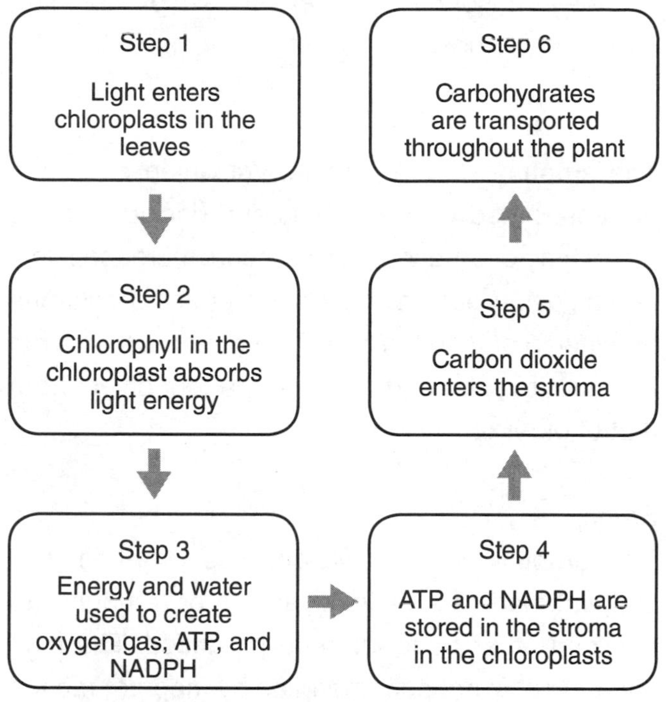

Figure 1

In plants, chlorophyll absorbs photons of sunlight, which are then used in the photosynthesis process. The net reaction for photosynthesis is shown below.

$$6CO_2 + 6H_2O + \text{light} \longrightarrow C_6H_{12}O_6 + 6O_2$$

Only certain wavelengths of sunlight are absorbed well by chlorophyll. Figure 2 shows this profile.

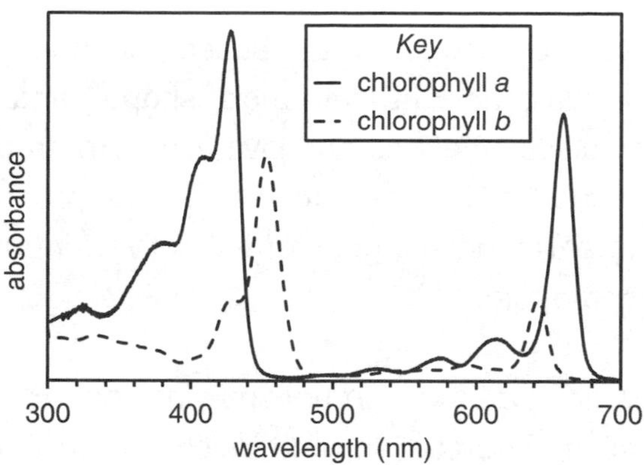

Figure 2

In an experiment, a type of tree, the *Fraxinus pennsylvanica*, is grown in an isolated greenhouse and exposed to different wavelengths of light. Its ATP production varies based on these wavelengths, and the results appear in Figure 3.

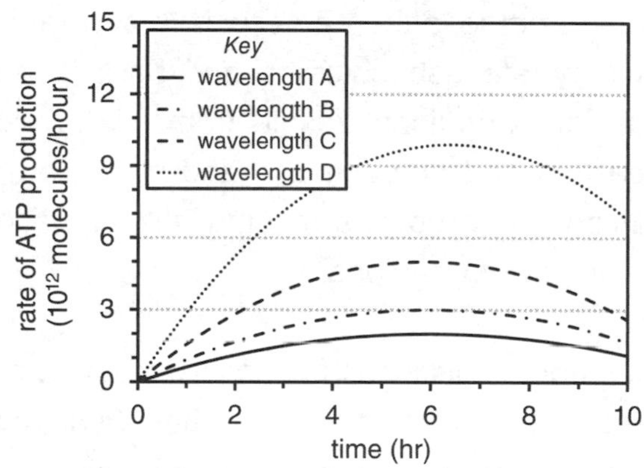

Figure 3

F. Nucleus
G. Chloroplast
H. Cell membrane
J. RNA

11.3.1 Context Clues

Introduction
Volcanic eruptions differ based on the size of the volcano, the volcano's shape, and the volcaniclastic material and lava flows. An eruption happens when a sudden release of energy occurs, due to earthquakes, geothermal activity, intrusion of magma, etc.

Common types of eruptions include Plinian, Hawaiian, Strombolian, and Vulcanian. In Plinian eruptions, high eruption columns are typically produced. Most result from the explosion of dacitic, trachytic, and phonolitic magmas whose temperatures can be as high as 750 to 1000°C. In Hawaiian eruptions, basaltic and highly fluid lavas are produced, and most start from fissures that concentrate at central vents. Strombolian eruptions are explosions separated by periods ranging from less than a second to several hours and generate ash columns and ballistic debris. Vulcanian eruptions result from hydrovolcanic processes and produce ash and steam eruption columns. All eruptions result in the formation of igneous rock formations.

Four students discuss the possible origin and type of the 2009 eruption in Sarychev Peak, which caused ash plumes of up to 14 km high.

Student 1
The eruption was Strombolian. The explosion lasted less than a year and produced material including bombs, scoriaceous lapilli, and ash.

Student 2
The eruption was Plinian. These eruptions typically produce eruption columns that transport volcaniclastic particles from beneath the ground into the atmosphere. They are known for their high eruption columns.

Student 3
The eruption was Vulcanian. Vulcanian eruptions are associated with andesitic and dacitic magma. In this type of eruption, gas pressure increases until an explosion occurs, typically producing columns between 5 and 10 km high. The material they eject has a unique, recognizable shape that differs from that of other explosions.

Student 4
The eruption was Hawaiian. The eruption was concentrated at one vent, and large amounts of ash and other material were produced. The high ash plumes were accompanied by magma, molten rock in the Earth's crust, that also erupted and spread down the peak, eventually cooling and hardening into rock.

A. Igneous
B. Metamorphic
C. Grained
D. Sedimentary

11.3.2 Examining Root Words

1. **Invasive species**

    a. ______________________________

    b. ______________________________

2. **Frequency**

    a. ______________________________

    b. ______________________________

3. **Amplitude**

    a. ______________________________

    b. ______________________________

4. **Wavelength**

    a. ______________________________

    b. ______________________________

5. **Genus**

    a. ______________________________

    b. ______________________________

6. **Homogeneous, homozygous**

    a. ______________________________

    b. ______________________________

11.3.2 Examining Root Words

Radar observations of a certain section of the ocean floor in the Atlantic have shown a surface that resembles longitudinal mountain ranges found on land. Such ridges are formed when magma emerges from the crust and spreads outward, cooling as it goes and depositing material in linear, parallel piles (see Figure 1). Figure 2 shows the average ridge spacing and average ridge height for each of a number of areas of the ridge in this section of the Atlantic and in 4 mountain ranges on land (Ranges A–E).

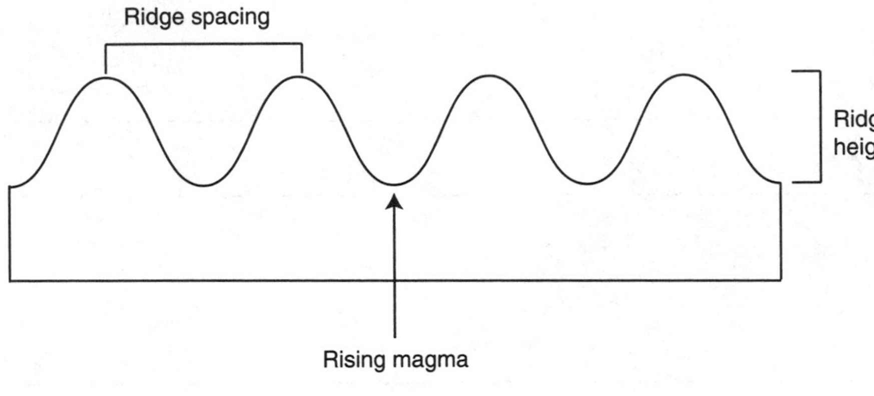

Figure 1

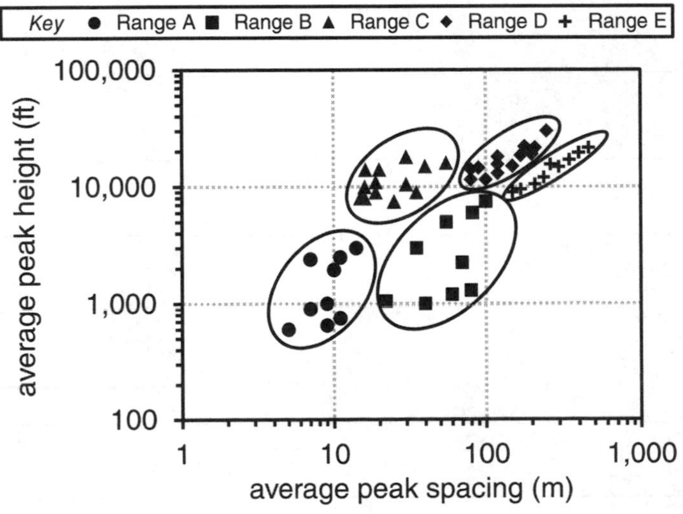

Figure 2

1. In Figure 1, ridge spacing and ridge height are directly analogous to which 2 quantities for transverse waves?

	ridge spacing	ridge height
A.	wavelength	amplitude
B.	frequency	amplitude
C.	wavelength	frequency
D.	amplitude	wavelength

11.3.3 Code Breaking

#1

Astronaut
Asteroid
Astronomy
Asterisk

A. Space
B. Rock
C. Star
D. Risk

#2

Logic
Dialogue
Analogy
Ontological

A. Thought
B. Speech
C. Describe
D. Real

#3

Diction
Dictate
Predict
Contradict

A. Guess
B. Say
C. Study
D. Argue

#4

Photograph
Photon
Photovoltaic
Photogram

A. Picture
B. Energy
C. Recreate
D. Light

#5

Export
Portable
Deport
Report

A. Carry
B. Leave
C. Package
D. Letter

#6

Evacuate
Vacate
Vacuum
Vacuole

A. Release
B. Empty
C. Clean
D. Hole

#7

Cranium
Craniectomy
Craniotomy
Amphicrania

A. Head
B. Spine
C. Skull
D. Face

1. ______ **2.** ______ **3.** ______ **4.** ______ **5.** ______ **6.** ______ **7.** ______

What field of study is the branch on top of which all other natural sciences are built?

Science Tip

Use What You Know: If you see an unfamiliar word in a science question, think of similar words you do know and try to guess the meaning of the word. Then try to answer the question based on your guess.

11.4.1 Set One

Passage I

A physics class is given the following information about Jupiter's moons: Jupiter's four largest moons are called Io, Europa, Ganymede, and Callisto (called its Galilean moons). Io is the most volcanically active and is covered in sulfur. It travels in a slightly elliptical orbit, and as a result, the large gravity exhibited by Jupiter leads to "tides" on Io's surface that rise 300 feet high. Europa has a surface predominantly consisting of water ice, which may cover even more water beneath. Scientists speculate about the potential of "habitable zones" on Europa, given some of the harsh conditions that organisms on Earth live under and the prevalence of water on the moon. Ganymede is the largest moon in our solar system, and is even larger than the planet Mercury. It also has its own internally generated magnetic field. Callisto has a heavily cratered surface, and may still have some surface activity today. It appears to be mainly a mixture of ice and rock.

Table 1 provides measurements on 16 of Jupiter's moons.

Two students discuss the orbit of Io. Io is the closest of the Galilean moons to Jupiter, and the third largest, with a diameter of 2,264 miles. Its mass is 8.93×10^{22} kg, and it takes 1.77 days to orbit Jupiter. Jupiter has a cloud around it near Io's orbit, called a torus.

Student 1

The torus around Jupiter is doughnut-shaped. It is caused by Jupiter's strong magnetic field, which strips ions from Io during its orbit. Therefore, Io acts like an electrical generator to produce a plasma torus.

Student 2

The torus around Jupiter is one of its rings, produced by the volcanic ash that is created by Io's numerous explosions. This ash is attracted to Jupiter's orbit, pulled in by its stronger gravitational pull. Jupiter is much larger than Io, with a radius of 43,441 miles and a mass that is 317.8 times that of Earth.

Table 1

Name	Distance from Jupiter (km)	Distance from Jupiter (Jupiter radii)	Orbital period (days)	Largest diameter (km)
Metis	128,000	1.79	0.29	40
Adrastea	129,000	1.80	0.30	20
Amalthea	181,000	2.54	0.50	260
Thebe	222,000	3.10	0.67	100
Io	422,000	5.90	1.77	3,640
Europa	671,000	9.38	3.55	3,130
Ganymede	1,070,000	15.0	7.15	5,270
Callisto	1,880,000	26.3	16.7	4,800
Leda	11,100,000	155	239	10
Himalia	11,500,000	161	251	170
Lysithea	11,700,000	164	259	24
Elara	11,700,000	164	260	80
Ananke	21,200,000	297	–631	20
Carme	22,600,000	316	–692	30
Pasiphae	23,500,000	329	–735	36
Sinope	23,700,000	332	–758	28

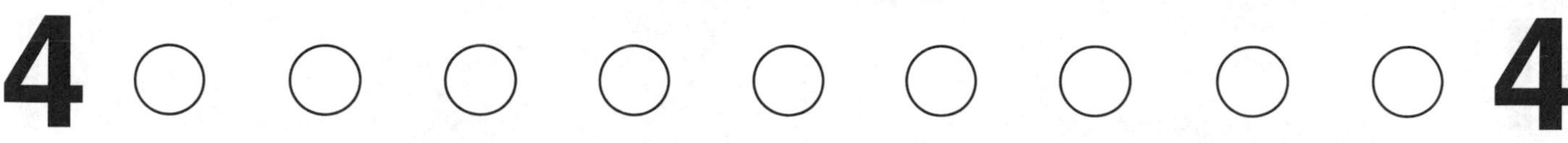

1. Based on Student 2's discussion, the torus around Io forms due to which of the following forces exerted on Io by the planet Jupiter?

   A. Nuclear force
   B. Friction force
   C. Electrostatic force
   D. Gravitational force

2. Based on the passage and Table 1, a moon orbiting Jupiter with a diameter of between 3,000 and 6,000 km is called which of the following?

   F. Athenian moon
   G. Thebe moon
   H. Galilean moon
   J. Carme moon

3. A scientist decides to study only those moons that are less than 1,000,000 km from Jupiter. Based on the table, how many moons is he going to study?

   A. 2
   B. 4
   C. 6
   D. 8

END OF SET ONE
STOP! DO NOT GO ON TO THE NEXT PAGE
UNTIL TOLD TO DO SO.

11.4.2 Set Two

Passage II

Coastlines are affected by a wide variety of forces. One of the most significant of these is waves, which can be either constructive or destructive to the coastline. When a wave breaks against the shore, water washes up on the beach (called the swash). The water that runs back down the beach is called the backwash. In constructive waves, the swash is stronger than the backwash, but in destructive waves, the backwash is stronger than the swash. Destructive waves tend to erode the coast and are high and steep with a short wave length. Constructive waves deposit material, building up beaches, and are low in height with a long wavelength. Table 1 provides data on the erosion of seven major pensisulas.

Three students hypothesize about the gradual loss of land near the Mississippi delta region in Louisiana, near the coast.

Student 1

Deltas increase in size due to the deposition of sediment. A slow increase occurs, offset by the sinking of the delta due to the consolidation of deeper sediments. These deltas are increasing in size despite the loss of nearby coastal lands.

Student 2

The delta is rapidly sinking below sea level; sediment is not being deposited by the river (due to changes made by man-made structures), and wind produces waves that, along with storm surges, lead to a process that removes rock and soil from the shore.

Student 3

Longshore drift moves the material sideways along the delta, transferring it from the delta to further along the shore. This transportation is helped along by the waves that carry material along the coast.

Table 1

Location	Country	Erosion time period	Average erosion rate (m/yr)
Yugorsky Peninsula, Kara Sea	Russia	1947–2001	0.6–1 (scarp) 1.3–1.6 (bluff)
Herschel Island, Beaufort Sea	Canada	1954–1970	0.7
		1970–2000	1.0
		1954–2000	0.9
Barrow, Alaska, Chukchi Sea	United States	1948–1997	0.4–0.9 (Elson Lagoon)
		1948–2000	1–2.5 (Holocene terrace)
Pesyakov Island, Pechora Sea	Russia	2002	0.5–2.5
Varandei, Pechora Sea	Russia	2002	1.8–2.0
Varandei Island, Pechora Sea	Russia	1970–1980	7–10
		1980–1990	1.5–2
		1987–2000	3–4
Maly Chukochy Cape, East Siberian Sea	Russia	1984–1988	3.5
		1988–1990	1.5
		1990–1991	3
		1991–1994	5
		1994–1999	4.4
		1984–1999	4.3

4. The process described by Student 3 is an example of which of the following geological processes?

   F. Tectonics
   G. Cementation
   H. Metamorphism
   J. Erosion

5. The table includes data from regions in how many different countries?

   A. 2
   B. 3
   C. 4
   D. 5

6. Which of the following terms best describes the type of waves that are breaking against the Yugorsky Peninsula in the Kara Sea and the type of waves that are breaking against the Maly Chukochy Cape in the East Siberian Sea?

	Yugorsky Peninsula	Maly Chukochy Cape
F.	destructive	destructive
G.	destructive	constructive
H.	constructive	destructive
J.	constructive	constructive

END OF SET TWO
STOP! DO NOT GO ON TO THE NEXT PAGE
UNTIL TOLD TO DO SO.

11.4.3 Set Three

Passage III

Recent observations of the ocean surface in the Atlantic have revealed longitudinal waves that are formed by the wind whipping across the water (see Figure 1). Figure 2 shows the average wave spacing and wave height for a number of areas in the Atlantic, as well as 4 additional oceans. Figure 3 plots the average height (measured from crest to trough) across a 10-mile perpendicular cross section of waves in Ocean B.

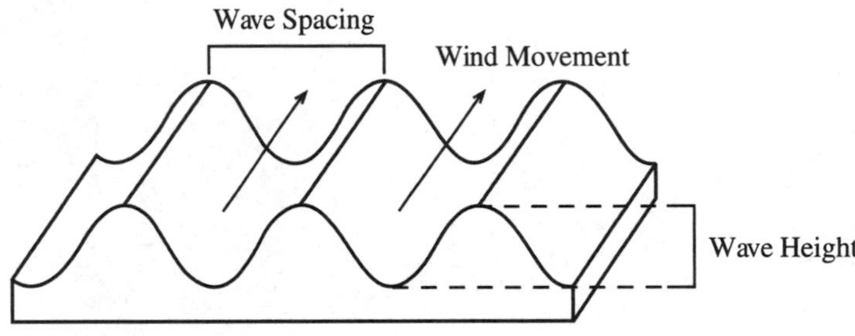

Figure 1

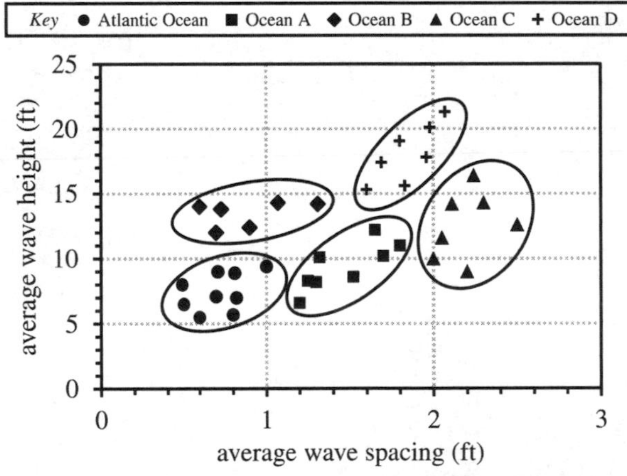

Figure 2

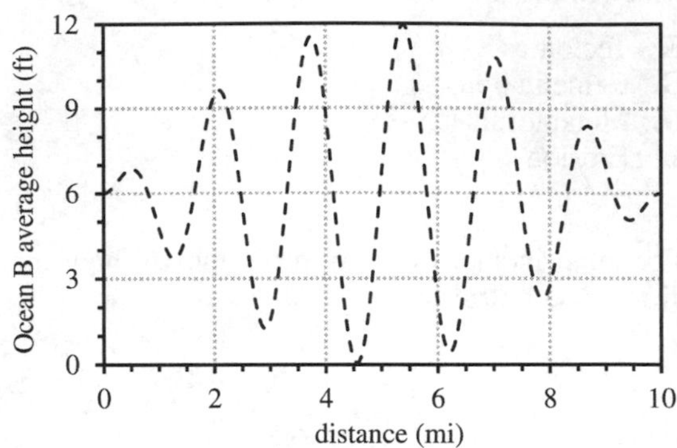

Figure 3

7. The two quantities for waves that are defined in Figure 1—wave height and wave spacing—are directly analogous to which two quantities for electromagnetic waves?

	wave height	wave spacing
A.	frequency	wavelength
B.	amplitude	frequency
C.	wavelength	amplitude
D.	amplitude	wavelength

8. How many wave features were directly measured in Figure 2?

   F. 1
   G. 2
   H. 3
   J. 4

9. Based on Figure 2, waves that average about 0.5 feet apart and 7 feet high are most likely to be in which ocean?

   A. Ocean A
   B. Ocean B
   C. Ocean C
   D. The Atlantic Ocean

END OF SET THREE

STOP! DO NOT GO ON TO THE NEXT PAGE UNTIL TOLD TO DO SO.

11.4.4 Set Four

Passage IV

A teacher showed two test tubes to a chemistry class. One test tube contained vegetable oil and the other contained water (H_2O). The teacher then added solid iodine (I_2) to each test tube. The solid iodine dissolved quickly in the vegetable oil but stayed undissolved at the bottom of the test tube with water. The test tube with the vegetable oil also turned purple, but the test tube with water remained colorless. The teacher asked three students to explain these results.

Student 1

Vegetable oil (Figure 1) is made up of atoms joined together in a linear structure, while water (Figure 2) is made of atoms that have a different, bent structure. The solid iodine was able to bond more easily to the linear molecules of the vegetable oil, while it was not able to bond as easily to the bent structure of water.

For a solid to dissolve in a solvent, its molecules must be able to align easily with the solvent molecules. The molecular structure of a substance indicates whether it will be able to dissolve in a solvent (the solvent and substance should be of a similar structure). Since iodine has the same linear structure as vegetable oil, it dissolved in the vegetable oil but not the water.

Student 2

A water molecule is polar because it has both regions of positive charge and regions of negative charge. By contrast, nonpolar molecules like those that make up vegetable oil do not have differently charged regions. Both compounds may contain covalent bonds. Polar molecules are attracted to polar molecules, and nonpolar molecules are attracted to nonpolar molecules. However, polar and nonpolar molecules repel each other. Therefore, polar substances dissolve in polar solvents, and nonpolar substances dissolve in nonpolar solvents. So the iodine dissolved in vegetable oil but not water. Molecular structure itself does not explain solubility but requires knowledge of the distribution of electrons as well.

Student 3

The explanation given by Student 2 is correct, except that nonpolar molecules are actually strongly attracted to polar molecules. However, nonpolar molecules do not dissolve in polar substances because the polar molecules are too strongly attracted to each other to allow nonpolar molecules to come between them. If a drop of vegetable oil is placed on top of a dish of water, the drop will spread to form the thinnest possible layer in order to maximize contact with the polar water molecules.

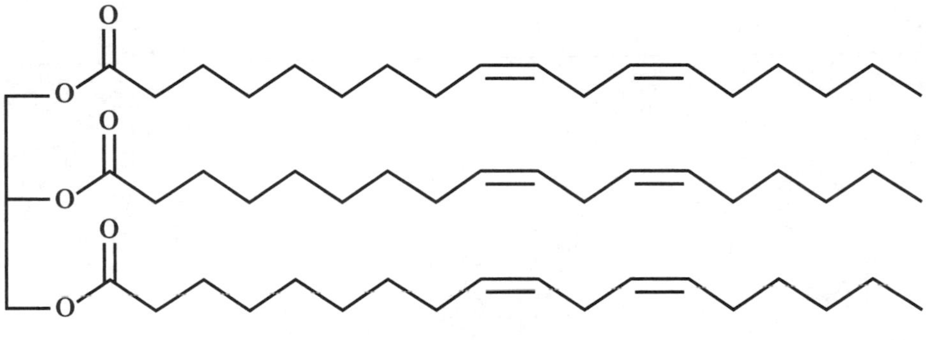

Figure 1

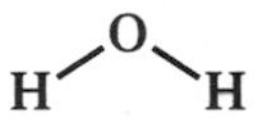

Figure 2

10. Which of the following terms best describes the mixture of iodine and solvent in each of the test tubes described in the teacher's demonstration?

	iodine and vegetable oil	iodine and water
F.	homogeneous	homogeneous
G.	homogeneous	heterogeneous
H.	heterogeneous	homogeneous
J.	heterogeneous	heterogeneous

11. Based on Student 2's discussion, the atoms of a single water molecule are held together by which of the following types of atomic bonds?

A. Metallic
B. Quantum
C. Nuclear
D. Covalent

12. In polar molecules, the type of chemical bonding described in the passage is typically governed by which of the following parts of an atom?

F. Protons
G. Electrons
H. Neutrons
J. Quarks

END OF SET FOUR

STOP! DO NOT GO ON TO THE NEXT PAGE
UNTIL TOLD TO DO SO.

11.4.5 Set Five

Passage V

The chemical reaction associated with energy production in some aerobic eukaryotes can be represented by the following chemical equation:

$$C_6H_{12}O_6 + 6O_2 \longrightarrow 6CO_2 + 6H_2O + \text{energy}$$

Table 1 lists the ways that different eukaryotes obtain energy.

Table 1

Energy source	Oxidizing donor source	Carbon source	Name
Sunlight *photo-*	organic *-organo-*	organic *-heterotroph*	photoorganoheterotroph
		carbon dioxide *-autotroph*	photoorganoautotroph
	inorganic *-litho-*	organic *-heterotroph*	photolithoheterotroph
		carbon dioxide *-autotroph*	photolithoautotroph
Chemical compounds *chemo-*	organic *-organo-*	organic *-heterotroph*	chemoorganoheterotroph
		carbon dioxide *-autotroph*	chemoorganoautotroph
	inorganic *-litho-*	organic *-heterotroph*	chemolithoheterotroph
		carbon dioxide *-autotroph*	chemolithoautotroph

Figure 1 shows the relative production of energy by eukaryote A and eukaryote B when exposed to differing levels of sunlight during the day.

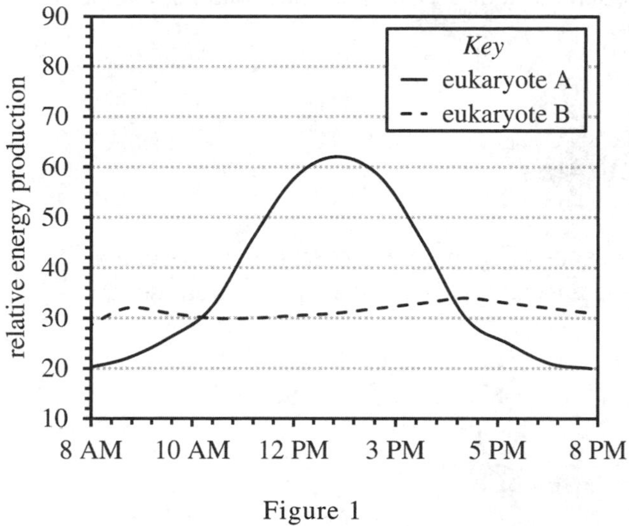

Figure 1

Figure 2 shows the average rate of energy production of eukaryote A at various times as a percentage of the average rate of production at 4:00 PM.

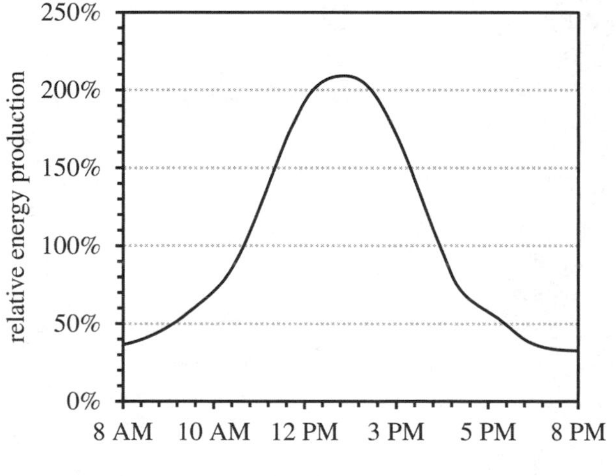

Figure 2

13. In eukaryotic organisms, the chemical reactions associated with the chemical equation shown in the passage typically occur using which of the following structures?

A. Cytoskeleton
B. Mitochondria
C. Vacuoles
D. Endoplasmic reticulum

14. Based on Figure 1 and the data presented in Table 1, the energy source of eukaryote A is most likely to be:

F. sunlight, while the energy source of eukaryote B is most likely to be chemical compounds.
G. sunlight, while the energy source of eukaryote B is also most likely to be sunlight.
H. chemical compounds, while the energy source of eukaryote B is also most likely to be chemical compounds.
J. chemical compounds, while the energy source of eukaryote B is most likely to be sunlight.

15. The two types of organisms listed in Table 1—photoorganoautotrophs and chemoorganoheterotrophs—are analogous to which of the following organisms?

	<u>photoorganoautotrophs</u>	<u>chemoorganoheterotrophs</u>
A.	fungi	animals
B.	animals	plants
C.	fungi	plants
D.	plants	animals

END OF SET FIVE

STOP! DO NOT GO ON TO THE NEXT PAGE UNTIL TOLD TO DO SO.

Sum It Up

Terminology

Context: The surrounding circumstances or details of an event, statement, or idea that inform its meaning

---

Root Word: The most basic part of a word, what is left without a suffix or prefix; in science, often of Greek or Latin origin

Tips and Techniques

Use What You Know: If you see an unfamiliar word in a science question, think of similar words you do know and try to guess the meaning of the word. Then try to answer the question based on your guess.

Lesson 12

Compare Models

CAPTION:

12.1 Entrance Ticket

Many nutritionists have different ideas about dieting—whether low-carbohydrate diets or low-fat diets are most effective for weight loss. Write a short paragraph (5–7 sentences) describing which method you think would be more effective. Do you think low-carbohydrate diets or low-fat diets help people lose weight faster? Be sure to include details to support your stance. What information would you need to know to prove your hypothesis?

12.2 Learning Targets

1. Analyze varying viewpoints on scientific facts, theories, and experiments

2. Identify the similarities and differences between multiple scientific viewpoints

Self-Assessment

Circle the number that corresponds to your confidence level in your knowledge of this subject before beginning the lesson. A score of 1 means you are completely lost, and a score of 4 means you have mastered the skills. After you finish the lesson, return to the bottom of this page and circle your new confidence level to show your improvement.

Before Lesson

1 2 3 4

After Lesson

1 2 3 4

12.3.1 Compare and Contrast Experiments

Hypothesis: ____________________

____

____

____

Experiment: ____________________

____

____

____

Results: ____________________

____

____

____

Conclusion: ____________________

____

____

____

12.3.1 Compare and Contrast Experiments

Compare and Contrast: ______________________________

Science Tip

Skim and Scan: Comparing models questions almost always come from passages that have no graphs, tables, or diagrams, so it is important to do a one-minute skim of the passage and circle the key similarities and differences with your pencil. Then, scan to locate answers as you solve each question.

12.3.2 Similarities and Differences

An astrophysics class received the following information about the death of a massive star.

The death of a massive star is classified into 3 phases: *red supergiant* (RSG), *supernova* (SN), and *black hole* (BH).

Depletion of hydrogen in the core of a massive star causes the star to begin fusing helium, forming an RSG. The core of the RSG is surrounded by a shell of expanding, cooling gas.

When the RSG has completely fused the material in its core into iron, gravitational forces cause the star to collapse in on itself. This core collapse creates a powerful explosion called a supernova.

An SN becomes a BH if a sufficient amount of the dense core survives the explosion and exerts a gravitational force on other objects in space. The higher the mass of the original RSG, the stronger the resulting gravitational pull the BH will exert.

Two students discuss the evolution of three recently discovered features of the Whirlpool Galaxy, M51a: a central BH of 10 million solar masses (the Sun's mass is one solar mass); SN2005, a supernova caused by an RSG of 10 solar masses; and WP3, an RSG of 10 solar masses. The BH lies at the center of the Whirlpool Galaxy, and WP3, which was last observed by astronomers in 2005, orbits the central BH. SN2005 was recorded by astronomers in 2005.

Student 1

As the Whirlpool Galaxy was forming, the central BH, WP3, and SN2005 became RSG stars at the same time. The star with the highest mass rapidly underwent gravitational collapse, forming a BH at the center of the galaxy, while WP3 remained an RSG star. Because the star that produced SN2005 was located closer to the BH than WP3, this star lost most of its matter to the BH and rapidly progressed to the SN stage. As a result, WP3 remains an RSG star while the remnants of SN2005 are of too little mass to form a second black hole in the galaxy.

Student 2

WP3 was not a part of the original Whirlpool Galaxy. WP3 and what would eventually become the central BH progressed to RSG stars in separate galaxies at separate times, and so moved in two different orbits. When the BH formed at the center of the Whirlpool Galaxy, its gravitational force pulled WP3 into its orbit.

WP3 lost some of its mass to the central BH, and progressed from an RSG star to the SN stage. SN2005, seen by astronomers in 2005, was actually the SN stage of WP3, which has not been observed since 2005. WP3 must no longer be an RSG star and instead has formed a small BH.

12.3.2 Similarities and Differences

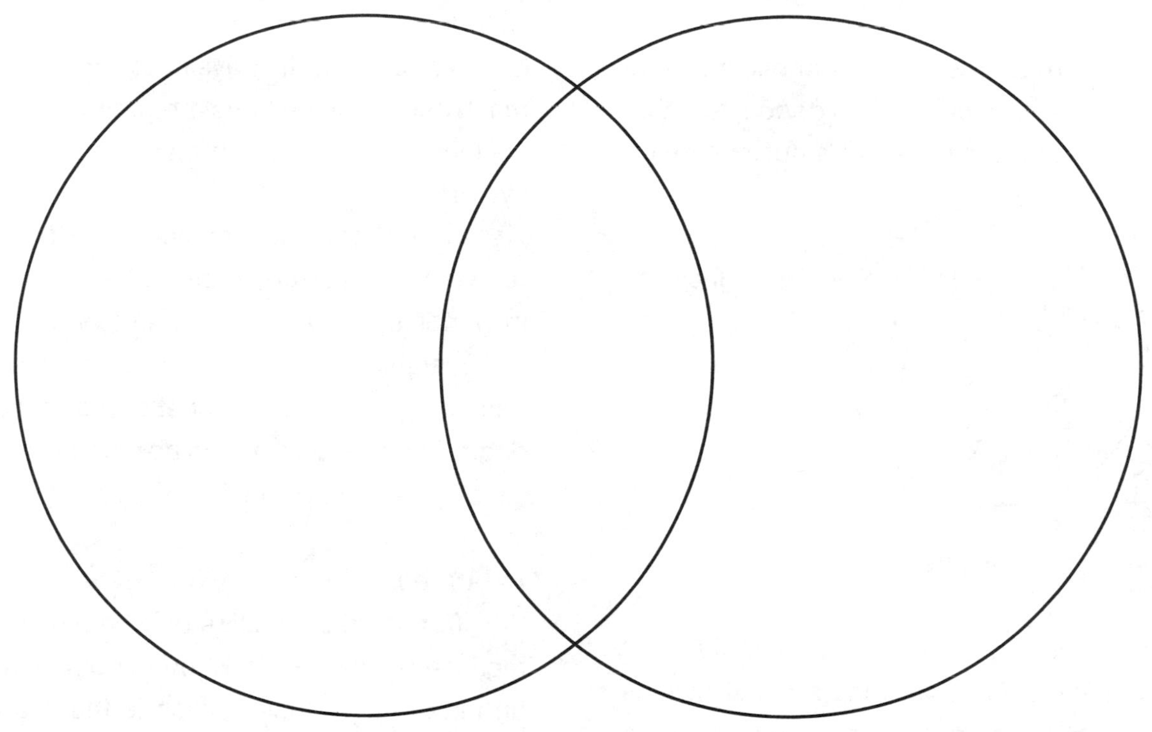

Similarities: ____

____

____

____

Differences: ____

____

____

____

12.3.2 Similarities and Differences

In the 1950s, biologists believed that the transmission and expression of genetic material was controlled by structures called *genes*, and that genes were located within the cell's nucleus only.

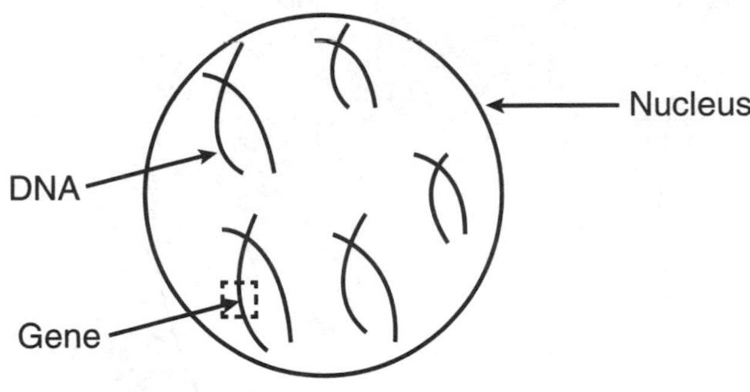

Figure 1

Genes are discrete segments of *deoxyribonucleic acid* (DNA) that give instructions for the production of certain proteins. When a gene is used to make a protein, the DNA is first copied in a process called *transcription*, which forms a messenger copy. This messenger copy is then used to make a protein in a process called *translation*. While DNA is a double-stranded molecule composed of units called *nucleotides*, a second molecule, called *ribonucleic acid* (RNA), is a single-stranded molecule that is involved in some aspects of both transcription and translation.

Two scientists in the 1950s discuss whether transcription creates an RNA or DNA messenger copy of the gene.

DNA Theory:

Transcription creates a DNA copy of the gene to carry the information to the site of protein synthesis. As DNA is always replicated when the cell divides, DNA replication machinery already in place can easily be used to create copies of DNA, which can then be used to make proteins. DNA is a very stable molecule, so it can maintain its structure as it travels to protein synthesis machinery. Proteins must be produced in the cell's nucleus, and from there they are exported to the cytoplasm.

In contrast, the creation of RNA from DNA requires specialized, non-DNA machinery, which may not exist within the nucleus. Further, RNA lacks stability: it cannot form the long strands necessary to transfer genetic information, and it degrades too quickly to reliably carry messages to sites of protein synthesis.

RNA Theory:

Transcription of DNA only creates RNA as the messenger copy. RNA is found both in the nucleus and in the cytoplasm, which is the site of protein synthesis, while DNA is only found in the cell's nucleus. Further, almost all cells within an organism have a constant amount of DNA, independent of the amount of protein the cell produces.

Though RNA is less stable than DNA, the amount of RNA produced by a cell is proportional to the amount of protein a cell produces, a relationship that has been best described for *hepatocytes* (cells in the liver). Hepatocytes make 10 times as much protein as do certain other cells, such as skin cells. Hepatocytes also have 10 times the amount of RNA at any one time as skin cells do. Thus the amount of RNA is consistent with the amount of protein produced by a cell. The amount of DNA, in contrast, does not vary with the amount of protein production in a cell.

12.3.2 Similarities and Differences

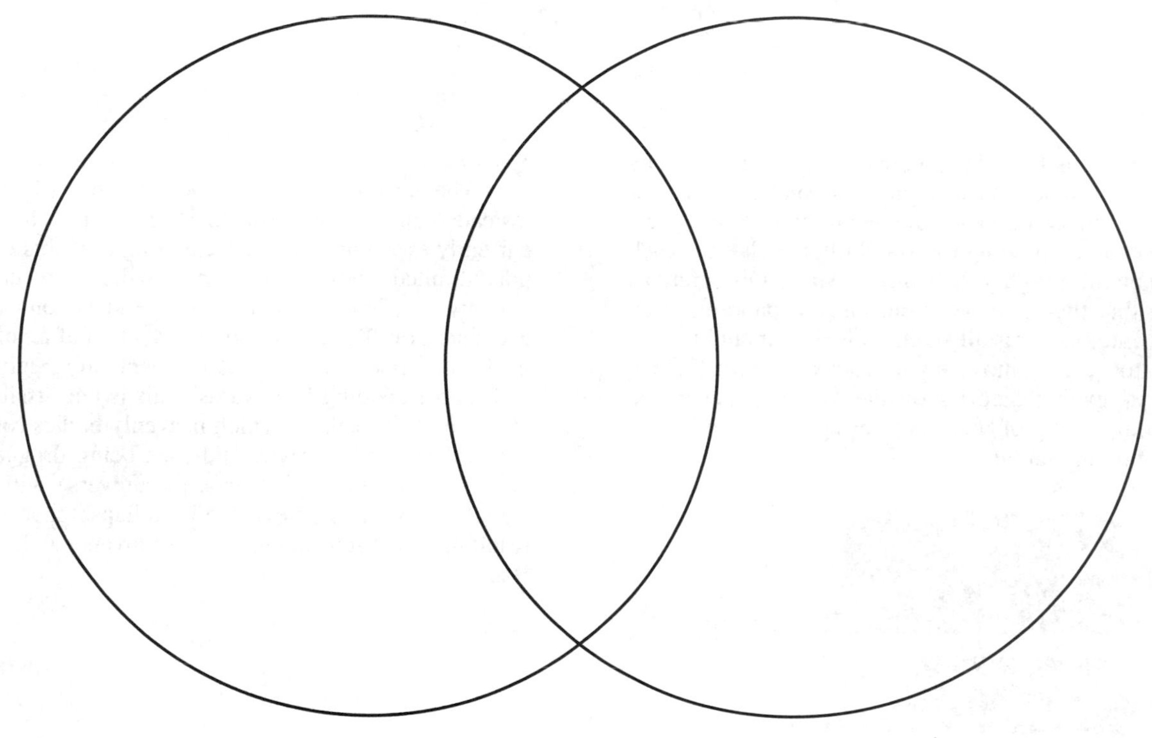

Similarities: ______________________________

____

____

____

Differences: ______________________________

____

____

____

Science Tip

Mental Venn Diagram: Every ACT has one passage with conflicting viewpoints. When you find that passage, make a mental Venn diagram to track the similarities and differences within the passage. Use your pencil to underline any key points to help you keep track of what you find.

12.4.1 Set One

Passage I

The universe is thought to be roughly 14 billion years old, having begun in a flash with an event known as the Big Bang. Our universe is composed of the totality of time, space, and matter, containing roughly 100 billion galaxies, each of which contains roughly 100 billion stars. Observations have shown that the universe is currently expanding at an accelerating rate, causing all of its galaxies, including our Milky Way, to quickly move away from each other. There are several competing theories on the ultimate fate of the universe, though none of them are yet agreed upon by the scientific community at large.

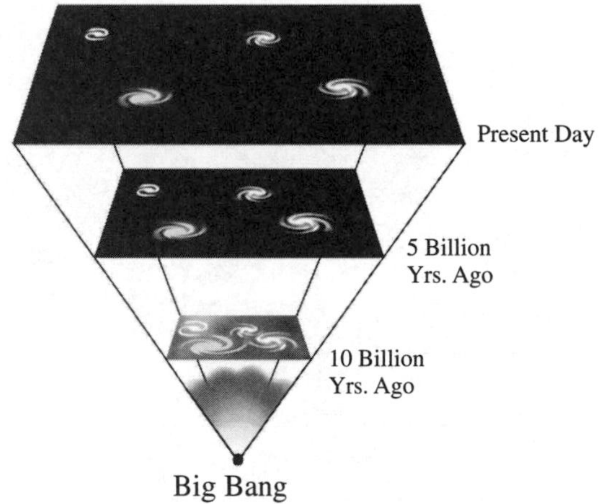

Two scientists present their viewpoints about how the universe will end.

Scientist A

The universe will end in what is known as the Big Freeze, when the accelerating expansion of the universe eventually causes the temperature of the universe to approach absolute zero. As the expansion of the universe will continue on forever, the entropy of the universe will increase at a rapid rate. The universe will grow darker and darker until there is no longer enough gas for stars to continue forming. At this time, the universe will only be populated by black holes, which will eventually die as well. After trillions of years of slowly fading out, the universe will die in a heat death, meaning that it will have exhausted all of the free thermodynamic energy remaining, preventing any work from being done and preventing all of the processes necessary for creating or sustaining life from continuing.

Scientist B

The universe will not end with the Big Freeze, but instead with the Big Crunch. Even though the universe is currently expanding at an accelerating rate, this expansion is not unlimited. The expansion speed will not exceed the escape velocity to allow expansion to extend beyond a universal event horizon. The gravitational attraction of all of the matter in the universe will cause it to eventually begin retracting and rubber-banding backwards. This is not dissimilar to the same elliptical path by which heavenly bodies rotate around each other, hurtling away and then being dragged back by gravitational pull. In this way, the universe will not end in a heat death, but will eventually collapse back in on itself, resulting in the reformation of the universe with another Big Bang.

1. Do Scientist A and Scientist B differ in their claims of the universe's potential for expansion?

   A. No; both scientists claim the universe will continue expanding forever.
   B. No; both scientists claim the universe will only expand to a certain extent.
   C. Yes; Scientist A claims the universe will expand forever, while Scientist B claims the universe can only expand to a certain extent.
   D. Yes; Scientist A claims the universe can only expand to a certain extent, while Scientist B claims the universe will expand forever.

2. The universe was 50% smaller 5 billion years ago than it is today. Assuming that the proportion of dark energy, a repulsive force between molecules, has remained constant, both scientists would most likely agree that the speed with which the universe was expanding 5 billion years ago was:

   F. higher than the speed with which the universe is expanding today.
   G. the same as the speed with which the universe is expanding today.
   H. less than the speed with which the universe is expanding today but above zero.
   J. less than the speed with which the universe is expanding today and below zero.

3. Which of the following statements will Scientists A and B most likely agree on?

   A. The universe will contract before reaching escape velocity.
   B. The universe will reach escape velocity.
   C. The universe is expanding.
   D. The Big Bang did not occur.

4. Scientists A and B would most likely agree on all of the following points, EXCEPT that:

   F. the universe was created by an event called the Big Bang.
   G. after the universe collapses on itself, it will reform with another Big Bang.
   H. the galaxies in the universe are moving away from each other.
   J. the universe is currently expanding at an accelerating rate.

5. Consistent with Scientist A's position, over time entropy in a closed system is known to increase. According to the laws of thermodynamics, this means a closed system will eventually exhaust all of the free energy capable of performing work. If Scientist A were to use this aspect of thermodynamics to support his position, how could another scientist attempt to refute it?

   A. By suggesting that the universe is not finite but instead infinite and, therefore, cannot be a closed system
   B. By stating that stars have only a limited life span
   C. By suggesting that gravitational force will prevent the universe from exceeding escape velocity
   D. By saying that dark energy fuels the acceleration of the universe's expansion

END OF SET ONE
STOP! DO NOT GO ON TO THE NEXT PAGE UNTIL TOLD TO DO SO.

12.4.2 Set Two

Passage II

In *Cucurbita* (squash plants), male flowers contain *anthers*, which produce pollen, and female flowers contain *stigmas*, which house the ovaries. When pollen from anthers is deposited on stigmas, the ovaries are pollinated and subsequently develop seeds. Two researchers debate the processes controlling pollination in *Cucurbita.*

Researcher 1:

In *Cucurbita,* honeybees are responsible for 95% of total pollination of the stigmas. *Self-pollination* (a process through which pollen travels from the anther of one flower to the stigma of an adjacent flower on the same plant) is responsible for 5% of pollination. *Cucurbita* uses only these two mechanisms for pollination.

Cucurbita has a *symbiotic* (mutually dependent) relationship with honeybees. Honeybees enter male *Cucurbita* flowers to collect nectar as male flowers release pollen. The pollen from the anthers covers the honeybees' bodies and pollen baskets (special structures on the legs for gathering pollen). Honeybees then visit female *Cucurbita* flowers and release pollen onto the stigmas. With the decline of honeybees in a region, less than 5% of female *Cucurbita* flowers are pollinated, meaning most plants fail to reproduce.

In *Cucurbita*, self-pollination is infrequent because of the relatively large distance between adjacent male and female flowers, which prevents the spread of pollen from anthers to stigma. Further, *Cucurbita* pollen grains can only survive if they remain hydrated (full of water), and so pollen is much too heavy to be transferred among flowers via air currents.

Researcher 2:

While honeybee pollination accounts for 40% of all Cucurbita pollination, self-pollination accounts for 60%. When self-pollination is prohibited, the amount of total pollination and subsequent seed production decreases by 60%, while when honeybee populations decline, the percent of pollination decreases by up to 40%. When both of these processes fail to occur, 0% of flowers are pollinated and no seeds are produced.

Observations of wild *Cucurbita* plants have revealed that male flowers are both more numerous and of greater height than are female flowers. In *Cucurbita,* each female flower is thus surrounded by several taller male flowers, and so the heavy, wet pollen is able to fall down onto the female flower. Additionally, female *Cucurbita* flowers have enlarged, two-lobed stigmas, a trait that is common in self-pollinating plants.

Experiments

The researchers developed 3 experiments using a *Cucurbita* sample maintained in an outdoor garden. The garden was constructed in a region with a wild honeybee population and in which, on average, 94% of *Cucurbita* flowers were successfully pollinated (Table 1).

Table 1

Experiment	Protocol
A	Individual female *Cucurbita* flowers were isolated within plastic bags to prevent entry of honeybees and pollen into the flower.
B	Individual female *Cucurbita* flowers were isolated within thin plastic nets to prevent the entry of honeybees while allowing pollen to enter the flower.
C	Individual male *Cucurbita* flowers were enclosed in plastic domes to prevent pollen from falling out of the flower, while allowing honeybees access to the flowers.

6. In reference to the experiments described in Table 1, Researchers 1 and 2 would most likely both hypothesize that the percent of pollination would be highest in *Cucurbita* plants that are:

   F. not covered with plastic bags, nets, or plastic domes.
   G. covered with nets that block honeybees.
   H. covered with plastic domes that prevent pollen from falling out of the male flowers.
   J. covered with plastic bags that prevent any material from entering the flower.

7. Researcher 1 claims that "pollen is much too heavy to be transferred among flowers via air currents." Of the statements below, which best describes how Researcher 2 would respond to this claim? Researcher 2 argues that the greater height of the:

   A. female *Cucurbita* flowers allows pollen to fall, increasing the probability that the flowers below will be pollinated.
   B. female *Cucurbita* flowers allows pollen to fall, decreasing the probability that the flowers below will be pollinated.
   C. male *Cucurbita* flowers allows pollen to fall, increasing the probability that the flowers below will be pollinated.
   D. male *Cucurbita* flowers allows pollen to fall, decreasing the probability that the flowers below will be pollinated.

8. Honeybees were 30% more abundant 50 years ago than they are today. Assuming that the relative importance of honeybee pollination and self-pollination in *Cucurbita* have not varied over this time, both researchers would agree that the percent of female flowers pollinated in *Cucurbita* populations 50 years ago was most likely:

   F. Higher than the percent of female flowers pollinated in *Cucurbita* today.
   G. Equal to the percent of female flowers pollinated in *Cucurbita* today.
   H. Lower than the percent of female flowers pollinated in *Cucurbita* today, but above 5%.
   J. Less than 5%.

9. Of the following statements about pollen in *Cucurbita*, with which would both researchers most likely agree?

   A. *Cucurbita* pollen is both heavy and wet.
   B. *Cucurbita* pollen is heavy but dry.
   C. *Cucurbita* pollen is both light and dry.
   D. Dehydration of pollen is necessary for self-pollination.

10. Researcher 1's model differs from Researcher 2's model in that Researcher 1 hypothesizes that total pollination in *Cucurbita* is:

   F. primarily from self-pollination, while Researcher 2 claims insect pollination is more frequent than self-pollination.
   G. primarily from insect pollination, while Researcher 2 claims that insects lack the ability to pollinate *Cucurbita*.
   H. primarily from insect pollination, while Researcher 2 claims that self-pollination is more important than pollination by insects.
   J. primarily from self-pollination, while Researcher 2 claims that the *Cucurbita* lacks the ability to self-pollinate.

END OF SET TWO
STOP! DO NOT GO ON TO THE NEXT PAGE
UNTIL TOLD TO DO SO.

12.4.3 Set Three

Passage III

In a biology laboratory, a research professor removed a flask containing a dark purple liquid from a freezer and placed it on a bench top. During the next 15 minutes, vapor rose from the flask as the liquid bubbled, decreased in volume, and lightened in color. After 15 minutes, the liquid had become colorless, and a brown solid formed and sank to the bottom of the flask. After 20 minutes, only the brown solid remained in the bottom of the flask. The research professor then asked four students to provide hypotheses for their observations of the liquid over the 20 minutes.

Student 1

The flask initially contained a solution made by dissolving a brown solid in a mixture of purple and colorless solvents with boiling points below room temperature. When the liquid was removed from the freezer, the purple solvent evaporated, leaving the colorless solvent and increasing the concentration of the solid. After 15 minutes, the colorless solvent began evaporating; the volume of the solvent then decreased such that the solid could no longer be dissolved, so the solid precipitated from the solution. All of the solvent had evaporated by 20 minutes.

Student 2

The solution in the flask had been made by dissolving a brown solid protein in a colorless, pure solvent. Solvent molecules surrounded, but did not react with, each molecule of protein to form a purple-colored enzyme-substrate complex (ESC). Throughout the first 15 minutes the solvent, because of its low boiling point, evaporated; loss of the solvent increased the concentration of the ESC. At 15 minutes, there were too few solvent molecules remaining to surround each solid molecule, and the nonreactive ESCs dissociated, leaving a brown precipitate and a colorless solvent. All of the solvent had evaporated by 20 minutes.

Student 3

The solution in the flask had been made by dissolving a purple solid in a pure, colorless solvent with a low boiling point. This solvent evaporated during the first 15 minutes, causing the concentration of the solid to increase. After 15 minutes, the concentration and temperature of the solution caused the solid to react with the remaining solvent, forming an insoluble brown solid and a colorless solvent. All of the solvent had evaporated by 20 minutes.

Student 4

The solution in the flask was initially a pure purple liquid with a low boiling point. During the 15 minutes, some of this liquid evaporated while its molecules decomposed into a brown, soluble solid and a colorless liquid. After 15 minutes, the volume of liquid was too low for the brown solid to remain soluble, and so it precipitated from the colorless solvent. All of the solvent had evaporated by 20 minutes.

11. Do Students 3 and 4 provide different hypotheses for the cause of the liquid's purple color?

A. No; both students hypothesize the color was from a dissolved solid.
B. No; both students hypothesize the color was from a pure liquid.
C. Yes; Student 3 hypothesizes the color was caused by a dissolved solid, while Student 4 hypothesizes the color was from a pure liquid.
D. Yes; Student 3 hypothesizes the color was from a pure liquid, while Student 4 hypothesizes the color was caused by a dissolved solid.

12. Student 2 claims that "the nonreactive ESCs dissociated, leaving a brown precipitate and a colorless solvent." How would Student 3 respond to this statement? Student 3 claims that:

F. the purple solid was formed by a reaction caused by the increasing concentration and heat of the solution.
G. the purple solid was formed by a reaction caused by the decreasing concentration and heat of the solution.
H. the brown solid was formed by a reaction caused by the increasing concentration and heat of the solution.
J. the brown solid was formed by a reaction caused by the decreasing concentration and heat of the solution.

13. Students 1 and 2 would most likely agree that the precipitation of a solid would have occurred sooner if:

A. less solvent had been added to the beaker.
B. less solid had been added to the beaker.
C. more solvent had been added to the beaker.
D. more solvent and less solid had been added to the beaker.

14. Decreasing the atmospheric pressure decreases the boiling point of a solution. Assuming a change in atmospheric pressure would only affect the boiling point of the solution and not any reaction within the flask, the four students would most likely agree that if the experiment were to be repeated at a decreased atmospheric pressure, the amount of time until the solid precipitated would be:

F. fewer than 20 minutes.
G. exactly 20 minutes.
H. more than 20 minutes.
J. zero minutes.

15. Do Students 1 and 4 offer different explanations for the source of the solid precipitate's brown color?

A. No; both students hypothesize the cause is a solid being dissolved.
B. No; both students hypothesize the cause is decomposition of a liquid.
C. Yes; Student 1 hypothesizes the source is a dissolved solid, while Student 4 hypothesizes the source is a decomposed liquid.
D. Yes; Student 1 hypothesizes the cause is decomposition of a liquid, while Student 4 hypothesizes the cause is a solid being dissolved.

END OF SET THREE
STOP! DO NOT GO ON TO THE NEXT PAGE
UNTIL TOLD TO DO SO.

Sum It Up

Compare Models

Hypothesis
A proposed explanation based on evidence

Experiment
A test to see if a hypothesis is true

Results
What happened or changed when a hypothesis is tested

Conclusion
A statement, backed up by data analysis, which supports or refutes a hypothesis

Tips and Techniques

Skim and Scan: Comparing models questions almost always come from passages that have no graphs, tables, or diagrams, so it is important to do a one-minute skim of the passage and circle the key similarities and differences with your pencil. Then, scan to locate answers as you solve each question.

Mental Venn Diagram: Every ACT has one passage with conflicting viewpoints. When you read a conflicting viewpoints passage, make a mental Venn diagram to track the similarities and differences within the passage. Use your pencil to underline any key points to help keep track of your findings.

Lesson 13

Text and Experiments

CAPTION:

13.1 Entrance Ticket

Write a paragraph (5–7 sentences) describing an experiment you have done. It can be something from science class, something you did for a project, or something completely unscientific you did at home. Be sure to include why you carried out this experiment and your findings.

13.2 Learning Targets

1. Understand the scientific method and explain the significance of each step

2. Find information in text that describes both simple and complex experiments

Self-Assessment

Circle the number that corresponds to your confidence level in your knowledge of this subject before beginning the lesson. A score of 1 means you are completely lost, and a score of 4 means you have mastered the skills. After you finish the lesson, return to the bottom of this page and circle your new confidence level to show your improvement.

Before Lesson

1 2 3 4

After Lesson

1 2 3 4

13.3.1 Describing an Experiment

Solubility gives the amount of solute that can be dissolved in a given solvent, and it can be affected by temperature and pressure. Increases in temperature have varying effects on any given solute, largely dependent on whether or not the solute has an endothermic or exothermic reaction process. These processes are often measured by changes in heat, or kilojoules per mole, where 1 mole is 6×10^{23} discrete units of a compound. Solutes may also be affected by *the common ion effect*, which occurs when a salt solute shares an ion in common with a solvent. Figure 1 shows one example of this effect. Gases will typically show decreased solubility with increasing temperatures. Figure 2 shows how temperature affects the solubility of various salts and Figure 3 shows how temperature affects the solubility of gases.

Example of the common ion effect:

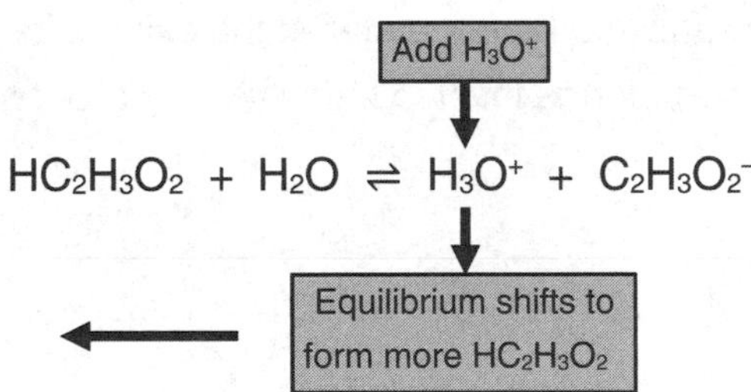

Figure 1

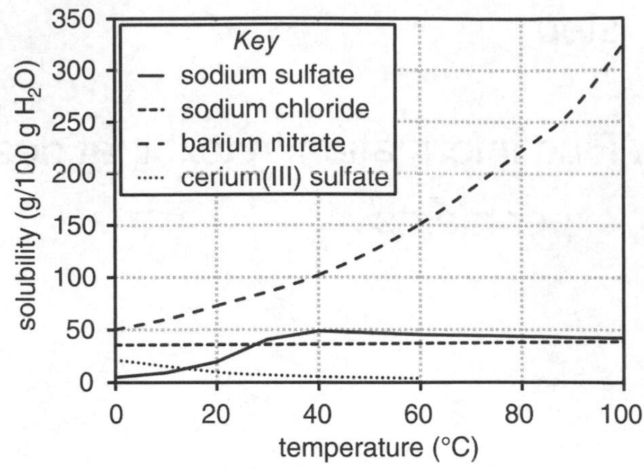

Figure 2

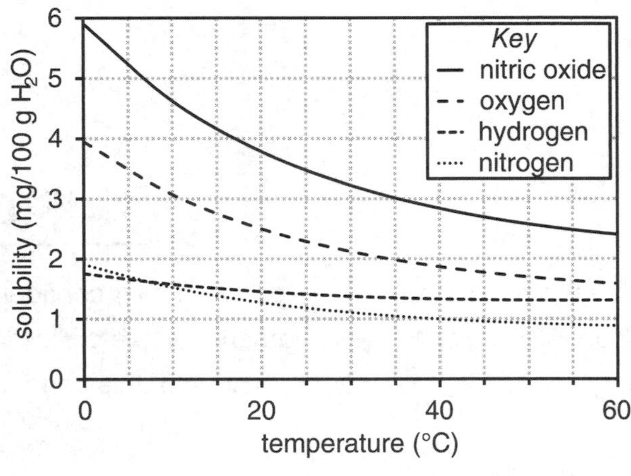

Figure 3

13.3.1 Describing an Experiment

13.3.1 Describing an Experiment

1. A solution contains two solutes: NaCl and $Ba(NO_3)_2$. It has a concentration of 10 mol/L of NaCl and 5 mol/L of $Ba(NO_3)_2$. Based on the passage, the number of molecules of NaCl in the solution is:

A. half the number of molecules of $Ba(NO_3)_2$ in the solution.

B. equivalent to the number of molecules of $Ba(NO_3)_2$ in the solution.

C. double the number of molecules of $Ba(NO_3)_2$ in the solution.

D. 5 times the number of molecules of $Ba(NO_3)_2$ in the solution.

This page is intentionally left blank.

13.3.1 Describing an Experiment

When gases dissolve in a solvent, they are affected by both temperature and pressure. The effects of pressure on the solubility of gases in liquids can be represented by Henry's Law:

$P = k_H c$

where P is the partial pressure of the gas above the liquid, k_H is the Henry's Law constant, and c is the concentration of the gas in the liquid.

The constant given in the equation depends on the type of gas. For example, for helium (He) the value is 2,700, and for Neon (Ne) the value is 2,200, when the units are $\frac{L \cdot atm}{mol}$, where 1 mole is 6×10^{23} discrete units of any substance. Typically, the solubility of gases goes down with an increase in temperature. Figures 1 and 2 show two examples of the solubility of different gases as a function of temperature. Figure 1 shows the solubility of noble gases while Figure 2 shows the solubility of hydrogen gas.

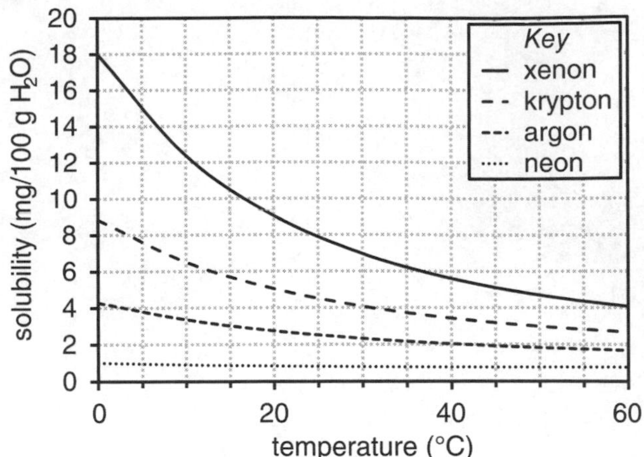

Figure 1

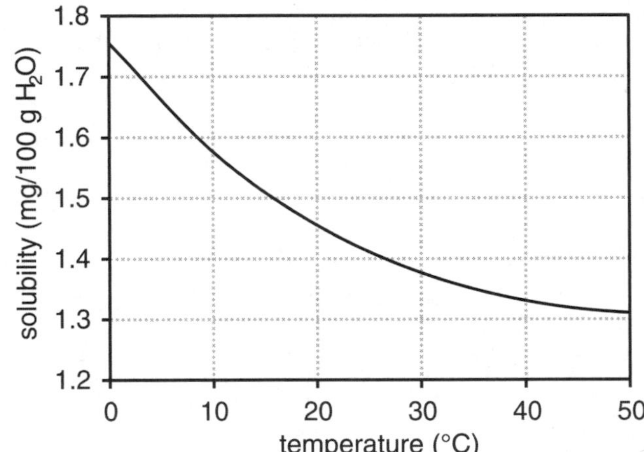

Figure 2

13.3.1 Describing an Experiment

13.3.1 Describing an Experiment

2. Which of the following statements best describes the solubility of hydrogen gas?

F. The solubility of hydrogen gas is not affected by temperature.

G. The solubility of hydrogen gas is not affected by pressure.

H. The solubility of hydrogen gas is affected by temperature and pressure.

J. The solubility of hydrogen gas is affected by temperature only.

Science Tip

Road Signs: All of the clues you need are already in the passage—you will rarely need any outside knowledge to answer ACT science questions. Use the questions to guide you to the appropriate information in the passage.

This page is intentionally left blank.

13.4.1 Set One

Passage I

Female finches employ varying strategies in the selection of their mates. Given a choice, females' selection should improve their evolutionary fitness, so long as they have a wide selection of potential mates to choose from.

Scientists recently looked at the mating selections of a group of female zebra finches *Taeniopygia guttata*, who chose between the mating songs of males in different conditions. Typically, zebra finches from smaller broods fare better than zebra finches from larger broods. However, female finches did not uniformly select male zebra finches from smaller broods as their mates. Instead, they preferred the songs of males who originated from broods similar to themselves, large or small.

Experiment

The scientists tested male and female choice, linked to brood size, in a multiple, interactive choice set-up. Male and female finches set in the focal, or center, could express their preferences in an 8-way choice arena by perching near their selected mate. Figure 1 shows a map of this apparatus, with the left side showing a test with a focal female and the right side showing a test with a focal male.

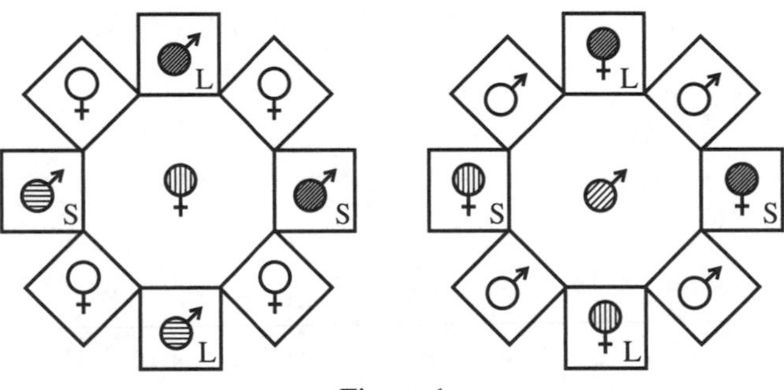

Figure 1

In the experiment, stimulus birds were presented with four same-sex birds picked randomly and four opposite-sex birds from manipulated brood sizes. Halfway through the test period, the stimulus birds were rotated 180 degrees.

Using the 8-way choice arena, scientists tested female mating preferences by allowing females to choose between four males from both large and small brood sizes, along with a few same-sex competitors, and to visually and vocally interact with these finches.

The experiment showed that females from small broods spent a greater amount of time near males from small broods, while females from large broods preferred to associate with males from large broods. The experiment was then repeated using males in the focal position, with reverse results: males spent more time with females from broods of opposite size. Figure 2 shows a graph of the preferences of finches for mates from small and large broods.

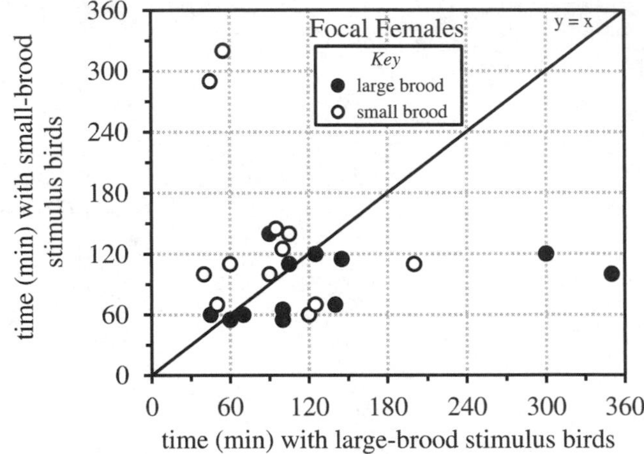

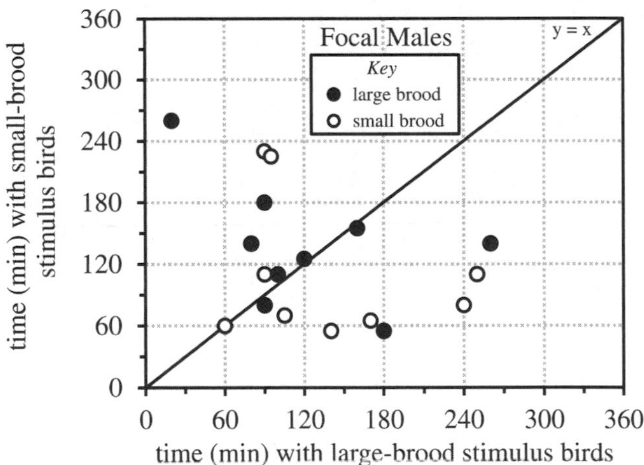

Figure 2

1. Which of the following best describes the female zebra finches studied in the experiment?

   A. They preferred mates who came from larger brood sizes.
   B. They preferred mates who came from smaller brood sizes.
   C. They preferred mates who came from similar brood sizes to themselves.
   D. They preferred mates who came from different brood sizes from themselves.

2. In the passage, the sentence, "female finches did not uniformly select male zebra finches from smaller broods as their mates" implies that:

   F. females preferred the more evolutionarily fit males from larger broods.
   G. females did not always select mates based on straightforward evolutionary fitness.
   H. females preferred larger to smaller males when selecting their mates.
   J. female finches chose randomly without paying attention to other factors, such as song quality, age, or brood size.

3. Based on the experiment, is it likely that a male from a large brood would show any preference for females from large broods?

   A. Yes, because males would be most interested in approaching broods with the greatest number of females.
   B. Yes, because the experiment and associated graph show that males also preferred mates from similar brood sizes.
   C. No, because the experiment and graph indicate that males preferred mates from opposite sized broods.
   D. No, because only female finches were recorded as having any mate preferences based on brood size.

4. In the experiment with focal females, approximately what was the largest recorded amount of time that a female from a small brood spent with males from a small brood?

   F. 60 minutes
   G. 150 minutes
   H. 320 minutes
   J. 360 minutes

5. What is the evidence from the experiment that female finches preferred mates from similar brood sizes?

   A. The female finches in the focal position spent more time with male finches of a similar brood size.
   B. Female finches sorted themselves naturally into groups based on brood size.
   C. Female finches' recorded mating calls were of a longer duration towards finches of a similar brood size.
   D. Female finches took a shorter amount of time to approach male finches of a similar brood size.

END OF SET ONE
STOP! DO NOT GO ON TO THE NEXT PAGE
UNTIL TOLD TO DO SO.

13.4.2 Set Two

Passage II

A teacher displayed two different mixtures to her chemistry class. One was a beaker containing water (H_2O), while the other was a beakcr containing vegetable oil. She informed the class that they would be studying the solubility of a certain solute in these two distinct solvents. The teacher then took a dropper containing a small amount of dyed toluene, with a concentration of 0.5 mol/L, and added it to each beaker (a mole is 6×10^{23} molecules of a compound). The toluene dissolved in the vegetable oil, but remained floating on top of the water. The teacher asked three students to explain these results.

Student 1

Nonpolar molecules are able to mix with one another, and polar molecules are able to mix with one another. However, polar molecules cannot dissolve in nonpolar molecules. Polar molecules have a positively charged pole and a negatively charged pole due to an unfair sharing of electrons (based on the attraction and pull of the different atoms). Since both vegetable oil and toluene are polar, they mix easily. Since water is nonpolar, however, toluene is not able to dissolve in water and instead spreads thinly over the top.

Student 2

Water molecules are bonded to one another by weak hydrogen bonds, which form between the oxygen atoms and the hydrogen atoms in each molecule. Vegetable oil and toluene, on the other hand, contain no hydrogen atoms and instead are made up of long carbon backbones with branching chains. Thus, they cannot bond to water molecules and are even repelled by the stronger hydrogen bonds linking the water molecules.

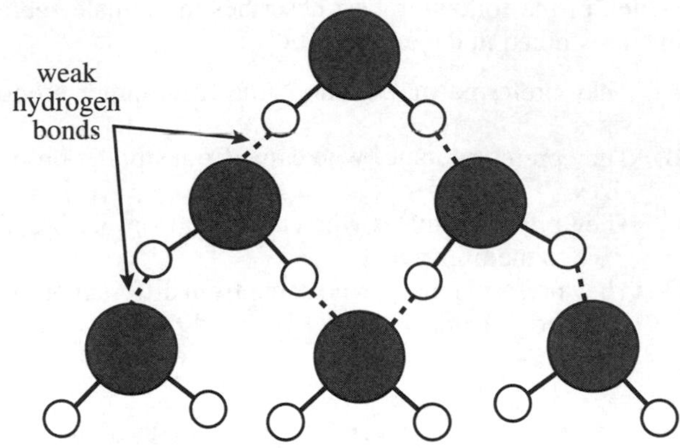

Student 3

Student 1 is correct that nonpolar molecules mix with nonpolar molecules and polar molecules mix with polar molecules, but he confused which substances were which. Water is a polar molecule, which has regions of positive and negative charge and is composed of two hydrogen atoms and an oxygen atom. Toluene and vegetable oil are both nonpolar molecules, which do not have differently charged regions and dissolve easily with one another.

6. The teacher repeated her experiment using the same volume of toluene solution, but with a concentration of 0.25 mol/L. According to the passage, the number of molecules of toluene used in this second experiment is:

F. half the number of molecules of toluene used in the first experiment.
G. equal to the number of molecules of toluene used in the first experiment.
H. twice the number of molecules of toluene used in the first experiment.
J. three times the number of molecules of toluene used in the first experiment.

7. In the experiment with vegetable oil, which was the solvent and which was the solute?

	solvent	solute
A.	toluene	vegetable oil
B.	vegetable oil	toluene
C.	vegetable oil	water
D.	water	vegetable oil

8. Based on Student 3's explanation, which of the following statements best describes water?

F. It is a nonpolar compound with strong hydrogen bonds.
G. It is a nonpolar molecule with regions of different charge.
H. It is a polar molecule with branching carbon chains.
J. It is a polar molecule with regions of different charge.

9. In Student 1's explanation, the sentence, "Since water is nonpolar, however, toluene is not able to dissolve in water and instead spreads thinly over the top" implies that toluene is:

A. nonpolar.
B. polar.
C. more positively charged than H_2O molecules.
D. more negatively charged than H_2O molecules.

10. Based on Student 2's explanation, is it likely that water molecules would be soluble in vegetable oil?

F. Yes, because both substances are nonpolar and would thus be similar enough to mix with each other.
G. Yes, because vegetable oil has strong hydrogen bonds that would be attracted to the strong hydrogen bonds in water.
H. No, because vegetable oil is nonpolar and water is polar and the two unlike substances would not mix.
J. No, because vegetable oil would be repelled by the hydrogen bonds linking water.

END OF SET TWO

STOP! DO NOT GO ON TO THE NEXT PAGE UNTIL TOLD TO DO SO.

13.4.3 Set Three

Passage III

A *capacitor* is the name for a device that stores electrical charge. *Capacitance* is the amount of charge that a capacitor can hold at a given voltage. In a science class, a teacher instructed her students to determine the charge on a parallel-plate capacitor with a fixed capacitance. Students conducted a few different studies with this capacitor.

Study 1

Students constructed an electrical circuit with the capacitor, as shown in Figure 1. The capacitor was initially uncharged.

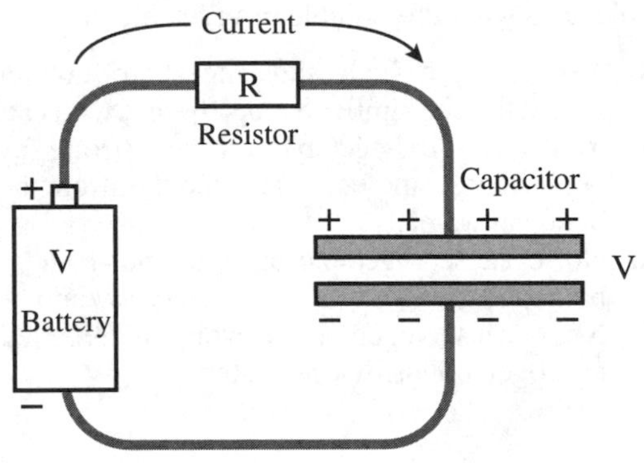

Figure 1

Students then charged the capacitor and recorded the voltage at specific time intervals. They then used a computer program to help them graph this information, which is recorded in Figure 2.

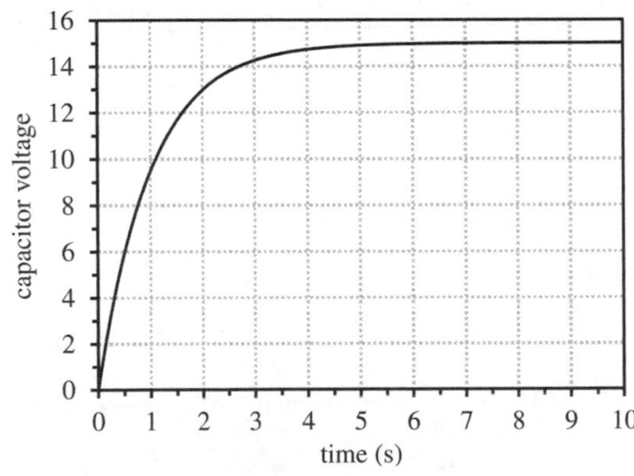

Figure 2

With this data, students then calculated the current at each time interval and recorded this information in Table 1. The students noted any trends and determined that voltage and current initially change rapidly before leveling out.

Table 1

Time (seconds)	Battery voltage	Capacitor voltage	Current
0	15 V	0 V	1500 uA
0.5	15 V	5.902 V	909.8 uA
1	15 V	9.482 V	551.8 uA
2	15 V	12.970 V	203.0 uA
3	15 V	14.253 V	74.68 uA
4	15 V	14.725 V	27.47 uA
5	15 V	14.899 V	10.11 uA
6	15 V	14.963 V	3.718 uA
10	15 V	14.999 V	0.068 uA

Study 2

The teacher then introduced students to an *inductor* and explained that, contrary to capacitors, which store energy in an electric field, inductors store energy in a magnetic field produced by the current running through the wire. As a result, inductors oppose changes in current and act opposite of capacitors, which oppose changes in voltage. She then drew a diagram on the board for students, Figure 3.

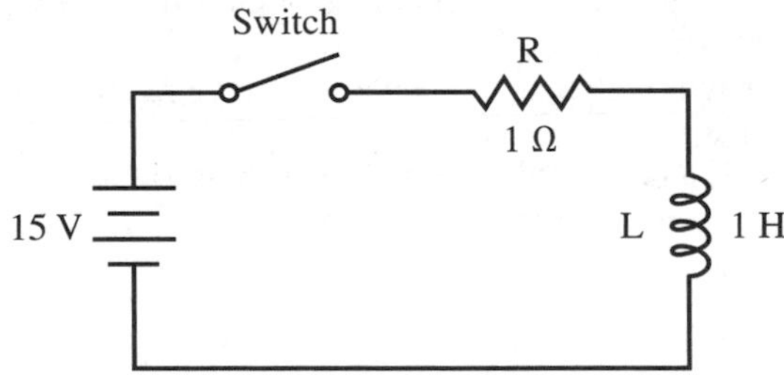

Figure 3

The teacher then recorded the decay in voltage over time and represented this in a graph for students, as shown in Figure 4.

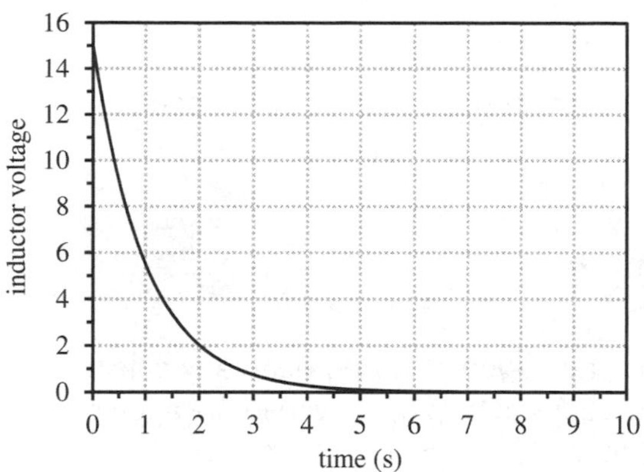

Figure 4

Finally, she plotted the drop in voltage and increase in current in a chart similar to the one that the students had produced in Study 1 (see Table 2).

Table 2

Time (seconds)	Battery voltage	Inductor voltage	Current
0	15 V	15 V	0 A
0.5	15 V	9.098 V	5.902 A
1	15 V	5.518 V	9.482 A
2	15 V	2.030 V	12.97 A
3	15 V	0.747 V	14.25 A
4	15 V	0.275 V	14.73 A
5	15 V	0.101 V	14.90 A
6	15 V	0.037 V	14.96 A
10	15 V	0.001 V	14.99 A

11. In Studies 1 and 2, what was the maximum voltage for both the capacitor and inductor?

A. 5 V
B. 10 V
C. 14 V
D. 15 V

12. What is the evidence from Studies 1 and 2 that capacitors and inductors worked in opposite ways?

F. As time progressed, capacitor voltage increased while inductor voltage decreased.
G. As time progressed, capacitor voltage decreased while inductor voltage increased.
H. As time progressed, capacitor current increased while inductor current decreased.
J. As time progressed, battery capacity for the capacitor increased and battery capacity for the inductor decreased.

13. A capacitor similar to the one used in Study 1 is charged, and its voltage at various time intervals is recorded. The voltage readings after 5, 6, and 10 seconds are 29.888 V, 29.945 V, and 29.998 V. Based on the information given, the voltage on the capacitor is:

A. half that on the capacitor used in Study 1.
B. twice that on the capacitor used in Study 1.
C. equal to that on the capacitor used in Study 1.
D. three times that on the capacitor used in Study 1.

14. An identical experiment is conducted, mimicking Studies 1 and 2. Which of the following represents the expected direction in voltage recordings for capacitors and inductors over time?

	capacitors	inductors
F.	increase	increase
G.	decrease	increase
H.	increase	decrease
J.	decrease	decrease

15. Based on the passage, which of the following best describes the way that inductors store energy?

A. A magnet creates a charged field where inductors store energy.
B. A battery charges an electric field where inductors store energy.
C. A current running through the wire produces a magnetic field where inductors store energy.
D. A current running through the wire produces an electric field where inductors store energy.

END OF SET THREE
STOP! DO NOT GO ON TO THE NEXT PAGE UNTIL TOLD TO DO SO.

Sum It Up

Text and Experiments

Scientific Method
A set of techniques used to test hypotheses, develop new knowledge, and correct and build upon previous theories

Tips and Techniques

Road Signs: All of the clues you need are already in the passage—you will rarely need any outside knowledge to answer these questions. Make sure to use the questions to help guide you to the appropriate information in the passage.

Lesson 14

New Information

CAPTION:

14.1 Entrance Ticket

Write a paragraph (5–7 sentences) describing how scientific discoveries affect our world today. What does it mean when scientists come upon new information? Think of an example of a historic breakthrough or write creatively about a future one you predict or imagine.

14.2 Learning Targets

1. Understand how to relate new information presented in questions to data already available in the passage, charts, and graphs

2. Use new information to draw conclusions or read data from charts and graphs

Self-Assessment

Circle the number that corresponds to your confidence level in your knowledge of this subject before beginning the lesson. A score of 1 means you are completely lost, and a score of 4 means you have mastered the skills. After you finish the lesson, return to the bottom of this page and circle your new confidence level to show your improvement.

Before Lesson

1 2 3 4

After Lesson

1 2 3 4

14.3.1 Identifying New Information and Clues

Table 1					
Color	Average lifespan (years)	Average adult snout size (inches)	Reaction to humans	Percentage of diet consisting of seashells	Percentage of diet consisting of coconuts
Blue	14.4	6.14	mild aggression	22.5%	77.5%
Green	11.0	8.92	neutral	37.3%	62.7%
Yellow	19.6	7.74	moderate aggression	25.8%	74.2%
Purple	15.9	6.22	friendly	41.0%	59.0%
Red	21.2	6.05	avoidance	32.2%	67.8%

1. Assume that for dolosaurs, as average weight increases, average snout size increases. Do blue or red dolosaurs have a greater average weight?

Clue Location: ______________________________

____

Answer: ______________________________

____

2. A dolosaur has a 5.5 inch snout as a juvenile and an 8.8 inch snout as an adult. Based on this information, how long will the dolosaur likely live?

Clue Location: ______________________________

____

Answer: ______________________________

____

14.3.1 Identifying New Information and Clues

3. Scientists find that a dolosaur's diet affects the likelihood that females in each subspecies will give birth to twins. A dolosaur that consumes a higher percentage of seashells has a greater chance of having twins. Based on this information and the table, which dolosaur color is most likely to have twins?

Clue Location: ____

____

Answer: ____

____

4. A dolosaur consumes 58 pounds of coconuts one week and 36 pounds of coconuts the following week. If the dolosaur consumes 32.0% of its diet in seashells, what is the dolosaur's likely reaction to humans?

Clue Location: ____

____

Answer: ____

____

Science Tip

Road Signs: When a question presents new information, figure out how it is relevant to the passage and data. Be confident that you can find the answer with the given information because the science test is an open-book test. Use the new information as a clue that points to where you need to look for the answer.

14.3.2 Create Your Own Clue Questions

Two measures of water quality are the amount of *dissolved oxygen* (the concentration of oxygen in the water) and the *salinity* (the total concentration of all salts in the water). These measures can both be affected by temperature.

Dissolved oxygen concentration is an important factor in a river's ability to sustain fish, with lower concentrations indicating a lower level of fish sustainability.

Figure 1 shows the average dissolved oxygen concentration for different months at Sites 1 and 2 of a river.

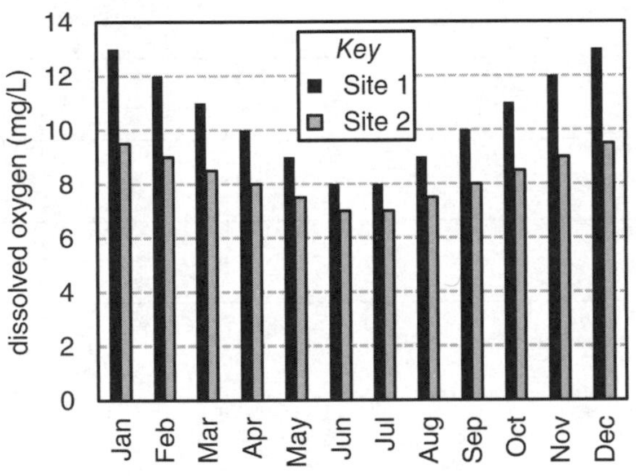

Figure 1

Table 1 shows the salinity values for different types of water. Table 2 shows the average salinity value at each site over the course of the year.

Table 1	
Salinity (ppt)	Type of water
0 to 0.5	freshwater
0.5 to 17	brackish/estuary
16	Black sea
32 to 37	ocean range
35	ocean average

Table 2	
Location	Average salinity (ppt)
Site 1	0.05
Site 2	0.20

Figure 2 shows the average monthly water temperature at each site across the year.

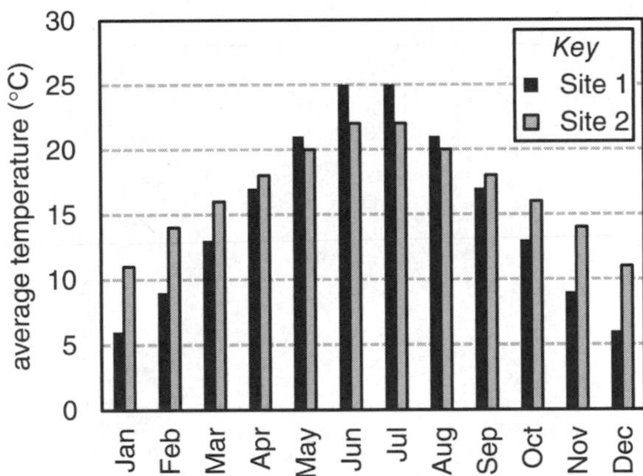

Figure 2

14.3.2 Create Your Own Clue Questions

1. ____

____

____

A. ____

B. ____

C. ____

D. ____

2. ____

____

____

F. ____

G. ____

H. ____

J. ____

14.3.2 Create Your Own Clue Questions

More than 20% of the surface of Titan, Saturn's largest moon, is covered by giant sand dunes. The dunes located at the equatorial belt exhibit the feature of sand being deposited eastward. However, the wind direction suggested by atmospheric circulation models is the opposite (westward). Scientists examining recent data from the Cassini space probe have proposed an explanation for this phenomenon. Although the westward winds are the most frequent, these winds lack the speed to lift and move the sand. The Cassini data suggests that at regular intervals there are strong gusts of eastward wind. The mystery would be solved if these winds possessed sufficient speed to move the sand on Titan. Figure 1 shows the average wind speeds for eastward and westward winds, with eastward speeds represented as a negative value.

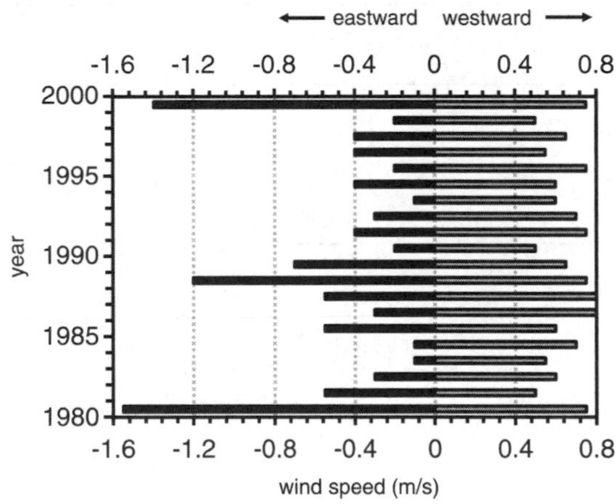

Figure 1

Unfortunately, one major issue remains that must be addressed. While Cassini has revealed much about Titan, it has yet to gather data on the size or moisture content of the sand comprising these dunes. Both of these attributes factor heavily in determining the speed necessary to move sand.

The point at which sand will move by wind alone is known as the fluid threshold, and the point at which sand will move when struck by another particle already in motion is known as the impact threshold. Figure 2 shows the thresholds, based on grain size, for dry material (moisture content 0%). As moisture affects these thresholds, it is necessary to modify the dry number. Figure 3 shows a graph of the multiplier, for moisture content, which is applied to the dry value to obtain a wet threshold value.

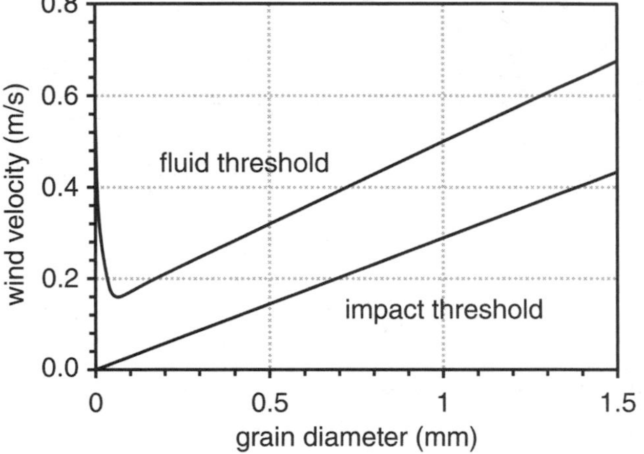

Figure 2

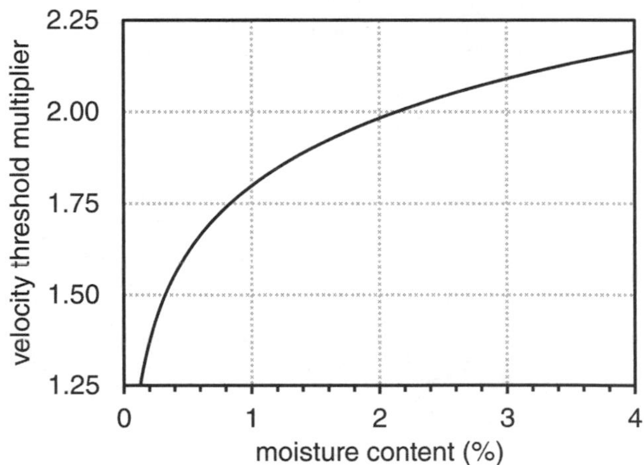

Figure 3

14.3.2 Create Your Own Clue Questions

1. Consider the wind profile shown in Figure 1. If the westward wind speeds consistently measured between 1.0 and 1.6 m/s, in which direction might we expect the sand to deposit?
   A. Westward, because the wind to the west more often meets or exceeds the fluid threshold.
   B. Eastward, because the wind to the east more often meets or exceeds the fluid threshold.
   C. Eastward, because the wind to the west more often meets or exceeds the fluid threshold.
   D. Neither, because both directions meet or exceed the impact threshold, therefore dunes would not form.

14.4.1 Set One

Passage I

Depending on where fish live, their diets may vary, especially if the area is subject to human disturbances. Researchers investigated this phenomenon in groups of winter flounder captured from two different locations. All of the flounder were between 100 mm and 300 mm in length.

Location 1

During September and November, winter flounder were collected from New Haven Harbor, an area subject to human disturbances such as dredging, shipping traffic, and sewage disposal. A 30-foot otter trawl with 2-inch 15-lb nylon mesh and a 1.5-inch mesh cod end was towed for 15 minutes along a single transect line. The stomach contents of the captured fish were fixed at sea in a 10% formalin solution and later examined in detail in the laboratory. Table 1 shows the relative weight (w), number (n), and frequency (f) of categories of prey, along with the index of relative importance ($IRI = f(w + n)$) at Location 1.

Table 1: Diet of winter flounder showing index of relative importance of prey from Location 1

Taxon	Weight (%)	Number (%)	Frequency (%)	IRI
Mollusca	17.25	17.21	13.87	478
Polychaeta	12.22	31.72	12.57	552
Crustacea	46.25	50.70	67.50	6544
Teleostei	2.67	0.35	1.98	6
Hydrozoa	16.28	0.01	7.84	128
unidentified	5.30	0.01	5.73	30

Location 2

At the same time, winter flounder were also collected from Clinton Harbor, a site with similar geographic qualities, but not subject to human disturbances. Samples were collected using a 3-foot beam trawl made of ¼ inch nylon mesh with one tickler chair and an 11-foot shrimp trawl with 1-inch nylon mesh. The stomach contents of the captured fish were prepared and analyzed as per Location 1. Table 2 shows the relative weight, number, and frequency of different categories of prey, along with the calculated relative importance at Location 2.

Table 2: Diet of winter flounder showing index of relative importance of prey from Location 2

Taxon	Weight (%)	Number (%)	Frequency (%)	IRI
Mollusca	4.80	7.80	50.91	642
Polychaeta	87.07	82.78	100.00	16,985
Crustacea	2.68	9.45	78.55	953
Teleostei	--	--	--	--
Hydrozoa	--	--	--	--
unidentified	5.08	0.01	36.63	186

Figure 1 shows the stomach contents by percent weight and the percentage of the number of meals of each food source between the two locations.

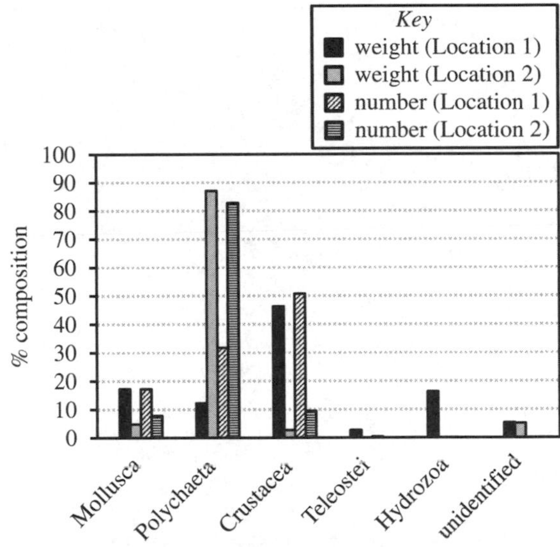

Figure 1

1. Scientists want to order the prey found in the flounder stomachs by percent weight. Of the six types of prey found in the stomachs, based on Table 1, which prey would be the third largest?

   A. Hydrozoa
   B. Polychaeta
   C. Crustacea
   D. Mollusca

2. The weight shown in Tables 1 and 2 is the percent of the total weight of the stomach contents that each type of prey represented. Based on Table 1, if the total weight of the stomach contents was 50 mg, the weight of the Crustacea would be closest to which of the following:

   F. 50.25 mg
   G. 46.3 mg
   H. 23.1 mg
   J. 7.8 mg

3. Previous studies involving the effects of human activity on winter flounder prey have shown that human activity can reduce the amount of Polychaeta in the environment by as much as 50%. Based on Table 2, if Clinton Harbor were subject to human disturbances, we might expect a new sampling of flounder to have Polychaeta at a relative weight of about:

   A. 12.2%
   B. 31.7%
   C. 43.5%
   D. 87.1%

4. Suppose a new species were introduced to the environment that fed on some of the same prey as winter flounder. Species X is smaller than the flounder, and better adapted to catching Mollusca than winter flounder. Species X denies the flounder all Mollusca, and the flounder makes up the difference with Teleostei. Based on Table 1, we might expect the relative weight of Teleostei to increase to:

   F. between 17% and 18%.
   G. between 19% and 20%.
   H. between 4% and 5%.
   J. between 2% and 3%.

5. Tables 1 and 2 show a distinct difference between the relative weight of Crustacea, Polychaeta, and Mollusca found in the flounder stomachs from Locations 1 and 2. This difference is most likely because:

   A. Crustacea are opportunistic feeders that thrive in areas disturbed by humans, whereas Polychaeta prefer undisturbed areas.
   B. Crustacea are opportunistic feeders that thrive in areas disturbed by humans, whereas Mollusca prefer undisturbed areas.
   C. Polychaeta are opportunistic feeders that thrive in areas disturbed by humans, whereas Mollusca prefer undisturbed areas.
   D. Mollusca are opportunistic feeders that thrive in areas disturbed by humans, whereas Crustacea prefer undisturbed areas.

END OF SET ONE
STOP! DO NOT GO ON TO THE NEXT PAGE
UNTIL TOLD TO DO SO.

14.4.2 Set Two

Passage II

Skeletal muscles commonly undergo four different types of activity during a workout: *isometric contraction*, in which the length of the muscle fibers does not change during the contraction; *concentric contraction*, in which the length shortens during contraction; *eccentric contraction*, in which the length increases during contraction; and *passive stretch*, where the muscle is lengthened without contracting. While all of these activities fatigue the muscle, they do so to differing degrees. Figure 1 shows the *maximum tetanic tension*, the maximum tension a muscle can apply and still relax under mental control, that a muscle can generate before and after a workout involving different types of muscle activity.

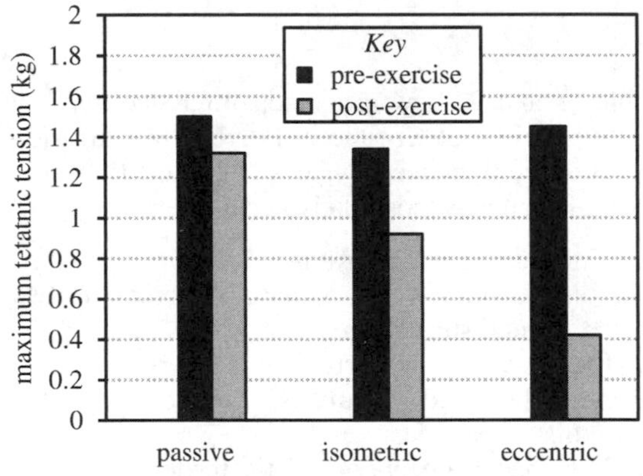

Figure 1

6. Figure 1 shows the effects of a single type of activity performed during a workout. However, most workouts are comprised of multiple activity types. If a workout is comprised of equal parts isometric and eccentric contractions, it might be expected that the maximum tension post workout would be:

   F. 0.38 kg.
   G. 0.65 kg.
   H. 0.96 kg.
   J. 1.42 kg.

7. Assume concentric contractions affect the muscle similarly to eccentric contractions. Based on Figure 1, after a workout composed of concentric contractions, the muscle's maximum tetanic tension would most likely be:

   A. less than or equal to 0.2 kg.
   B. between 0.2 kg and 0.6 kg.
   C. between 1.4 kg and 1.6 kg.
   D. greater than 1.6 kg.

8. A bodybuilder finds it difficult to do household chores after a workout composed of eccentric contraction exercises, whereas he has no trouble after a workout composed of isometric exercises. This difference is most likely because the maximum tetanic tension his muscles are capable of is:

   F. less than 1.0 kg after eccentric contractions, whereas it is less than 0.5 kg after isometric contractions.
   G. less than 0.5 kg after eccentric contractions, whereas it is greater than 0.5 kg after isometric exercises.
   H. greater than 1.0 kg after eccentric contractions, whereas it is less than 1.0 kg after isometric exercises.
   J. greater than 1.5 kg after eccentric exercises, whereas it is less than 1.5 kg after isometric exercises.

9. Figure 1 shows that each exercise type has different pre- and post-workout maximum tetanic tension. Which of the exercise types reduce the maximum tetanic tension by at least 50% from pre-workout to post-workout?

A. Eccentric and Isometric
B. Eccentric only
C. Passive and Isometric
D. Isometric only

10. A muscle is worked using isometric exercises only. Assuming tests are performed immediately post-workout, with no time given for recovery, the value of the maximum tetanic tension is closest to:

F. 0.46 kg.
G. 0.95 kg.
H. 1.32 kg.
J. 1.37 kg.

END OF SET TWO
STOP! DO NOT GO ON TO THE NEXT PAGE
UNTIL TOLD TO DO SO.

14.4.3 Set Three

Passage III

Satellite observations of the Himalayas have revealed mountain ranges that resemble longitudinal waves. These mountain ranges are produced over thousands of years from the movement of the Earth's crust. An approximation of these types of mountain ranges can be found in Figure 1. Figure 2 shows the average mountain spacing and average height for a few different areas in the mountain ranges in the Himalayas, along with the average spacing and height for areas in 4 other mountain ranges on Earth (Ranges A–D). Figure 3 is a graph of the *surface elevation* (elevation above a horizontal reference plane) across a 10-mi wide perpendicular cross section of mountains in the Himalayas and in Range A.

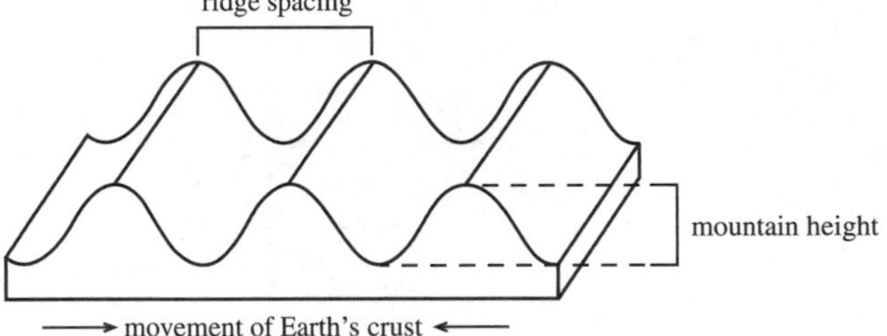

Perpendicular cross section through longitudinal mountain ranges

Figure 1

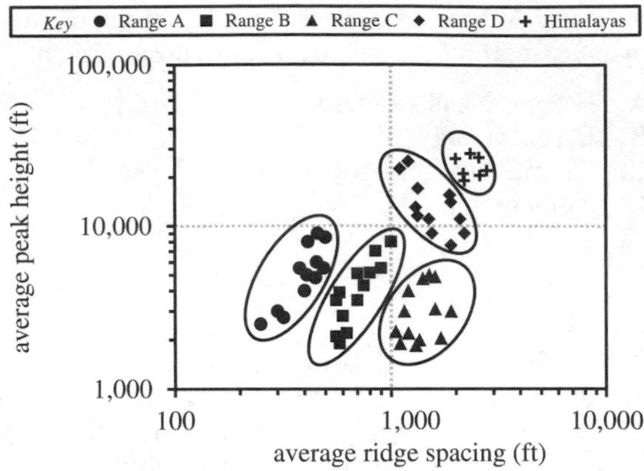

Figure 2

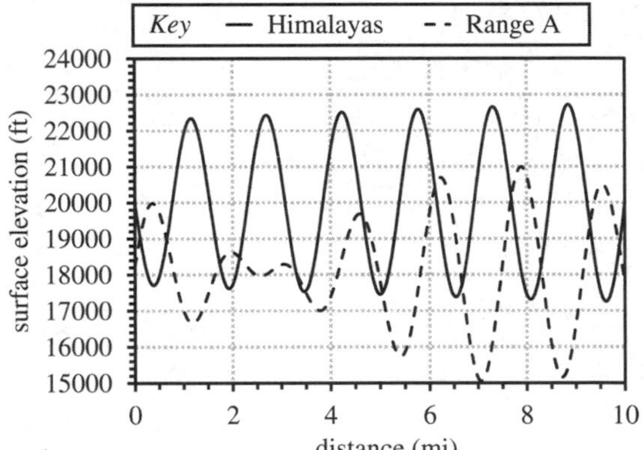

Figure 3

11. The climate and plant life on a mountain changes based on distance from sea level. Range C is covered mainly by conifer trees and rocky outcrops, while the top of Range D is covered mostly by ice and snow. The difference is most likely because:

    A. Range D has an altitude of 8–30 thousand feet, while Range C has an altitude of about 2–7 thousand feet.
    B. Range D an altitude of 2–7 thousand feet, while Range C has an altitude of about 8–30 thousand feet.
    C. Range D has an average ridge spacing of about 900–2,000 feet, while Range C has an average ridge spacing of about 500–1,000 feet.
    D. Range D has an average ridge spacing of about 500–1,000 feet, while Range C has an average ridge spacing of about 900–2,000 feet.

12. A group of scientists decide to classify mountain ranges by ridge spacing. They determine that mountain ranges with a short average ridge spacing, less than 1,000 feet, will be given a classification of 1.0. Based on Figure 2, which of the mountain ranges will be given a classification of 1.0 ?

    F. Range A only
    G. Range B only
    H. Ranges A and B only
    J. Ranges A, B, and C

13. A certain type of tree only grows near the lowest average peak elevation in Range A. Based on Figure 2, this type of tree grows at an elevation closest to:

    A. 2,500 feet
    B. 10,000 feet
    C. 15,000 feet
    D. 26,000 feet

14. Suppose that for the mountain ranges represented in Figure 2, as age of the range increases, elevation also increases. Is Range A or Range B likely older?

    F. Range A, because the areas in that range have greater average peak height.
    G. Range B, because the areas in that range have greater average peak height.
    H. Range A, because the areas in that range have lower average peak height.
    J. Range B, because the areas in that range have lower average peak height.

15. For the ranges represented in Figure 3, assume that as average surface elevation increases, temperature decreases. Will the Himalayas or Range A likely have a lower average temperature?

    A. Range A, because the surface elevation in that range is on average lower.
    B. Range A, because the surface elevation in that range is on average higher.
    C. The Himalayas, because the surface elevation in that range is on average lower.
    D. The Himalayas, because the surface elevation in that range is on average higher.

END OF SET THREE

STOP! DO NOT GO ON TO THE NEXT PAGE UNTIL TOLD TO DO SO.

Sum It Up

New Information

Title
States the purpose or main idea of the graphic or an axis

Legend
Shows how to categorize different parts of the graph

Axis
One of two sides of the graph (x-axis is horizontal, y-axis is vertical) that show the variables being compared or measured

---

Axis Labels
Show the units for each axis

Context
The parts that precede, follow, or surround other information and that help make sense of that information

Tips and Techniques

Road Signs: When a question presents new information, figure out how it is relevant to the passage and data. Be confident that you can find the answer with the given information because the science test is an open-book test. Use the new information as a clue that points to where you need to look for the answer.

Lesson 15

Science Strategy

CAPTION:

15.1 Entrance Ticket

Solve the questions below.

Serum secretory leukoprotease inhibitor (SLPI) is a protein that is synthesized by cells lining mucous membranes that can be found in both the mouth and throat. SLPI is currently being studied for its potential as a disease marker. Oral samples from volunteers were collected and the levels of SLPI measured; the percentage of volunteers who possessed certain levels of SLPI in their oral samples are listed in Table 1.

Table 1

Range of SLPI concentration (ng/mL)	% volunteers
0–50	12
51–100	12
101–150	1
151–250	35
251+	40

SLPI is thought to be a marker protein for respiratory diseases, such as chronic bronchitis (CB). SLPI concentrations above 100 ng/mL are often associated with patients exhibiting CB. Figure 1 shows the levels of SLPI in the serum of the same group of volunteers as a function of the amount of sputum expelled by the patients per day.

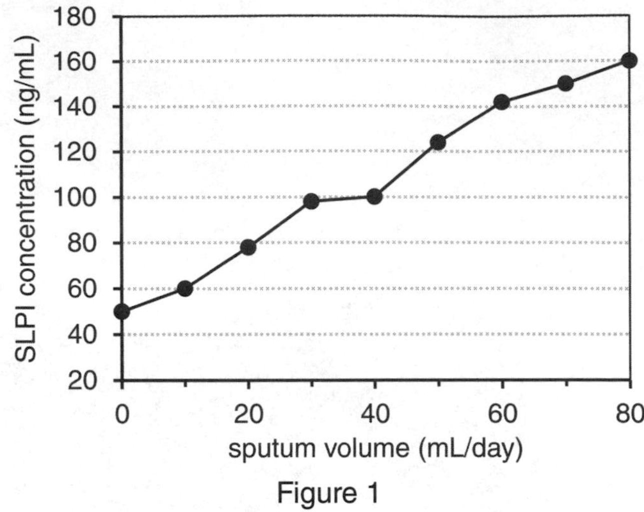

Figure 1

1. According to Table 1, what percentage of the volunteers had SLPI levels in their oral samples that were 250 ng/mL or below?
   A. 12%
   B. 24%
   C. 41%
   D. 60%

15.1 Entrance Ticket

2. Based on Figure 1, what volume of sputum is produced in patients who are likely to have CB?

F. Less than 20 mL/day

G. Between 20 mL/day and 30 mL/day

H. Between 30 mL/day and 40 mL/day

J. More than 40 mL/day

3. Suppose 70 mL per day of sputum volume and above indicates a higher risk of contracting an upper respiratory disease. Approximately what percentage of the volunteers shown in Table 1 are at risk of contracting an upper respiratory disease?

A. 12%

B. 24%

C. 75%

D. 88%

15.2 Learning Targets

1. Recognize when to use appropriate strategies to answer standard ACT questions

2. Develop a method to address difficult questions during the test

Self-Assessment

Circle the number that corresponds to your confidence level in your knowledge of this subject before beginning the lesson. A score of 1 means you are completely lost, and a score of 4 means you have mastered the skills. After you finish the lesson, return to the bottom of this page and circle your new confidence level to show your improvement.

Before Lesson

1 2 3 4

After Lesson

1 2 3 4

15.3.1 Process of Elimination

Due to industrial activity, the soil around areas such as mines and factories has elevated levels of trace metals; such high levels of these trace metals is harmful to plants and wildlife. A novel way to address this problem is by *phytoremediation*, which is the removal of chemicals and metals from the environment by using plants.

In the following study, researchers wanted to test the effectiveness of garlic in metal phytoremediation. This plant was chosen because of its ability to grow hydroponically (in water) in environments containing metal concentrations of 100 μM or more and because of the low cost of growing garlic.

Experiment 1

Garlic bulbs were incubated and grown for 3 weeks in a growth chamber with 14 hours of light and 10 hours of darkness. After this initial growth step, the garlic plants were given a salt solution containing 3 different concentrations (12.5, 50, and 100 μM) of a mixture of four metals—arsenic (As), selenium (Se), antimony (Sb), and tellurium (Te)—and allowed to incubate for 14 days. After exposure to the metals in the solution, the garlic plants were harvested and the weight of their leaves, bulbs, joints, and roots were measured (in grams). The results from Experiment 1 are shown in Figure 1.

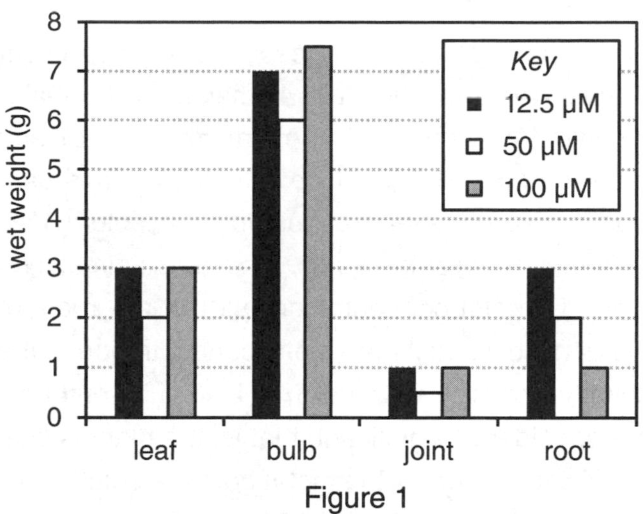

Figure 1

Experiment 2

In this experiment, the growing conditions in Experiment 1 were used except that the garlic plants were grown in 12.5 μM, 50 μM, and 100 μM of selenium-only solutions instead. After the 14-day growing period, the plants were harvested; the concentrations of selenium in the leaves, bulbs, joints, and roots of the garlic plants were measured (μmol/g DW, dry weight). The data from Experiment 2 are shown in Figure 2.

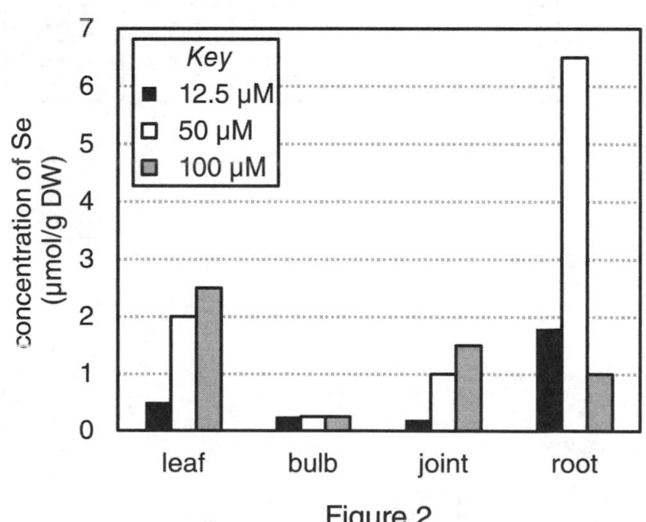

Figure 2

15.3.1 Process of Elimination

Experiment 3

The experimental setup described in Experiment 2 was repeated for all 4 metals individually: arsenic (As), selenium (Se), antimony (Sb) and tellurium (Te). The purpose of obtaining this data was to determine the bioaccumulation factor (BAF) of the 4 metals for garlic. The bioaccumulation factor is metal concentration (μM) in the roots of the garlic divided by the metal concentration of the solution the plant was grown in. BAFs higher than 1 are considered significant, that is, the plant is able to efficiently remove the metal from the solution (or soil) it was grown in. The BAF values of arsenic (As), selenium (Se), antimony (Sb), and tellurium (Te) for garlic are shown in Table 1.

Table 1				
	Bioaccumulation Factor (BAF)			
Treatment concentration (μM)	As	Se	Sb	Te
12.5	2.1	8.0	0.61	0.36
50	2.2	7.4	0.74	0.28
100	1.6	2.9	0.67	0.18

1. Is the statement "Garlic is efficient at removing antimony (Sb) and tellurium (Te) from metal-laden solutions" supported by the data shown in Table 1?

A. Yes; lower BAF numbers are indicative of an increased ability of the plant of to remove metal from the solution.

B. No; the lower BAF numbers (less than 1) for Sb and Te are indicative that garlic plants are not efficient at removing these metals from the solution.

C. Yes; Sb and Te have the highest BAF numbers of all 4 metals and thus the garlic plants are most efficient at removing Sb and Te from the solution.

D. No; Sb and Te have the highest BAF numbers of all 4 metals and thus the garlic plants are the least efficient at removing Sb and Te from solution.

2. Plants with an Se concentration of more than 1 μmol/g DW are considered hazardous to eat. If the concentration of the Se-growing solution in Experiment 2 were increased to 250 μM, which part of the garlic plants would be the most safe to eat?

F. Leaf

G. Bulb

H. Joint

J. Root

15.3.1 Process of Elimination

3. Why was the measurement unit for metal content in Experiments 1 and 2 different? In Experiment 1:
   - **A.** the incubation time was measured, whereas in Experiment 2, the bioaccumulation factor was measured
   - **B.** the Se concentration in plant parts was measured, whereas in Experiment 2, the weight of plant parts was measured.
   - **C.** the weight of plant parts was measured, whereas in Experiment 2, the Se concentration in plant parts was measured.
   - **D.** the bioaccumulation factor was measured, whereas in Experiment 2, the incubation time was measured.

4. Do the results in Experiment 3 indicate that the garlic plants are equally capable of removing all 4 metals—arsenic (As), selenium (Se), antimony (Sb), and tellurium (Te)?
   - **F.** Yes; all of the metals had BAF numbers between 0.18–8.0, indicating that the garlic plants are equally capable of removing them from the solution.
   - **G.** No; the BAF numbers indicate that the garlic plants are best at removing Sb and Te from the solution.
   - **H.** Yes; all metals have BAF numbers within 1 unit from one another.
   - **J.** No; the BAF numbers indicate that the garlic plants are best at removing As and Se from the solution.

Science Tip

Process of Elimination: The single most useful strategy on the science test is the process of elimination. Eliminate incorrect answers whenever possible. Some questions can be answered correctly simply by eliminating the wrong answers.

15.3.2 Contradictions

Scientists wanted to study proteins that decrease damage caused by environmental effects on bacteria, such as antibiotics. Learning more about these proteins could help scientists better understand the acquisition of bacterial antibiotic resistance. The scientists studied this by adding DNA fragments to selected genes in order to produce mutant bacteria. The mutation essentially disrupts the production of certain proteins. These mutant bacteria are known as *gene-disrupted bacteria*.

Table 1 lists some of the genes disrupted in this study.

Table 1

Disrupted gene	Protein disrupted by gene insertion
emrK	membrane fusion protein
ybcM	ARAC-type regulatory protein
ycjU	putative β-phosphoglucomutase
ycjW	putative LACI-type transcriptional regulator
yrbB	predicted NTP-binding protein

Experiment 1

Wild-type (WT) *E. coli* bacteria and bacteria containing gene disruptions were grown on agar plates and then treated with 2000 μJ/cm² of UV light for 15 minutes. The percentage of surviving colonies was determined by comparing the amount of treated bacteria to the amount of an untreated control. Figure 1 shows the percentage of surviving colonies for the WT bacteria and the gene-disrupted bacteria.

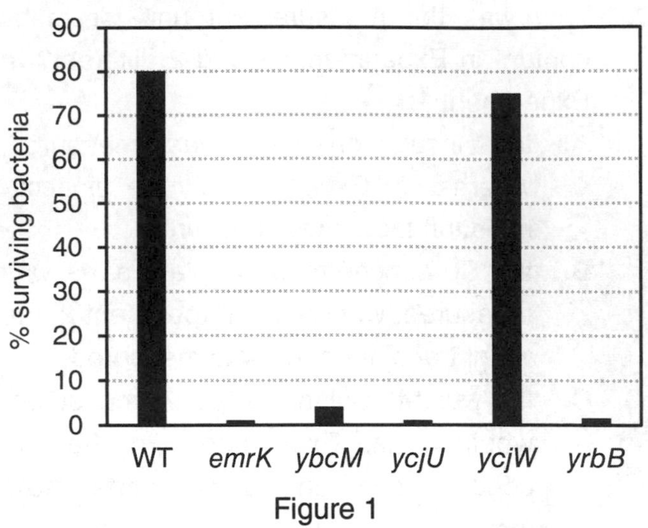

Figure 1

Experiment 2

Wild-type (WT) *E. coli* bacteria and bacteria containing gene disruptions were grown on agar plates and then treated with increasing amounts of the antibiotic tetracycline. The amount of tetracycline that was required to kill 90% of the bacteria was calculated for all the bacterial species and is shown as the LD_{90} value (μg/mL) in Figure 2.

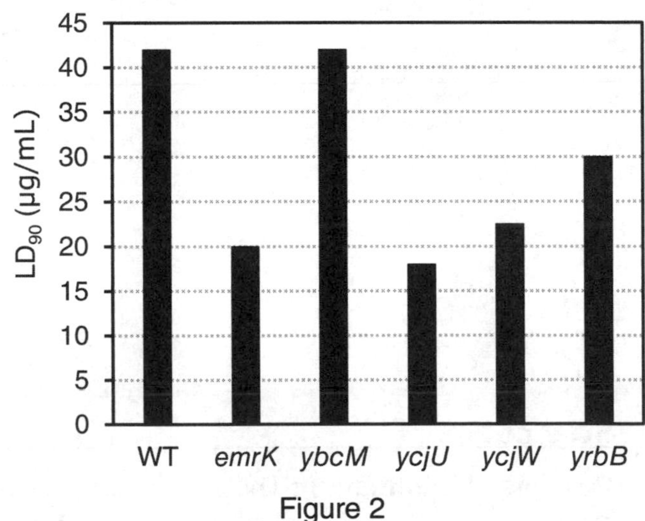

Figure 2

15.3.2 Contradictions

Experiment 3

To confirm that the bacterial mutant outcomes were due to a specific gene being disrupted, and not some side effect of the DNA insertion process, a new experiment was conducted. The disrupted genes were transferred to another strain of bacteria. If the outcomes were due to side effects of putting that disrupted gene into the bacteria, the resulting bacteria would have had a significantly different growth curve, that is, a higher mortality rate. For this experiment, WT and mutant bacteria were grown in increasing concentrations of nalidixic acid [NaI] (μg/mL) for two hours at 37°C. The percentage of surviving bacteria was calculated as before, and the results are shown in Figure 3. A lower percentage of surviving bacteria indicates a higher mortality rate.

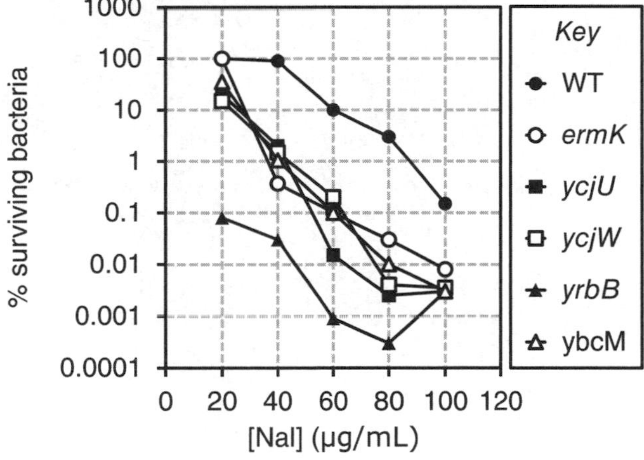

Figure 3

1. A scientific journal reviewer looked at the results of this study and surmised that the effects seen from the gene-disrupted bacteria are due to side effects from the gene insertions. Experiment 3 provided which of the following pieces of evidence in support of this hypothesis?
   - **F.** The growth curves of the WT bacteria and the mutant bacteria with the inserted gene are virtually identical, indicating the mortality rate of the WT bacteria is higher than that of the mutant bacteria.
   - **G.** The growth curves of the WT bacteria and the mutant bacteria with the inserted genes are different, indicating the mortality rate of the WT bacteria is higher than that of the mutant bacteria.
   - **H.** The growth curves of the WT bacteria and the mutant bacteria with the inserted gene are virtually identical, indicating the mortality rate of the mutant bacteria is higher than that of the WT bacteria.
   - **J.** The growth curves of the WT bacteria and the mutant bacteria with the inserted genes are different, indicating the mortality rate of the mutant bacteria is higher than that of the WT bacteria.

2. According to the results of Experiment 2, which of the 3 mutant genes exhibited an LD_{90} greater than 25 μg/mL?
   - **F.** *ybcM* only
   - **G.** *yrbD* and *ycjW* only
   - **H.** *ybcM* and *yrbB* only
   - **J.** *ybcM, yrbB,* and *ycjW*

15.3.2 Contradictions

3. Another scientist looked at the results of this study and surmised that the effects seen from the gene-disrupted bacteria are due to side effects from the gene insertions. Given what is shown in Figure 3, is this a correct conclusion, and why?
   A. No; the growth curves of the WT bacteria and the mutant bacteria with the gene insertions are virtually identical.
   B. No; all of the mutant genes yielded the same outcomes in the bacteria in Figures 1 and 2.
   C. Yes; all of the mutant genes had different growth curves than WT.
   D. Yes; none of the bacteria with the mutant genes were killed by the increasing amount of NaI.

4. According to the results of Experiment 3, as the concentration of NaI increased from 40 μg/mL to 80 μg/mL, how did the percentage of surviving bacteria vary?
   A. Increased only
   B. Decreased only
   C. Increased then decreased
   D. Decreased then increased

Science Tip

Contradictions: Narrow down your answer options by looking for choices that contradict the passage or the information in the question. Sometimes just eliminating the contradictions is enough to find the correct answer.

This page is intentionally left blank.

15.3.3 Use the Figures

There are several ways to decontaminate foods, such as dates, for long-term storage using the chemicals methyl bromide and phosphine. However, these chemicals are toxic at high concentrations and thus safer methods of food decontamination need to be found. The use of reactive oxygen, ozone (O_3), is currently being studied to determine if it causes a significant effect (decrease) on the number of mold and bacteria colonies that remain on dates during storage. In this experiment, dates were treated with ozone and stored in anaerobic (without oxygen) conditions for a period of several months. One set of dates was stored at 25°C, while another was stored at 40°C. Figures 1 and 2 show the mean colony counts of bacteria and molds on the dates over the duration of testing; Figure 1 shows the dates stored at 25°C, and Figure 2 shows the dates stored at 40°C.

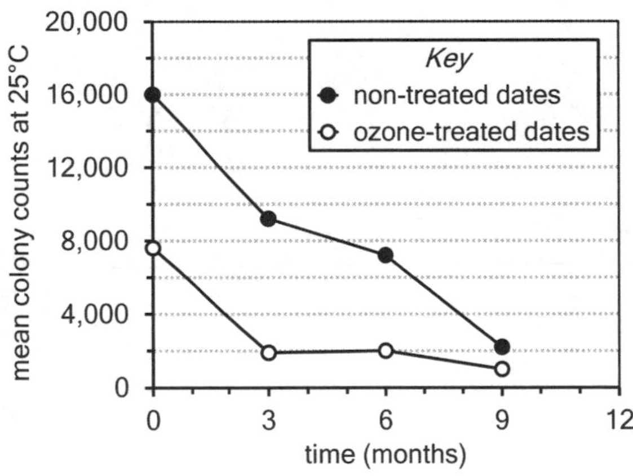

Figure 1

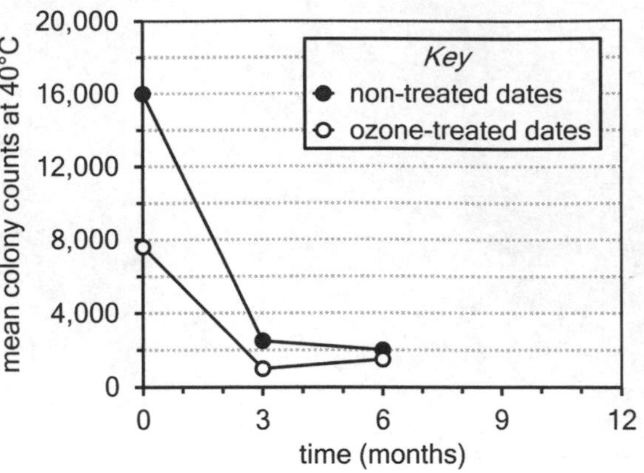

Figure 2

1. From the data shown in Figure 1, the difference in total number of microbes between the non-treated and the ozone-treated dates is the smallest in which of the following ranges?
   A. 0–2 months
   B. 2–5 months
   C. 5–7 months
   D. 7–9 months

2. According to Figures 1 and 2, what is the approximate minimum mean number of colonies on the dates stored at either temperature that were treated with ozone from 2 to 7 months?

	25 °C	40 °C
F.	1,000	1,750
G.	2,000	1,000
H.	2,000	2,000
J.	7,500	2,250

15.3.3 Use the Figures

3. After the dates were treated with ozone for 6 months, what was the difference between non-treated and ozone-treated mean colony counts on the dates?
   A. There was a small difference in the mean colony counts on the dates stored at 25°C.
   B. There was a large difference in the mean colony counts on dates stored at both 25°C and 40°C.
   C. There was a small difference in the mean colony counts on the dates stored at both 25°C and 40°C.
   D. There was a small difference in the mean colony counts on the dates stored at 40°C.

4. Suppose the time of testing at 40°C was extended to 9 months, as shown in Figure 1. Given the trends in both Figures 1 and 2, what would be the expected mean colony count on ozone-treated dates at 40°C after 9 months?
   F. Less than 4,000
   G. Between 4,000 and 7,000
   H. Between 7,000 and 10,000
   J. Greater than 10,000

Science Tip

Use the Figures: On the ACT science test, the passage text is not nearly as important as the figures. Start with the figures and answer as many questions as you can before going back to the text.

15.3.4 Road Signs

One way to characterize the role of an unknown enzyme in a biological process is to develop inhibitors to the enzyme and see what the biological effects are, either in a cell culture or an animal model. Capsase-5 is an enzyme known as a protease whose role in inflammation is still poorly understood. To learn more about this enzyme, an inhibitor to capsase-5 labeled Compound 8 (C-8) was synthesized and mixed in various ratios with capsase-5 and its substrate WEHD-AFC. Reaction rate profiles of these mixtures are shown in Figure 1.

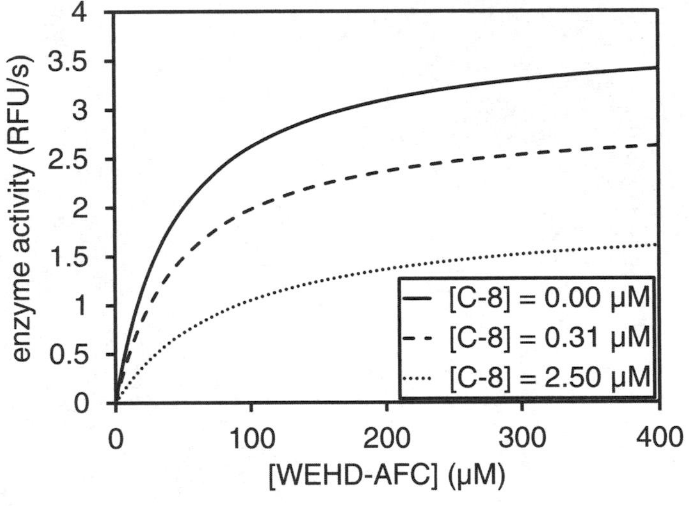

Figure 1

Table 1 shows the maximum reaction rates (v_{max}) and Michaelis coefficients (K_m) for a variety of C-8 concentrations [C-8]. In addition, the difference between K_m values when C-8 is present and when it isn't is also listed as ΔK_m to illustrate the decrease in enzyme activity.

Table 1

[C-8] (μM)	K_m (μM)	ΔK_m (μM)	v_{max} (RFU/s)
0.00	45.2	0.0	3.80
0.08	46.5	1.3	3.75
0.15	50.0	4.8	3.43
0.31	49.0	3.8	2.95
0.63	55.5	10.3	2.48
1.25	70.1	24.9	2.05
2.50	85.5	40.3	1.95

To determine if Compound 8 specifically acts on capsase-5, the same experiment was done using capsase-1 (an enzyme in the same family as capsase-5) instead of capsase-5. This data is shown in Figure 2.

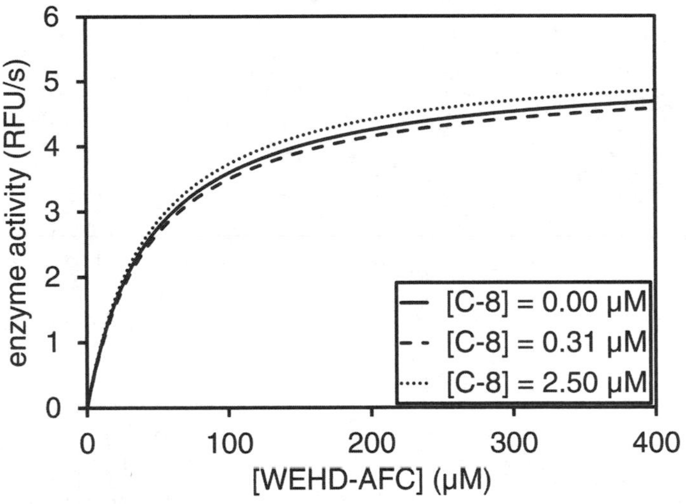

Figure 2

15.3.4 Road Signs

1. Based on the information in Table 1 and Figures 1 and 2, compared to v_{max} for capsase-5 when the concentration of C-8 is 0.00 μM, v_{max} for capsase-5 when the concentration of C-8 is 2.50 μM will be approximately:
   A. ½ as large.
   B. ¼ as large.
   C. the same.
   D. 2 times as great.

2. Based on Table 1, the relationship between [C-8] (in μM) and ΔK_m (in μM) for the inhibition of capsase-5 by Compound 8 is best represented by which of the following equations?
   F. $[\text{C-8}] = 16.8 \times \Delta K_m$
   G. $[\text{C-8}] = \frac{\Delta K_m}{16.8}$
   H. $[\text{C-8}] = 8.4 \times \Delta K_m$
   J. $[\text{C-8}] = \frac{\Delta K_m}{2.1}$

3. Based on the data in Table 1, half of the reaction rate of capsase-5 would be inhibited by which of the following concentrations of Compound 8?
   A. 1.25 μM
   B. 0.63 μM
   C. 2.50 μM
   D. 0.15 μM

4. Based on Table 1, v_{max} when using 0.30 μM C-8 with capsase-5 would be closest to which of the following values?
   F. 1.5 RFU/s
   G. 2.0 RFU/s
   H. 2.5 RFU/s
   J. 3.0 RFU/s

Science Tip

Road Signs: If you get lost, follow the road signs in the question to find the correct answer. If the question tells you exactly which figures or experiments to use, look at those first. If the question tells you something that can only be found in the passage text, read the text.

15.4.1 Set One

Passage I

A student conducted an experiment to determine the transepithelial electrical resistance (TEER) of canine kidney epithelial (CKE) cell monolayers in culture after exposure to proteases. Figure 1 shows the typical setup of a TEER experiment.

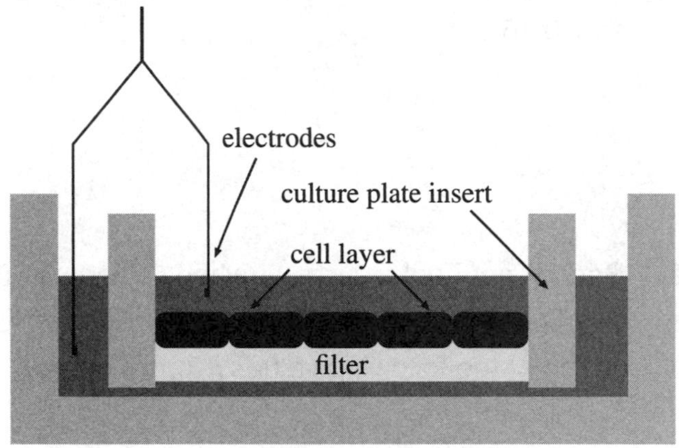

Figure 1

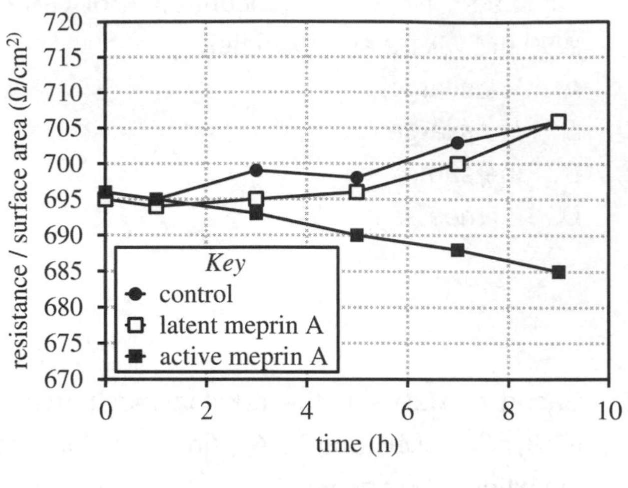

Figure 2

A TEER experiment involves determining the resistance (in Ω, using a volt-ohmmeter) between the solution and the cell monolayer. The greater the resistance value, the more resistance provided by the cells and thus the tighter the cells are packed together, that is, the stronger the bonds are between the cells.

In Figures 2 and 3, the student added latent (non-active) and active proteases meprin A and meprin B to CKE cells and monitored the resistance over a period of nine hours. Her hypothesis was that both the meprin A and meprin B would disrupt the tight junctions CKE cells make between themselves. The resistance provided by the cells under the various protease treatments is shown on the y-axis as resistance (Ω) per surface area of the cultured cells (cm^2).

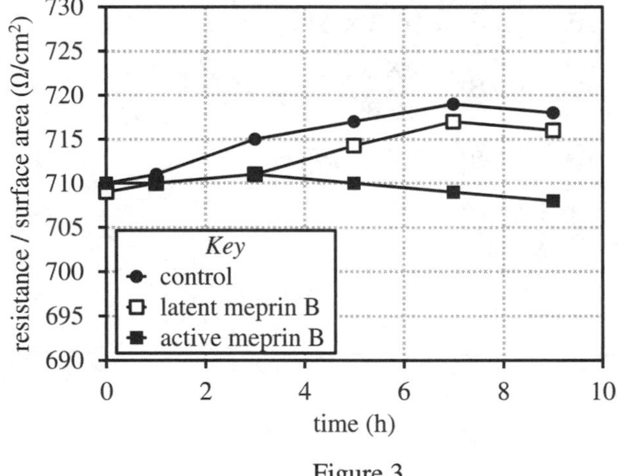

Figure 3

1. Based on Figure 2, at 11 hours, the resistance of the CKE cells given active meprin A would most likely be?

   A. Less than 685 Ω/cm^2
   B. Between 685 and 695 Ω/cm^2
   C. Between 695 and 705 Ω/cm^2
   D. Greater than 705 Ω/cm^2

2. For each of the proteases tested, as time increased, resistance:

   F. increased only.
   G. decreased only.
   H. varied but with no general trend.
   J. remained the same.

3. For a protease that disrupts the binding between CKE cells, the resistance provided by the cells will decrease. Based on Figures 2 and 3, which of the 4 proteases showed little effect on the binding between CKE cells for the duration of the experiment?

   A. Active meprin B only
   B. Active meprin A only
   C. Latent meprin A and latent meprin B only
   D. Active meprin B and latent meprin A only

4. Based on Figure 3, when the time equaled 5 hours for latent meprin B, the resistance of the CKE cells was closest to which of the following?

   F. 710 Ω/cm^2
   G. 715 Ω/cm^2
   H. 720 Ω/cm^2
   J. 725 Ω/cm^2

5. Based on Figures 2 and 3, the CKE cells best conducted electricity when treated with which of the following?

   A. Latent meprin A
   B. Latent meprin B
   C. Active meprin A
   D. Active meprin B

END OF SET ONE
STOP! DO NOT GO ON TO THE NEXT PAGE
UNTIL TOLD TO DO SO.

15.4.2 Set Two

Passage II

In the pursuit of quick and non-destructive ways to determine the freshness of fruit, researchers in China wanted to know if impact force analysis (IFA), where a fruit is dropped upon a force sensor, could be used for this purpose. In this study, the researchers used peaches to test their IFA theory. If you consider the peach a sphere and the force sensor as a stationary surface, the coefficient of restitution (R) can be calculated using the equation:

$$R = th\sqrt{\frac{g}{8h}}$$

The time (t) is the time between the first and second impact, that is, the time it takes for the peach to bounce and return to the sensor after it first strikes the sensor. The acceleration due to gravity is denoted as g, and h is the height from which the peach was dropped.

Experiment 1

The researchers calculated various R values of peaches with low firmness (ripe or rotten) and also the R values of peaches that were firmer (fresh or not ripened). Firmness was estimated by the force with which the peach impacted the force sensor. The curve of R as a function of firmness is shown in Figure 1.

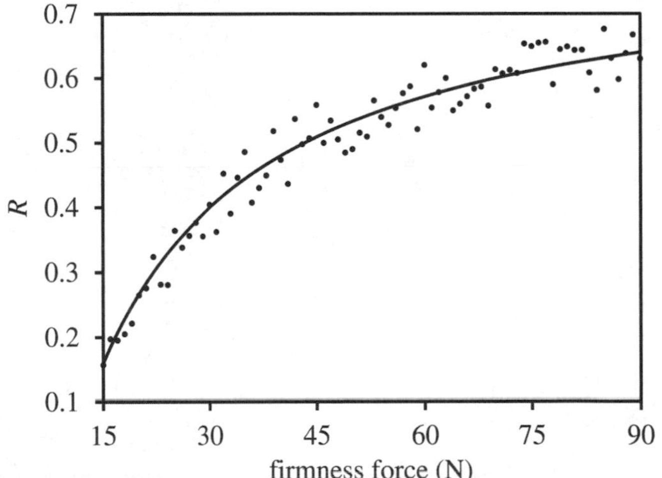

Figure 1

Experiment 2

After the data were collected in Experiment 1, the researchers decided to do additional tests. First, they selected peaches with three different masses (95 g, 120 g, or 145 g) and with varying firmness forces. The researchers then calculated the R values for these sets of peaches. The results are shown in Table 1.

Table 1

Firmness force	Mass (g)	Coefficient of restitution (R)
18–24	95	0.389
18–24	120	0.358
18–24	145	0.319
42–49	95	0.498
42–49	120	0.479
42–49	145	0.415
66–79	95	0.604
66–79	120	0.581
66–79	145	0.549

6. Suppose that, in an additional trial in Experiment 2, a 121-g peach had a firmness force of 45. Based on the results of the experiment, *R* would have been closest to which of the following values?

   F. 0.358
   G. 0.479
   H. 0.498
   J. 0.581

7. Suppose the researchers had changed the drop height from 1.0 cm to 0.5 cm, and there was no significant change in the coefficient of restitution. Which of the following statements would best explain this results?

   A. The acceleration due to gravity does not have an affect on *R*.
   B. The drop height in these experiments has little effect on the outcomes.
   C. The peaches stuck to the sensor board and did not bounce.
   D. The time between when the peach first struck the sensor board and the second time the peach struck the board was too quick to incorporate into the coefficient of restitution equation.

8. Suppose, in an additional trial in Experiment 2, the researchers had dropped a peach onto the sensor, and the peach stuck to the surface of the sensor without bouncing. *R* for this trial would have equaled what value?

   F. 0.000
   G. 0.250
   H. 0.500
   J. Cannot be determined from the given information

9. Two peaches have the same firmness force, but Peach A weighs 100 g and Peach B weighs 140 g. Which of the following is most likely to be their respective R values?

	Peach A	Peach B
A.	0.548	0.603
B.	0.501	0.422
C.	0.322	0.393
D.	0.612	0.381

10. Suppose that in Experiment 2 a 70-g peach in the lowest firmness force range had been tested. Approximately how much lower or higher would the calculated coefficient of restitution be compared to a 95-g peach in the least firm category?

   F. 0.036 lower
   G. 0.072 lower
   H. 0.036 higher
   J. 0.072 higher

END OF SET TWO

STOP! DO NOT GO ON TO THE NEXT PAGE UNTIL TOLD TO DO SO.

15.4.3 Set Three

Passage III

Phytoremediation, or the use of plants to remove toxic levels of heavy metals from contaminated soil, is a promising technique to decontaminate soils around sites of heavy industry. There are several species of plants that are currently being tested for their phytoremediation properties; however, the main flaw of most of the plants currently being tested is that they do not grow rapidly. Willow plants, genus *Salix*, are getting special attention in phytoremediation because not only are they good at removing heavy metals from soil, but they also grow quickly and have deep roots.

Another advantage of willow plants for phytoremediation targets is that they have a high genetic diversity, and thus it might be possible to find specific species of willows that are better at bioremediation than others without the need for genetic engineering. The purpose of this study was to characterize different willow plants and determine their efficiency at phytoremediation of the heavy metals copper (Cu^{2+}) and zinc (Zn^{2+}). Clones of a dozen willow species used in this study are listed in Table 1.

Experiment 1

One-year-old hardwood stems of willow plants were grown for 42 days in plastic buckets with a nutrient solution (1 mM $Ca(NO_3)_2$, 1.25 mM KNO_3, 0.5 mM $MgSO_4$, 0.5 mM $NH_4H_2PO_4$) and micronutrients including 25 μM FeEDTA, 23.1 μM H_3BO_3, 0.4 μM $ZnCl_2$, 0.18 μM $CuCl_2$, 4.57 μM $MnCl_2$, and 0.06 μM Na_2MoO_4. After this growing time, plants were selected and switched to growing in a waste analyte solution containing 50 μM Cu^{2+} or 50 μM Zn^{2+} (added as $CuSO_4$ or $ZnSO_4$) and grown for an additional 50 days. Some of the plants were maintained in nutrient solution throughout this testing period.

After the 50-day growing period, the plants were harvested, and the leaves, stems, and roots of the plants were separated. The plant parts were washed both with deionized water and EDTA. Next, the plant parts were dried and ground into powder. The metal content per dry weight (DW) in the plant parts was determined by first extracting with acid the metal and quantifying the metal concentration using atomic absorption spectrometry. Figures 1 and 2 show the concentration of Cu^{2+} and Zn^{2+} in the roots and shoots of the willow plant clones.

Table 1

Entry No.	*Clone*	Species/hybrid
1	SB7	*Salix babylolica*
2	SM16	*S. matsudana*
3	SM30	*S. matsudana*
4	SI63	*S. integra*
5	J9-6	*S. integra* × *S. suchowensis*
6	SI646	*S. integra*
7	J795	*S. matsudana* × *S. alba*
8	J844	*S. baylonica* × *S. alba*
9	J1011	*S. baylonica* × *S. alba*
10	J1052	*S. suchowensis* × *S. leucopithecia*
11	SI102-1	*S. integra*
12	SI102-2	*S. integra*

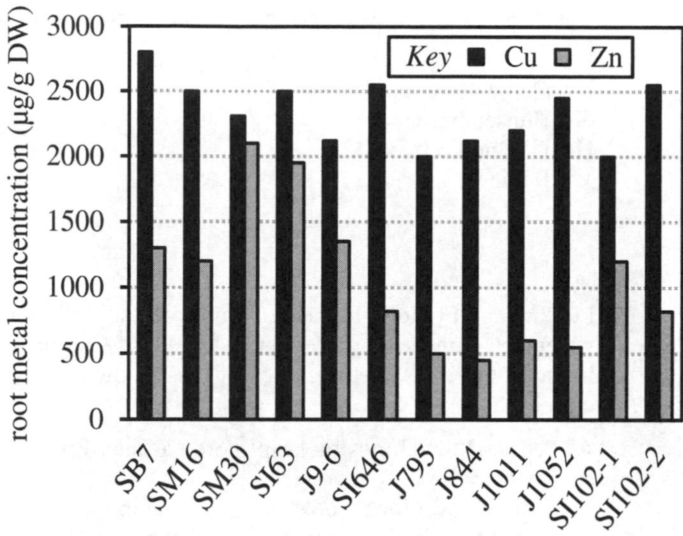

Figure 1

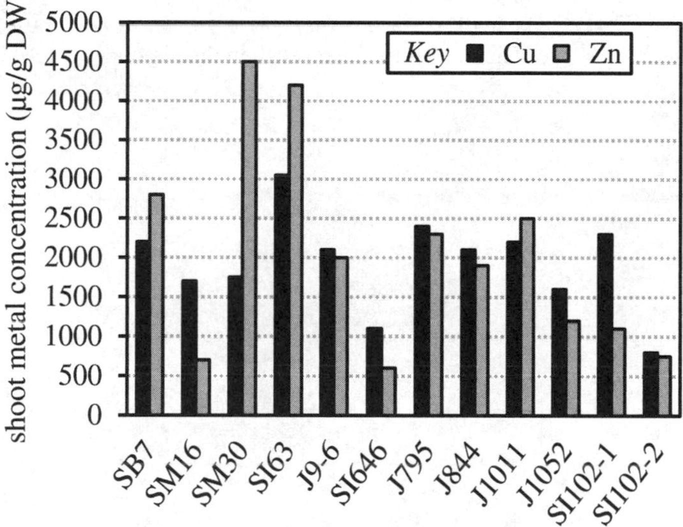

Figure 2

11. Which willow plant clone absorbed the highest amount of Zn in its shoots?

A. SM30
B. J795
C. J844
D. SM16

12. The plant parts were separated and washed twice, once with the metal chelator EDTA most likely to:

F. completely ensure the plants had stopped growing.
G. remove the metal that was not absorbed by the plant and thus should not be measured.
H. assist with drying the plant parts in the next step faster.
J. remove any microbes on the plant parts that might affect the quantification of the metals.

13. Given the data in Figure 1, overall, which metal are the willow plant clones more proficient at removing from their environment by their roots?

A. Cu; the J9-6 clone is the most proficient.
B. Zn; the J795 clone is the most proficient.
C. Cu; the SB7 clone is the most proficient.
D. Zn; the J844 clone is the most proficient.

14. Which of the following pieces of scientific equipment was most likely used to gather the data shown in both Figure 1 and 2?

F. Cell culture hood
G. Bunsen burner
H. UV light box
J. Balance

15. Looking at Figures 1 and 2, which of the following statements concerning the overall uptake of Cu and Zu in either the roots or the shoots of the willow clones is correct?

A. The willow clones took up more Cu than Zn in the roots.
B. The willow clones took up Cu and Zn in fairly equal quantities, both in the roots and the shoots of the plants.
C. The willow clones took up less Cu than Zn in the roots.
D. The willow clones took up a greater concentration of Cu and Zn in the roots than the shoots.

END OF SET THREE

STOP! DO NOT GO ON TO THE NEXT PAGE UNTIL TOLD TO DO SO.

Sum It Up

Tips and Techniques

Process of Elimination: The single most useful strategy on the science test is the process of elimination. Eliminate incorrect answers whenever possible. Some questions can be answered correctly simply by eliminating the wrong answers.

Contradictions: Narrow down your answer options by looking for choices that contradict the passage or the information in the question. Sometimes just eliminating the contradictions is enough to find the correct answer.

Use the Figures: On the science test, the passage text is not nearly as important as the figures. Start with the figures and answer as many questions as you can before going back to the text.

Road Signs: If you get lost, follow the road signs in the question to find the correct answer. If the question tells you exactly which figures or experiments to use, look at those first. If the question tells you something that can only be found in the passage text, read the text.

Lesson 16

Science Pacing

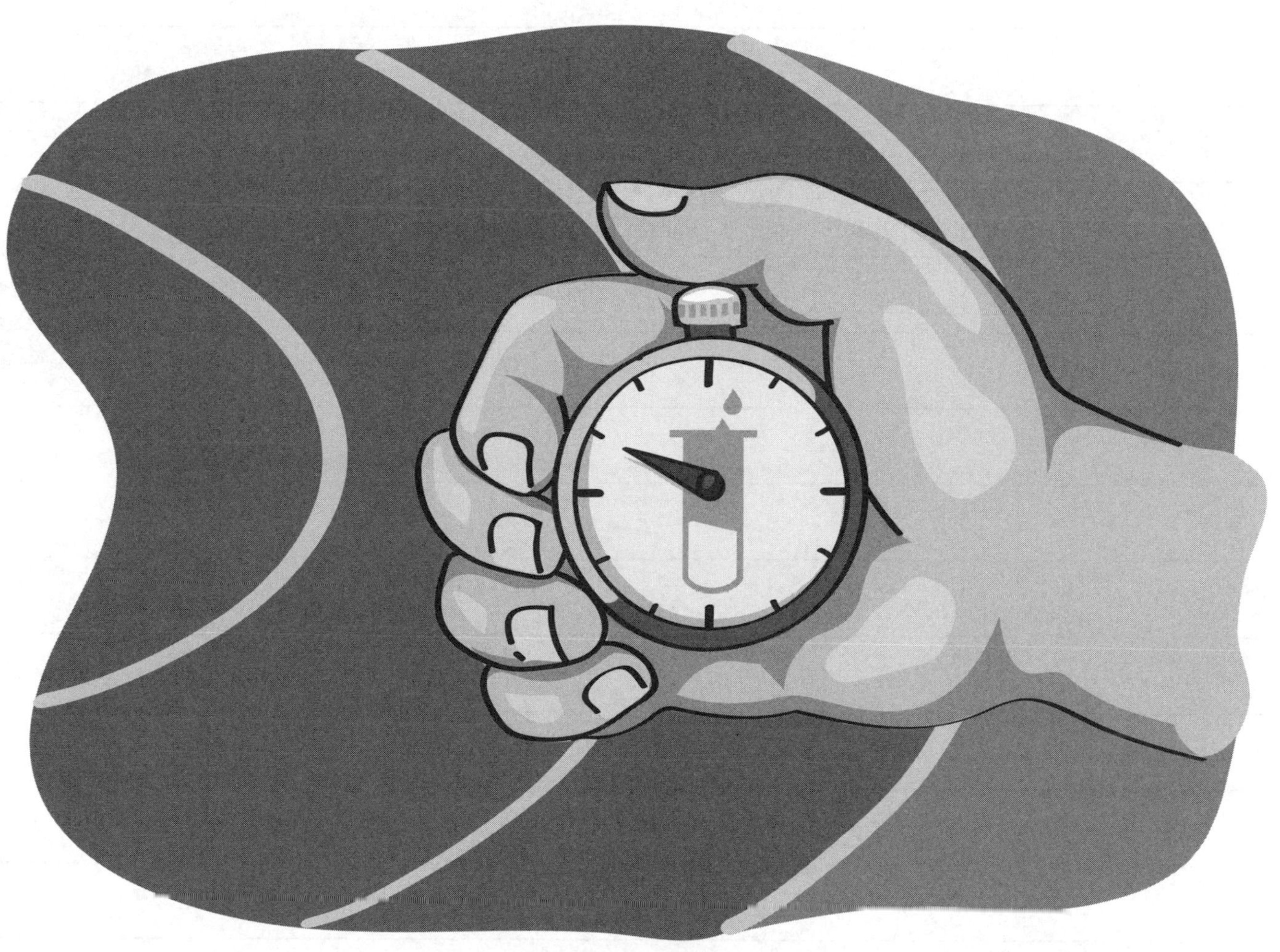

CAPTION:

16.1 Entrance Ticket

What are your goals for the ACT science test? How do you plan to achieve them? What could stand in your way? Answer these questions in complete sentences.

16.2 Learning Targets

1. Set a personalized pacing goal for the science test based on ACT scoring tables

2. Follow a personalized pacing plan for the science test

Self-Assessment

Circle the number that corresponds to your confidence level in your knowledge of this subject before beginning the lesson. A score of 1 means you are completely lost, and a score of 4 means you have mastered the skills. After you finish the lesson, return to the bottom of this page and circle your new confidence level to show your improvement.

Before Lesson

1 2 3 4

After Lesson

1 2 3 4

16.3.1 Setting a Pacing Plan

Scale Score	Raw Score (Correct answers)	Scale Score	Raw Score (Correct answers)
36	40	18	19
35	39	17	17
34	39	16	15
33	38	15	14
32	38	14	13
31	38	13	12
30	37	12	11
29	36	11	10
28	36	10	8
27	34	9	7
26	33	8	6
25	31	7	5
24	30	6	4
23	28	5	3
22	27	4	2
21	25	3	1
20	23	2	1
19	21	1	0

16.3.1 Setting a Pacing Plan

Goal Scale Score: ____________________

Overall Goal Raw Score: ____________________

Target Raw Score (1st Passage): ____________________
Actual Raw Score (1st Passage): ____________________

Target Raw Score (2nd Passage): ____________________
Actual Raw Score (2nd Passage): ____________________

Target Raw Score (3rd Passage): ____________________
Actual Raw Score (3rd Passage): ____________________

Target Raw Score (4th Passage): ____________________
Actual Raw Score (4th Passage): ____________________

Target Raw Score (5th Passage): ____________________
Actual Raw Score (5th Passage): ____________________

Science Tip

Mark and Move: Since the difficult questions are mixed throughout, you should be prepared to use the mark and move technique quite often. As soon as you get stuck on a question, eliminate what you can, mark your best guess, and move on. You probably will not have time to revisit these questions, but if you do, go back and check your work.

16.4.1 Mini-Test 1

Passage I

Attempts: ______ **Correct:** ______

A group of researchers attempted to develop a new technique for vertical farming by constructing three artificially heated and humidified chambers. The researchers found the weekly average air temperature in Celsius (°C) and the weekly average humidity in percent water vapor in each of the three chambers. The results for the first six weeks of their measurements are given in Table 1 and Table 2.

Table 1

Week	Weekly average air temperature (°C)		
	Chamber 1	Chamber 2	Chamber 3
1	20.01	19.12	18.87
2	20.13	19.13	18.85
3	20.36	19.13	18.88
4	20.68	19.15	18.92
5	20.95	19.22	18.98
6	21.02	19.20	19.03

Table 2

Week	Weekly average humidity (%)		
	Chamber 1	Chamber 2	Chamber 3
1	84%	83%	78%
2	84%	82%	77%
3	85%	81%	76%
4	86%	82%	76%
5	88%	80%	78%
6	87%	79%	79%

1. The highest weekly average humidity recorded during the first six weeks of the study was:

A. 86%
B. 87%
C. 88%
D. 89%

2. What was the average air temperature in the three chambers in Week 4?

F. 18.15
G. 18.59
H. 19.58
J. 20.69

3. Which of the following statements best describes the relative conditions of the three chambers in the first six weeks of the study?

A. Chamber 1 had high average air temperature and high average humidity, Chamber 2 had low average air temperature and low average humidity, and Chamber 3 had medium average air temperature and medium average humidity.
B. Chamber 1 had low average air temperature and medium average humidity, Chamber 2 had medium average air temperature and low average humidity, and Chamber 3 had high average air temperature and high average humidity.
C. Chamber 1 had high average air temperature and low average humidity, Chamber 2 had medium average air temperature and high average humidity, and Chamber 3 had low average air temperature and medium average humidity.
D. Chamber 1 had high average air temperature and high average humidity, Chamber 2 had medium average air temperature and medium average humidity, and Chamber 3 had low average air temperature and low average humidity.

GO ON TO THE NEXT PAGE

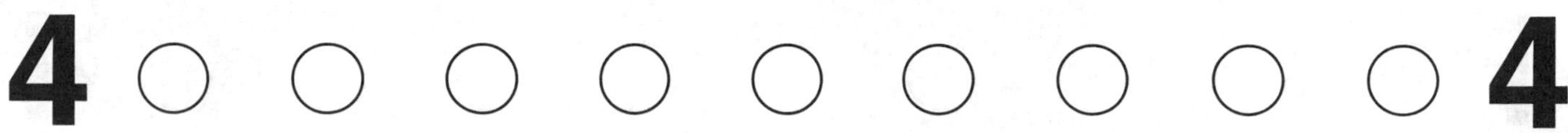

4. Which of the following statements best describes the change in weekly average air temperature in Chamber 2?

   F. The weekly average air temperature increased or stayed the same consistently from Week 1 to Week 6.
   G. The weekly average air temperature decreased from Week 1 to Week 3 and increased or stayed the same from Week 3 to Week 6.
   H. The weekly average air temperature increased or stayed the same from Week 1 to Week 5, and the weekly average air temperature decreased from Week 5 to Week 6.
   J. The weekly average air temperature decreased or stayed the same from Week 1 to Week 4 and increased from Week 4 to Week 6.

5. Suppose the rate of growth of crops in each of the vertical farming chambers is determined by either weekly average air temperature, weekly average humidity, or both. If the growth rate in Chamber 2 greatly exceeds the growth rate of Chambers 1 and 3, which of the following conclusions would be justified? Relative to the temperatures and humidity levels in the experiment:

   A. high weekly average air temperature or high weekly average humidity is ideal for plant life growth rate.
   B. medium weekly average air temperature or medium weekly average humidity is ideal for plant life growth rate.
   C. low weekly average air temperature or low weekly average humidity is ideal for plant life growth rate.
   D. all of the above conclusions can be justified.

END OF MINI-TEST ONE
STOP! DO NOT GO ON TO THE NEXT PAGE
UNTIL TOLD TO DO SO.

4 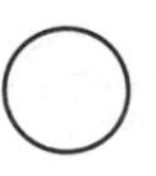         4

16.4.2 Mini-Test 2

Passage II

Attempts: _____ Correct: _____

Solar panels are assemblies of connected photovoltaic cells that harness solar energy to produce electricity. Photovoltaic cells can produce electricity from a range of light frequencies at varying efficiencies; however, current solar panel technology is incapable of capturing the entire solar range. Scientists have determined that illuminating photovoltaic cells with monochromatic light enables higher efficiency, but they have yet to develop the technology necessary to split light into its various wavelength ranges to make use of this higher efficiency.

Experiment 1

Photovoltaic cells show a decrease in efficiency at increased temperatures. A group of scientists wanted to determine which frequency range of light might produce the best efficiency in photovoltaic cells and how temperature might affect this efficiency. The results of their experiment are given in Table 1.

Table 1

Temp. (°C)	Photovoltaic cell efficiency (%)		
	Frequency Range 1	Frequency Range 2	Frequency Range 3
25	20.2%	20.0%	20.4%
26	19.7%	19.7%	19.7%
27	19.2%	19.4%	19.0%
28	18.7%	19.1%	18.3%
29	18.2%	18.8%	17.6%

Experiment 2

With mathematical models, the same group of scientists attempted to project the efficiencies of photovoltaic cells coupled with techniques that allowed for the splitting of wavelength ranges. They projected uniform increases in efficiencies for all frequency ranges, but they noted the continued decrease in efficiency at increased temperatures. The theoretical results of their models are given in Table 2.

Table 2

Temp. (°C)	Theoretical photovoltaic cell efficiency w/ wavelength splitting (%)		
	Frequency Range 1	Frequency Range 2	Frequency Range 3
25	47.2%	45.0%	50.4%
26	46.1%	44.3%	48.6%
27	45.0%	43.6%	46.8%
28	43.9%	42.9%	45.0%
29	42.8%	42.2%	43.2%

6. Do the results from Experiment 1 support the claim that photovoltaic cells capturing different frequency ranges function at varying efficiencies with changes in temperature?

F. Yes, because as temperature increases, so does efficiency.
G. Yes, because as temperature increases, efficiency decreases.
H. No, because there is no uniform change in efficiency as related to temperature.
J. No, because all photovoltaic cells function at the same efficiency regardless of frequency.

7. Based on the results from Experiment 1, photovoltaic cells capturing which frequency range of light would function best in environments that keep the cell temperatures at roughly 29°C?

A. Frequency 1
B. Frequency 2
C. Frequency 3
D. All frequency ranges will function the same.

GO ON TO THE NEXT PAGE

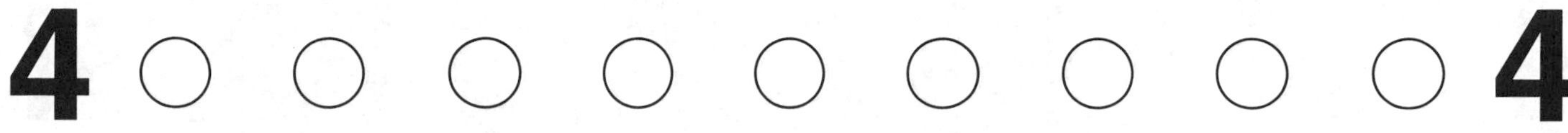

8. Based on the results from Experiment 1, photovoltaic cells capturing which frequency range of light would function best in environments that keep the cell temperatures at roughly 26°C?

   F. Frequency Range 1
   G. Frequency Range 2
   H. Frequency Range 3
   J. The cells would function the same with all three frequency ranges.

9. One of the scientists suggests that he can build a cooling system for the theoretical photovoltaic cells in Experiment 2, which will keep the cells 1°C cooler than normal but decrease their efficiency by 1%. The theoretical photovoltaic cells capturing which frequency ranges, if any, would benefit from this cooling system?

   A. Frequency Ranges 1 and 2
   B. Frequency Ranges 1 and 3
   C. Frequency Ranges 2 and 3
   D. None of the theoretical photovoltaic cells would benefit.

10. In Experiment 1, which of the following variables is held constant?

   F. The temperature of the environment
   G. The amount of sunlight shone on the photovoltaic cells
   H. The photovoltaic cells used
   J. The frequency range of light captured by the photovoltaic cells

11. Suppose the scientists note the temperature sensitivity of the photovoltaic cells in both experiments, defining sensitivity as the amount of change in efficiency as temperature increases. Which of the following best describes the changes in efficiency and temperature sensitivity of the photovoltaic cells in Experiment 1 to the theoretical photovoltaic cells with wavelength splitting in Experiment 2?

   A. Efficiency increases from Experiment 1 to Experiment 2, and sensitivity to temperature increases from Experiment 1 to Experiment 2.
   B. Efficiency increases from Experiment 1 to Experiment 2, but sensitivity to temperature decreases from Experiment 1 to Experiment 2.
   C. Efficiency decreases from Experiment 1 to Experiment 2, and sensitivity to temperature decreases from Experiment 1 to Experiment 2.
   D. Efficiency decreases from Experiment 1 to Experiment 2, but sensitivity to temperature increases from Experiment 1 to Experiment 2.

END OF MINI-TEST TWO

STOP! DO NOT GO ON TO THE NEXT PAGE UNTIL TOLD TO DO SO.

16.4.3 Mini-Test 3

Passage III

Attempts: _____ **Correct:** _____

Stars begin their lives composed of roughly 70% hydrogen. Nuclear fusion of hydrogen atoms into helium at the cores of stars drives the majority of energy and luminosity. After most of the hydrogen has been exhausted from the star's core, the star enters into the red giant branch and begins the fusion of hydrogen in the surrounding shell, as well as the fusion of helium in its core. The hydrogen in the surrounding shell is quickly exhausted, as is the helium in the core, and near the end of the star's life, it begins to fuse hydrogen and then helium in its outermost shell until all of it is exhausted. The figure below shows the percentage of hydrogen present in a star over the course of its life cycle.

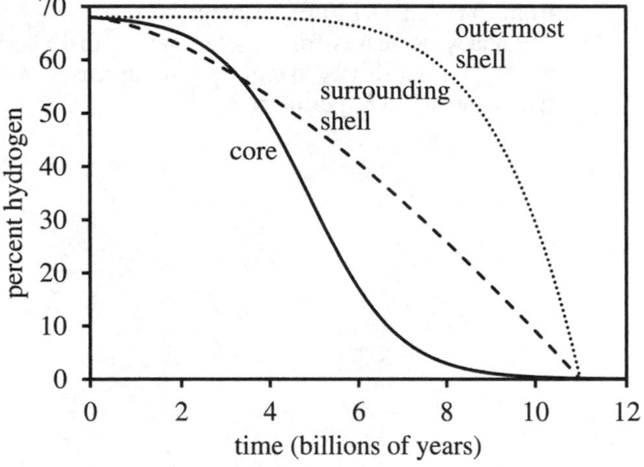

Figure 1

12. Based on the figure, the percentage of hydrogen in the surrounding shell after 8 billion years will be closest to which of the following:

F. 30%
G. 35%
H. 40%
J. 45%

13. Based on the figure, at how many billions of years will there be roughly 0% hydrogen remaining in the core?

A. Between 6 and 7
B. Between 7 and 8
C. Between 8 and 9
D. More than 9

14. After the fusion of hydrogen is exhausted in the core and fusion of hydrogen begins in the surrounding shell, the fusion of helium begins in the core. Which of the following is most likely true about the percentage of helium in the core as time increases after core hydrogen fusion is complete?

F. The percentage of helium decreases over time.
G. The percentage of helium increases over time.
H. The percentage of helium does not change over time.
J. The percentage of helium over time cannot be determined.

GO ON TO THE NEXT PAGE

15. A star's core is approximately 28% helium at the beginning of its lifetime. A scientist theorizes that the amount of helium present at first increases and begins to drop only after the percentage of hydrogen present in the core drops below 20%. According to this theory, which of the following is the best graphical representation of the percentage of helium over time?

A.

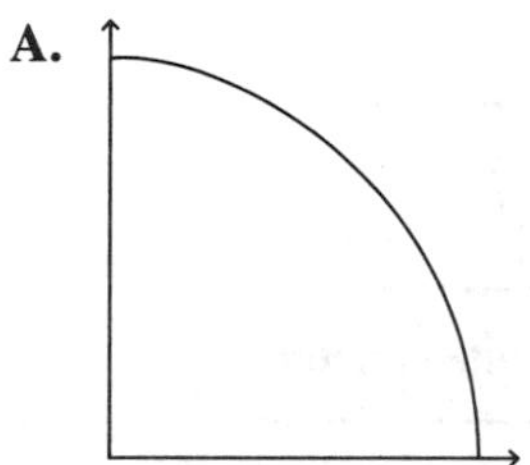

B.

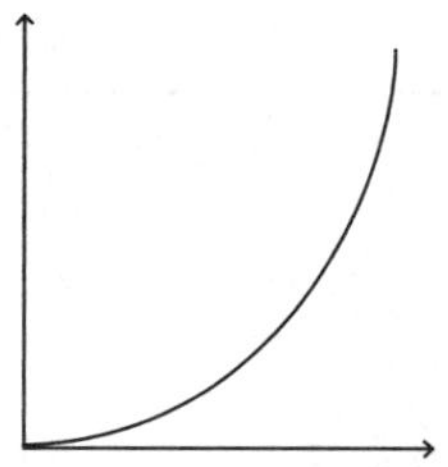

C.

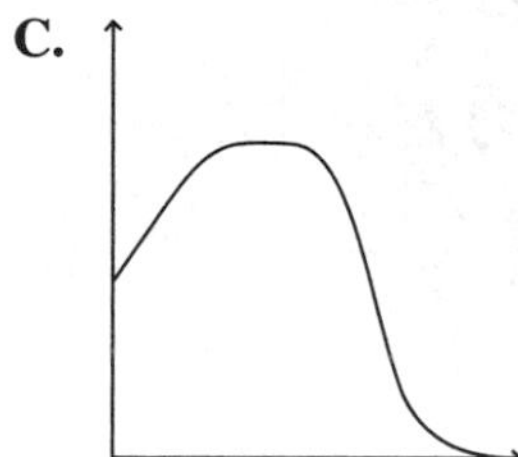

D.

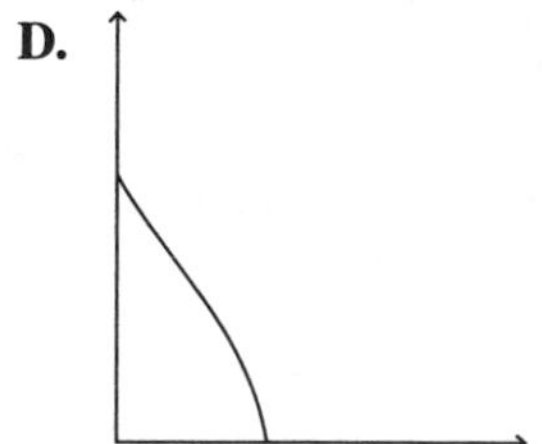

16. After 11 billion years, the star will shed nearly all of its mass and become a white dwarf, surviving for billions of years before fading out. Which of the following most likely catalyzes the transition from red giant to white dwarf?

F. The exhaustion of hydrogen in the core
G. The exhaustion of hydrogen and helium in the core
H. The exhaustion of hydrogen in the core and the exhaustion of helium in the shells
J. The exhaustion of hydrogen in the shells and the exhaustion of helium in the shells and core

END OF MINI-TEST THREE

STOP! DO NOT GO ON TO THE NEXT PAGE UNTIL TOLD TO DO SO.

16.4.4 Mini-Test 4

Passage IV

Attempts: _____ Correct: _____

Human blood cells allow for the influx and efflux of H_2O molecules through semipermeable membranes. Osmotic pressure is the phenomenon that drives this influx and efflux of water. Depending on the concentration of solutes in the blood plasma, it may be hypertonic, isotonic, or hypotonic when compared to the cells themselves. Figure 1 shows the three types of tonicity.

The plasma is *hypertonic* when it has a higher concentration of solute present outside of the cell than within the cell. Water flows out of the cell as it attempts to achieve homeostasis. This causes the cell to shrink and shrivel.

The plasma is *isotonic* when it has the same concentration of solute present both within the cell and outside it. This causes the cell to remain in equilibrium, or homeostasis, with water flowing both into and out of the cell evenly.

The plasma is *hypotonic* when it has a lower concentration of a solute present outside the cell than within the cell. Water flows into the cell as it attempts to achieve homeostasis. This causes the cell to bloat and burst.

A group of scientists is attempting to create synthetic plasma for hospital patients in need of transfusions. They realize a certain solute is key in the development of this synthetic plasma and use an initial set of solutions to approximate the amount of solute necessary for blood cells to achieve homeostasis. The composition of the four solutions (A, B, C, and D) in ppm (parts per million) is found in Table 1.

Table 1

Solution	Solute concentration (ppm)
Solution A	980
Solution B	1,150
Solution C	1,245
Solution D	1,350

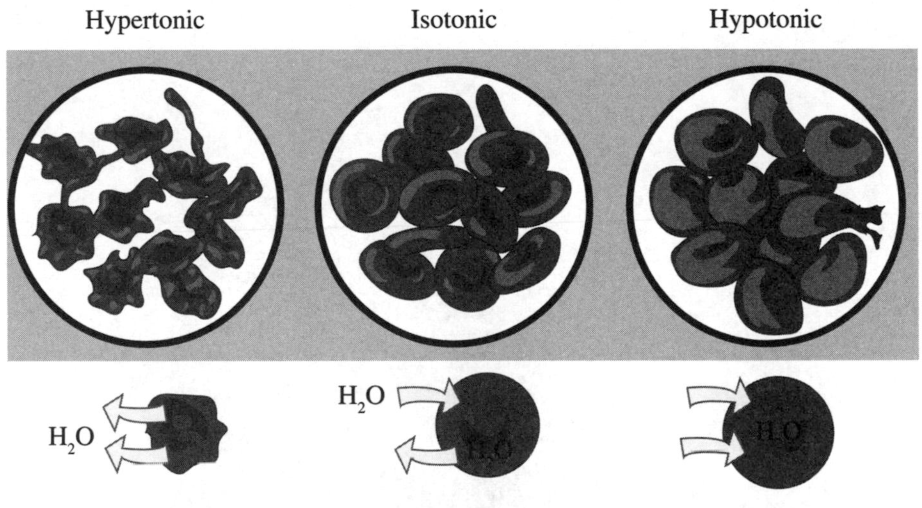

Figure 1

GO ON TO THE NEXT PAGE

17. If a cell is placed within a hypertonic solution, it will shrink and shrivel because:

A. water flows into the cell.
B. water flows out of the cell.
C. solutes flow out of the cell.
D. solutes flow into the cell.

18. If a cell is placed in an isotonic solution, it will remain in homeostasis because:

F. water flows into and out of the cell.
G. solutes flow into and out of the cell.
H. solutes flow into the cell, and water flows out of the cell.
J. solutes flow out of the cell, and water flows into the cell.

19. Which of the following solutions will best maintain homeostasis for a blood cell with a solute concentration of 1,250 ppm?

A. Solution A
B. Solution B
C. Solution C
D. Solution D

20. If a blood cell with a solute concentration of 1,250 ppm is placed within Solution D, the plasma will be which type of tonicity compared to the cell, and how will this affect the cell?

F. Hypertonic; it will shrink and shrivel.
G. Hypertonic; it will bloat and burst.
H. Isotonic; it will remain in homeostasis.
J. Hypotonic; it will bloat and burst.

21. If a blood cell with a solute concentration of 1,250 ppm is placed within Solution B, which type of tonicity will occur, and how will this affect the cell?

A. Hypertonic; it will shrink and shrivel.
B. Hypertonic; it will bloat and burst.
C. Isotonic; it will remain in homeostasis.
D. Hypotonic; it will bloat and burst.

22. Suppose one of the scientists has a blood sample from a patient but only needs a sample of the plasma. She places the blood sample in one side of a U-shaped tube, separated from the other side of the tube with a semipermeable membrane through which the blood cells and solute cannot pass. She uses a device to produce slight pressure on the filled side of the tube and watches the plasma flow through the semipermeable membrane to the other side, which increases the concentration of the solute in the remaining plasma. This process caused the remaining plasma in the blood sample to be which type of tonicity compared to the blood cells?

F. Hypertonic
G. Hypotonic
H. Isotonic
J. The type of tonicity cannot be determined.

END OF MINI-TEST FOUR

STOP! DO NOT GO ON TO THE NEXT PAGE UNTIL TOLD TO DO SO.

16.4.5 Mini-Test 5

Passage V

Attempts: _____ **Correct:** _____

A particular area's soil horizons can be broken down into three distinct layers: permeable topsoil, highly plastic clay, and limestone bedrock. A company engineer is attempting to collect calcium carbonate, $CaCO_3$, from the area in order to produce a range of industrial materials. He projects calcium carbonate to be present in varying levels throughout the various soil horizons, as shown below in Table 1. In order to ensure stable mining conditions, he additionally collects information on the average water capacity of the various soil horizons, as shown in Table 2.

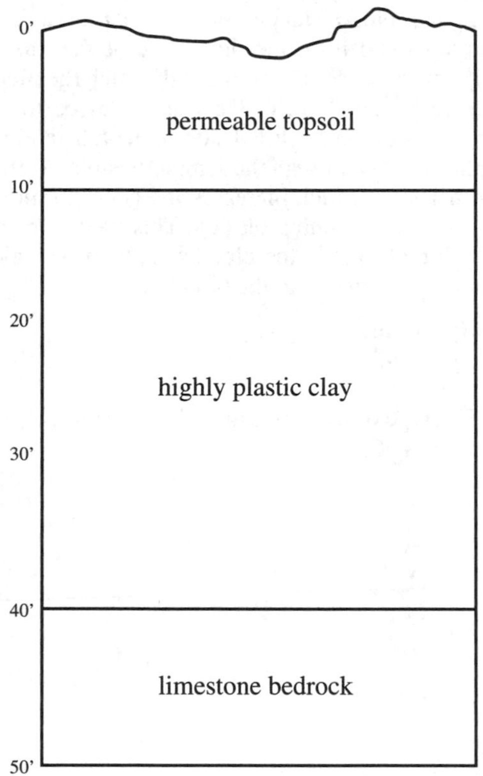

Figure 1

Table 1

Soil texture	% $CaCO_3$
Permeable topsoil	5%
Highly plastic clay	32%
Limestone bedrock	88%

Table 2

Soil texture	Water capacity (in^3/ft^3)
Permeable topsoil	0.9
Highly plastic clay	1.4
Limestone bedrock	0.3

GO ON TO THE NEXT PAGE

23. Highly plastic clay causes significant problems for heavy structures because it is prone to liquefaction. The engineer determines that for a stable foundation, there must be at least 10 feet of permeable topsoil under any heavy structure the company will be using. Can the company build on this area?

A. Yes, the company can build everywhere in this area.
B. Yes, but the company can only build on a portion of the area.
C. No, the company cannot build anywhere on the area.
D. This cannot be determined.

24. A sample is taken of minerals 18 feet below the surface. What is the projected percentage of calcium carbonate content in the sample?

F. 5%
G. 18%
H. 32%
J. 85%

25. Suppose $CaCO_3$ cannot be collected from permeable topsoil or highly plastic clay but can only be collected from limestone bedrock. How far must the company dig in order to begin the collection of calcium carbonate?

A. 10 feet
B. 30 feet
C. 40 feet
D. 50 feet

26. Suppose that actual water capacity varies uniformly according to depth and soil texture, with the values given in Table 2 representing the actual water capacities at the middle portions of the three soil horizons. The engineer takes a sample of soil and finds that it contains 1.1 in^3/ft^3 of water. Which of the following is the least likely depth from which he could have taken this sample?

F. 12 feet
G. 20 feet
H. 25 feet
J. 45 feet

27. Soil liquefaction occurs when stress or pressure is applied to soil with water content too high to allow for the soil to remain in a dry solid state. Highly plastic clay is itself prone to liquefaction due to its high average water capacity. Based on the information in the passage, which of the following is least likely to contribute to the highly plastic clay soil horizon's potential to liquefy?

A. The low average water capacity of limestone bedrock, because water cannot enter the bedrock and becomes stuck in the permeable topsoil and highly plastic clay
B. The high calcium carbonate content of limestone bedrock, because it makes the bedrock more porous
C. The plasticity of highly plastic clay when the clay mixes with water, which causes it to move more freely
D. The permeability of the permeable topsoil, because it allows water to flow through it and become absorbed more quickly

END OF MINI-TEST FIVE

STOP! DO NOT GO ON TO THE NEXT PAGE UNTIL TOLD TO DO SO.

Sum It Up

Tips and Techniques

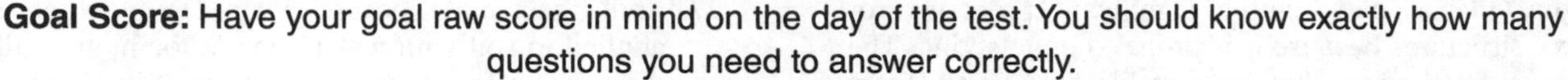

Goal Score: Have your goal raw score in mind on the day of the test. You should know exactly how many questions you need to answer correctly.

Pacing Plan: Have your plan in place before you take your ACT science test. Know how many minutes you should spend on each passage and how many questions you need to attempt in order to get to your goal score.

Mark and Move: Since the difficult questions are mixed throughout, you should be prepared to use the mark and move technique quite often. As soon as you get stuck on a question, eliminate what you can, mark your best guess, and move on. You probably will not have time to revisit these questions, but if you do, go back and check your work.

Notes

Science Glossary

Bar graph
A graphical representation of data that uses either vertical or horizontal bars to display data in discrete intervals

Claim
An assertion of the truth, typically one that is disputed or in doubt

Conclusion
A judgment or decision reached by reasoning

Connection questions
Questions with the connection not explicitly explained in the passage; these require critical thinking to determine the missing connections

Constant
Something that remains unchanged in an experiment

Control
The standards against which the experimenter compares results; the group or test subject that does not have a variable

Data
Facts or information often used to calculate, analyze, or plan something

Direct questions
Questions with the missing information clearly pointed to in the question

Direct trend
An upward sloping line, or a line sloping toward the direction in which the units are increasing

Evidence
Something that shows that something else exists or is true

Experiment
A test to see if a hypothesis is true

Extrapolate
To extend (a graph, curve, or range of values) by inferring unknown values from trends in the known data

Hypothesis

A supposition or proposed explanation made on the basis of limited evidence as a starting point for further investigation

Inverse trend

A downward sloping line, or a line sloping toward the direction in which the units are decreasing

Line graph

A graphical representation of data in which each data point is connected to the rest of the data points with a line that runs from point to point

Prediction

A statement about what might happen or what will happen in the future

Result

A consequence or conclusion that is caused by something else

Stagnant

A straight, non-sloping line

Statement

A definite or clear expression of something in speech or writing

Table

A non-graphical way to relay information about a system, in which columns or rows are used to display data

Variable

An element or factor that is liable to change during an experiment

Science Citations

Select Data and Features Part 2

Shukla, B. P., et al. *Theor Appl Climato*, 2009.

Support or Contradiction of Hypotheses and Conclusions Part 1

Campbell, N. A., et al. *Biol.* 6th ed.

Variables and Mathematical Relationships

Meade, F. C., et al. *Nat Commun.* 5, no. 4199 (2014).

Ludlow, F., et al. *Environ Res.* Let. 8 (2013).

Creating Figures

Hiller, B., et al. CyDas. 2004. Accessed 2015. http://www.cydas.org/OnlineAnalysis/.

Controls

Noller, H. F., et al. *Sci.* 256, no. 5062 (1992): 1416-419.

Mangal, M., et al. *Bul of Volcan*, 2010. doi:10.1007/s00445-010-0411-6.

Pamukcu, A., et al. *J Petrology*, 2012. doi:10.1093/petrology/egr072.

Harris, D. C. *Exploring Chem Analysis*. 5th ed. 2012.

Hendry, A. P., et al. *Evolution* 56, no. 6 (2002): 1199-216.

Keller, G., et al. *Palaeogeo, Palaeoclim, Palaeoeco*, no. 21 (2004): 19-43.

Science Strategy

Yukiko, A., et al. *The Tohoku J of Exptal Med* 182, no. 4 (1997): 319-25.

Han, X., et al. *BMC Microbiol.* 10 (2010): 35.

Ogra, Y., et al. *Bull Environ Contam Toxicol* 94, no. 5 (2014): 604-08.

Farajzadeh, D., et al. *J Res Med Sci*. 18, no. 4 (2013): 330-4.

Wells, J., et al. *Chem Biol Drug Des*. 79, no. 2 (2012): 209-15.

Bao, J., et al. *Am J of Phys: Renal Phys* 305, no. 5 (2013): F714-726.

Wang, Y., et al. *J of Zhejiang Uni* 10, no. 12 (2009): 883-89.

Yang, X., et al. *J of Zhejiang Uni* 15, no. 9 (2014): 788-800.

Contributors

Chief Academic Officer
Oliver Pope

Lead Content Editor
Lisa Primeaux-Redmond

Assistant Content Editors
Eric Manuel

Layout
Jeff Garrett, Elaine Broussard, Jeffrey Cappell, Ryan Herringshaw, Shannon Rawson, Nicole St. Pierre, Eliza Todorova, Lisa Primeaux-Redmond, Eric Manuel

Lesson Writers
Lisa Primeaux-Redmond, Stephanie Bucklin, Chad Sziszak, Lori Martin

Question Editors
Douglas K McLemore, Kristina Weatherhead, Irit Maor, Lisa Primeaux-Redmond

Question Writers
Stephanie Bucklin, Timothy Keiffer, Chad Sziszak, Lisa Primeaux-Redmond, Rebecca Anderson, Lauren Pope, Danielle Reid, Brett Roberts, David Glardon, Douglas K McLemore

Art
Nicole St. Pierre, Eliza Todorova, Roland Parker, Kayla Manuel, Anne Lipscomb, Douglas K McLemore

Proofreaders
Kristen Cockrell, Elaine Broussard, Allison Eskind, Jillian Musso, Lisa Primeaux-Redmond, Oliver Pope, Chrissy Vincent, Dan Marchese, Rhett Manuel, Catherine Tall, Jerelyn Pearson, Liz Baron, Jordan Sermon, Megan Reitzell, Diana Pietrogallo, Marcia Willis, Stephanie Bucklin, Chad Sziszak, Michael Laird

Interns
Kaitlyn Mattox, Rashaud Red, Jamaica Rhoden, Chelsey Smith

ACT® Mastery created by Craig Gehring

Contributors